W9-AOG-850

# Nicaragua:
# America's New Vietnam?

*Also by Karl Grossman*

*COVER UP: What you* ARE NOT *supposed to know about Nuclear Power*
*The Poison Conspiracy*

# Nicaragua: America's New Vietnam?

*Text and Photos*

By Karl Grossman

The Permanent Press
Sag Harbor, N.Y. 11963

Edited by Janet Grossman

International Standard Book Number: 0-932966-46-2
Library of Congress Catalog Card Number: 83-63242

The Permanent Press, Sag Harbor, New York 11963

Printed in the United States of America

*For Kurt and Adam*

"Revolutionary movements grow in the soil of exploitation and injustice . . . The danger in treating local revolutions as part of a worldwide conspiracy and not as expressions of nationalistic feeling and indigenous political sentiment is that so faulty an analysis cannot be the basis of a practical strategy. That lesson became clear in Vietnam and, I fear, will be taught to us again. Where the greatest power in the world scares itself with a set of beliefs that have at best only a tangential connection with the reality of revolution, that nation becomes a menace to itself and to others."

*Intervention and Revolution,*
*America's Confrontation with Insurgent Movements Around the World*
By Richard J. Barnet

# CONTENTS

# INTRODUCTION

Sandinista, Nicaragua, *contra*, Honduras, intervention, CIA, Somoza, human rights, *desaparecidos*, Big Pine II, Managua, Jalapa, Tegucigalpa. They are words involved in the volcanic mix of events, the upheaval underway today in Central America—centrally involving the United States.

To most Americans, the situation is confusing. What is it all about? What of these warnings about the "covert war" the U.S. is waging against the government of Nicaragua, of the American military build-up in Honduras, of "another Vietnam" in the making?

I have been a journalist for over twenty years, specializing in investigative reporting: trying to get past the layers of confusion to find out, as best I can, what is "really" happening—and telling that story. I have received a number of awards for this work. I've written two earlier books, concerning nuclear power and toxic chemicals. I am also a TV news anchor, a radio commentator and a journalism professor at the State University of New York, College at Old Westbury.

With two draft-age sons, 20 and 18, to whom I dedicate this book, I have been especially interested in finding out what is happening in Nicaragua, since I don't want them forced to risk their lives for specious causes. My attempts to clarify the reasoning and consequences of our Central American policy led me to the leadership of the Nicaraguan Sandinista revolution, to the war zone and urban *barrios* and countryside of Nicaragua, to a U.S. military base camp in Honduras, to U.S. officials in the region, and to, in Miami, a top leader of the Central Intelligence Agency-supported counterrevolutionaries.

The following is a record of a journey and an investigation. I invite the reader to share my impressions and discoveries. We received the facts far too late when it came to the Vietnam War. If we had known earlier what we learned late, perhaps that disaster might have been avoided.

Here, then, is an attempt to give light on what some say could be a new Vietnam.

KARL GROSSMAN

New York
1984

# "THE FIRE DOESN'T SPREAD TO WHERE THERE IS NO DRY WOOD"

The 737 jet from Miami makes a sharp dive zooming through the high mountains towards a city in their midst: Tegucigalpa (Tey-góos-i-galpa).

Ask 10,000 Americans what the capital of Honduras is and if one names Tegucigalpa, I'd be surprised.

Down there, beyond the tin-roofed shacks and grinding poverty that flashes before you as the plane makes its abrupt descent, is a place which most Americans don't know about, but it surely knows about America.

The first thing you see past the entrance of the shabby airport building, past the police who are part of the army and are dressed in antique U.S. military garb, including Sam Browne gunbelts, and with some brandishing automatic weapons, is the sign: "Holiday Inn © Plaza, Welcome to Tegucigalpa Honduras C.A."

Waiting for bags to be searched, inch by inch, by inspectors, I notice that a C-130 U.S. Air Force Military Air Command camouflaged cargo plane has landed, following the Tan Sahsa Honduran jet I came in on. I glance back through the window on the airport runway several minutes later, and there is another U.S. Air Force Military Air Command camouflaged C-130 landing. I do not spot the American I boarded with in Miami who said he was in "the grain distribution management business" and lives in Tegucigalpa, and was commenting about "an invasion" of Tegucigalpa by the U.S. military and CIA. He told of going to a favorite restaurant and coming upon a U.S. "Airborne general and his staff, Honduran brass and a bunch of CIA sitting there."

I asked how could he tell people were with the CIA?

"The CIA is crawling all over the place," he replied. "You get to be able to recognize them." He went on about how his appearance caused the group to speak quietly, and then several in it left. He expressed concern about the U.S. military "having a war within commuting range. They'll be able to fly from [Fort] Bragg in the morning, be in Central America in three hours, and be back for cocktails at the Officers Club that night to tell the other fellows about the war down there. It'll be damn convenient. They didn't have anything like that in Vietnam."

He asks why I am going to Honduras. I tell him I am a journalist. He looks unsettled, sorry for having spoken. He advises "write about food," as he drifts away in the line for the plane.

Behind me on the slow-moving Honduran customs line is an affluent Honduran, also arriving on the flight from Miami. He comments on airport service. "It takes a long time to get your bags here because the people are very dumb."

Behind him is a Nicaraguan expatriate, William Chirip, who lives in Miami where he is a salesman for OTC Pharmaceutical Products, Inc. of Miami. He says that now in Nicaragua "there's no opportunity to do business." The Sandinista government "says it is exploitation to sell medicine"

*UPON ENTERING HONDURAS: The first thing you see.*

and has gone into the wholesale distribution of medicine itself, complains the 44-year-old Mr. Chirip. "Well, medicine is a business like food," he says. The Sandinistas "are just puppets of Cuba. This is the truth." Chirip says the attitude of the Sandinistas toward the people of Nicaragua is "give them a gun, a meal and a promise." He is in Honduras to do business.

So is Donald J. Jasieniecki, assistant director of sales and international operations for Pan American Life, a New Orleans-based insurance company who is in front of me on the customs line as the Honduran inspectors, backed by the stern-looking police, keep going slowly through everyone's bags. I watch as they take apart a box of Fruit Loops a boy farther up the line has brought in his suitcase from Miami. "We're one of the first life insurance companies established in Latin America," Mr. Jasieniecki is saying. But there has been increasing "competition from local companies," says the U.S. insurance man. "That's why I'm here."

Finally through customs, I am in a taxi heading for Tegucigalpa. The billboards fly by: Zenith, Coca-Cola, Pepsi, American Express. It would seem we are in a subsidiary of the United States.

"The U.S. ambassador to Honduras lives in an enormous mansion on a hill overlooking the city," says a former Peace Corps volunteer sharing the taxi. "It's fitting. He's the Big Man in town."

After registering at the Hotel Alameda, leaving my luggage in a room, flipping on the television for a minute and being greeted by a commercial for General Electric, I am off to interview Dr. Ramón Custodio, a doctor, a founder and former president of the medical college in Tegucigalpa and president of the Committee for the Defense of Human Rights in Honduras.

"Our government is being expounded as an example of what a democratic regime is," says Dr. Custodio. "The strongest ally for the Reagan administration in Central America is Honduras."

But the nation is far from a democracy, says the physician, sitting in his apartment in the center of Tegucigalpa. "In the last two years, there has been an increase in *desaparecidos* (disappeared persons). It is a disturbing pattern." There have been thirty to forty disappearances a year in Honduras in

*DR. CUSTODIO: "An increase in* desaparecidos*"*

recent times. "Some were politically active, some not," but mainly the aim is to "repress dissident people." Some bodies have been found in "clandestine cemeteries." The judicial system refuses to investigate the disappearances or take any action against the "sustained systematic suppression" going on in the nation. Honduran police will often keep people in custody without a trial for weeks, and there have been numerous cases of torture by police. Meanwhile, the government is "trying to control every organized group in the country: the trade unions of workers, of teachers, student associations, peasant groups." The year before, four trade union leaders, "people who the government couldn't control," were killed. Now the government has its supporters in these positions.

The government, Dr. Custodio continues, has steadfastly insisted that there had been no disappearances even after a former chief of Honduran military intelligence, Colonel Leonidas Torres Arias bolted to Mexico in 1982 and declared "there is a preventive war that is going on to suppress every dissident in Honduras," and "that war is being led by General Alvarez." (General Augusto Alvarez Martinez is the chief of the armed forces of Honduras.) Dr. Custodio says the mother of a disappeared man took a tape of the Torres press conference, held in Mexico City, to a Honduran judge to press her search for her son. "The judge told her that was not proof in Honduras."

There has been a "rise in power" of General Alvarez, says Dr. Custodio, and the general works closely with the U.S. ambassador to Honduras who is usually "behind the people in power" in the country.

The Honduran armed forces are being rapidly expanded. The army gets its recruits often "by force," according to the doctor, taking youngsters "as they come out of schools, cinemas, offices." As to a need for a military build-up in Honduras, Dr. Custodio says intensely: "We have many political problems, many social problems, many economic problems. We don't have military problems." But the rapidly accelerating U.S. military build-up in Honduras is "weakening the democratic structure of Honduras."

Dr. Custodio, 53, whose education includes medical school in England and research in pathology in the United States, is asked why he puts himself at risk leading the 100-

member private human rights group. "It's my duty to defend human rights where very few speak out," he answers. "I know how to say it, write it; maybe I have the guts for it. I have the moral duty. I'd hate to be living in this country and be silent and be in the position of the many German people when Hitler came to power."

Driving back to the Hotel Alameda, I see graffiti scrawled over the side of a building suggesting that although many don't speak out publicly, there is an undercurrent of protest in Honduras. The words say: *No Bases Militares Yankis* (No Yankee Military Bases).

Waking up the following morning at the Hotel Alameda, I feel placed in a scene out of the film: "Missing." It is the episode where the American couple find themselves in a hotel just before the socialist government in Chile is overthrown, a hotel full of U.S. military who are obviously involved in the coup in Chile. It takes little analysis to spot the American military at the Hotel Alameda. Many are wearing, along with their civilian shirts and dungarees or chinos, shoes that one often sees these days in army/navy stores in the United States labeled "Vietnam jungle boots"—combat boots of black leather and khaki nylon first produced for the Vietnam war.

I follow the first two men who leave the hotel to their car in

*There is an undercurrent of protest.*

the parking lot. It is a new Ford station wagon with, inexplicably, decals for Mastercard and Visa on the rear window. I ask to speak to them; they wave me away.

A man with a plastic case with the name T. Sgt. Wallace on it appears next. I ask him where he's from. "From Ohio," he says. I ask what he is doing in Honduras. He realizes I am a journalist and says, "Can't speak," and hurries off.

Another U.S. military man appears. He has a nametag reading Major McGovern, U.S. Readiness Command. "Can't say a thing," he says, jumping into a car, a walkie-talkie in his hand.

There is what looks like an American at the hotel desk, but he isn't wearing Vietnam boots and it turns out he is an Englishman who works for the United Nations "doing flood control work here." He asks me about the U.S. government's military presence in Honduras.

"Think they'll have a go at it?" he muses.

We talk. He guesses that the U.S. might introduce its military into the area for combat "after your Presidential election in 1984."

An obvious American turns up at the hotel's front door. He is carrying an attaché case and looks like he is selling something. He introduces himself as "Jeff R. Ingram of the Inter American Geodetic Survey," and hands me his card. The Houston, Texas-based firm is part of the U.S. Defense Mapping Agency, he notes, and does "automated cartography" for the Department of Defense. He is in Honduras to work on "new maps" for the U.S. military of the Central American region.

"Looks like those will be needed?" I inquire.

"It's possible," he replies.

Later in the morning I interview Gautama Fonseca, a Honduran attorney and historian long involved in attempts at land reform in Honduras. He was the nation's minister of labor in the early 1970s. He prefaces his remarks with some history:

Honduras was discovered by Columbus on his fourth and last trip to the New World. It was a colony of Spain's until 1821 when it and the other Central American Spanish colonies gained independence. For a year those countries were part of Mexico but then split off and formed the Central American Federation, a dream of Francisco Morazán, a Honduran and early leader of what is still the country's Liberal

Party. Another dream of Morazán was having poor farmers share in the riches of the country. But the federation was broken up by local leaders in Central America "wanting control over local provinces" and by the Catholic Church "which owned vast land and held a lot of political influence as well, and did not want the federation.

"Throughout history there have been repeated attempts to join our countries again, but they never have been successful."

Morazán ended up being killed after a general "overthrew the government here. He wanted to take control of the precious wood business," the export of Honduran mahogany, cedar and pine, then done "in conjunction with the British."

Through the nearly century-and-a-half since, it has been a constant case of the military ruling Honduras, up front or behind the scenes, and foreign domination of the nation—with the United States replacing the British.

The U.S., through the years, has pointed to Honduras as being democratic because of elections. But these are typically "fraudulent," says Fonseca. "I am 51. From the time I was born up until today, I have never believed that there were honest elections in this country." U.S. citizens must "realize that elections in this country are very different than elections in the U.S. So when North Americans speak of elections as necessary first steps in democracy, they are speaking about something nobody believes in down here because they are a farce." When President Reagan and John D. Negroponte, the current U.S. ambassador to Honduras, now say they "consider" Honduras "a democratic country, they are only interested in the formal process," the veneer, not the reality.

As a result, there are "young people who are disenchanted with this and would rather go to the mountains and fight as guerrilleros" for political and social change.

Along with the military, the large landowners of Honduras govern the political process. U.S. corporations, including the banana giants United Brands and Standard Fruit, constitute four of the five main industries in Honduras and have "great influence" as well. U.S. companies have long made wide use of "corruption" to manipulate the Honduran system, Fonseca adds. American technical advisors attached to "public offices in the Honduran government" exert a "very decisive influence" on the country.

Fonseca's area is land reform. But, there is "no political will behind agrarian reform," and this is due to the resistance of landowning Honduran families central to politics and the U.S. multinationals.

He confirms Dr. Custodio's account of how the Honduran Army collects its soldiers. "The way they are recruited is very brutal. They take them by force, violently. They're kidnapped."

He speaks of disappearances and kidnappings of suspected government critics such as a "professor from the university" and "the dean of the medical college" both released weeks later in "lamentable physical condition."

Of his own safety, he says: "It is very likely that [being kidnapped] will happen any day, or they will kill me. We are

*FONSECA: "It is very likely . . . they will kill me."*

all mortals" and no one wants to die, but he feels he must live "according to my convictions." To be silent under the circumstances, "that would be a cowardly act."

Fonseca, educated in Honduras, Ecuador and Chile, says he is a believer in Abraham Lincoln's precept that government should be for the people, of the people, by the people, and in Honduras it is "government of the aristocracy, not the people." The consequent effects, he continues, are felt in hunger, illiteracy and malnutrition and an "insecurity" among Hondurans.

"Reagan is mistaken" in saying that revolution in Central America is being caused by forces from outside the region. "The fire doesn't spread to where there is no dry wood.

"Neither the Marines nor the Army nor any armed force is going to stop the revolutions if the social injustice continues." Several times in the early 20th Century, the U.S. Marines invaded Honduras. The nation's plight "is not a military problem," Fonseca concludes. "It is a social justice problem."

Ephraim Díaz, the only Christian Democrat in the Honduran Congress, and Carlos Roberto Reina and his brother, Jorge Arturo Reina, both attorneys and both leaders of the reform wing—called *Alianza Liberdad del Pueblo* or ALIPO (Liberal Alliance of the People)—of the ruling Liberal Party, are interviewed together later that day.

"We live in a formal democracy. We have the forms of a democratic system but we don't have a real, working democracy," says Díaz, 39, a graduate of Georgetown and Kansas State Universities with degrees in economics. In 1981, after eighteen years of military rule, elections were held but the "military has not diminished its influence. It has become stronger." He speaks of "widespread abuses: illegal detentions, an atmosphere of fear—more fear than we had before, selective repression not only of individuals but of organizations. The government and military have a strategy of control of organizations. Congress has become a rubber stamp." When it came to the "increased military presence" of the U.S. in Honduras in recent months, "Congress played no role at all. The country has lost all autonomy in foreign affairs. This country has become an occupied country . . . a base of military operations for the U.S."

It is "increasingly difficult to have a dissident view here," Díaz continues. It means "being called Communist. We have become a testing ground for the military and we don't really know where that policy is leading us to."

*DIAZ: "We don't have a real, working democracy."*

Carlos Reina, president of the Inter American Human Rights Court of the Organization of American States, adds that "the whole problem of Central America started with the shooting of Francisco Morazán in 1842." Five "very small countries" became vulnerable to outside manipulation. The United States, particularly with the construction of the Panama Canal and the development of giant banana planations in Honduras by U.S. companies, took that role. "Formally, we have a democracy," but in fact the military reigns and "at this moment" it is "led by the most conservative leaders. How to become a real democracy is the main problem we have." The political situation has worsened, the potential for democracy diminished, Reina says, by the new U.S. military involvement in Honduras. "We are an occupied country." Reina, 53, projects that in coming months a total of 20,000 U.S. troops would participate in military exercises and associated undertakings in Honduras. What is going on, he claims, "is a Vietnamization in this region."

Jorge Arturo Reina, former chancellor of the National

*Jorge Arturo Reina and Carlos Roberto Reina*

University, declares: "The Reagan administration says democracy is in danger in Central America. It seems to me the real crisis in Central America is not democracy but the lack of democracy." He speaks of systemic "violations of human rights" and "fraud in elections" in the Central American region. "The Central American people have to eat and have a right to live with dignity," and strive for this. But the United States, now hell-bent on stopping the Sandinista revolution by "restoring the Pretorian Guard of Somoza" in Nicaragua and halting the guerrilla movement in El Salvador, "has no interest in the needs and aspirations of the people of Central America." By its actions it has "opened the door to revolutionary movements" including "movements with Communist influences." It sidles up to figures like General Alvarez. "General Alvarez is not interested in hunger in Honduras. Poverty, misery, backwardness are not important." By blinding itself to social realities and being only concerned with stamping out revolution, the United States, "instead of moderating the Sandinista revolution, is producing a radical Sandinista revolution. Instead of cutting the influence of the Cubans, it has strengthened it. Instead of giving more strength to democracy, it is weakening it . . . Instead of helping Central America have peace, it is pushing Central America to war. Consequently, Central America can develop into a new Vietnam."

"One way out," he says, is the position of the Contadora Group—of Mexico, Venezuela, Panama and Colombia—which has been trying to develop negotiated programs for the problems of Central America. "It is urgent to have electoral processes that are really free and democratic." The extreme lack of balance in the distribution of wealth "has produced conditions" ripe for revolution. "When a very few become oligarchists, the very many become guerrillas. That's the position we are now in. We can stop that crisis . . . Honduras can become a real factor of peace in Central America, not an arsenal of war."

Jorge Reina, 46, continues: "From more war we will have more poverty, more destruction, more backwardness. So we would like to produce here a cry for peace, a revision of Ronald Reagan's policy toward Central America. Reagan calls it 'America's backyard.' It is a yard plagued by misery, hunger and poverty. It's not a garden. It's a desert that can be turned into a cemetery."

The Reinas speak of their own Liberal Party, the party of the Honduran president, Roberto Suazo Córdova, being dominated by extremely conservative elements, its functioning highly manipulated. They complain about a Liberal Party primary, held just the day before, being riddled with fraud. Between the two major parties in Honduras, the Liberal and Conservative parties, there is little choice. It is the military, and behind the military the U.S., they repeat, where the true power lies.

I leave the interview and return to the hotel's lobby. Out at the desk, a U.S. soldier, Sgt. Weller, is checking in. He is interested that I am a journalist. "I'm a journalist, too," he declares, "here to start on an army newspaper for Big Pine II," the massive U.S. military exercise beginning in Honduras. He won't say anymore.

# *APOCOLIPSIS AHORA*

I am approaching a U.S. military base camp in Honduras. Low, dark clouds hang above the camp which is spread out on a plain, mountains in the background. Honduran military bubble-domed helicopters dart around overhead. American soldiers in tropical uniforms can be seen working on tents. U.S. Army vehicles are rolling in and out.

I have been able to get out to the U.S. encampment being set up at the Honduran *Escuela Military de Aviación* (Military Aviation School) at Palmerola, about an hour-and-a-half from Tegucigalpa, with a crew from KMGH-TV in Denver, Colorado.

The American camp is mainly for the 1,000-member 43rd Logistics Support Group, from Fort Carson, Colorado, near Denver. The TV crew had asked permission to tape some interviews with local GI's, to show back home. Military brass at the U.S. Embassy in Honduras said they could interview some Fort Carson soldiers, but only in front of the gate to the base.

However, upon arriving, the crew is welcomed in. Indeed, the commanding officer of the 43rd and soldiers in the unit are waiting to be interviewed.

Says Colonel Roger Benson of East Jordan, Michigan, the CO of the 43rd, "This is very beautiful country. The people are very friendly." He explains how his unit is "responsible for logistic support" of Big Pine II which includes transportation duties and maintenance functions, "setting up showers, a fire department, water purification." The TV reporter, Tom Bearden, asks him about a comparison between the military undertaking in Honduras and that in Vietnam. "I have no comment," says the colonel.

But others seem better prepared for that question.

Specialist Lea Flute, 20, of Oakland, California, a chaplain's assistant, answers the question in front of the camera by saying, "I don't really think it's going to be another Vietnam" because "we are here for humanitarian reasons."

A few minutes later, I'm interviewing Sgt. First Class Glenn Meyers of Moorhead, Minnesota, a public affairs representative, and he answers that question with, "I served in Vietnam and I personally can't equate this particular situation to Vietnam. And I wouldn't want people in Minnesota or anywhere to think this is going to turn into another conflict. We're here for humanitarian purposes only."

*COLONEL BENSON: "The people are very friendly."*

I ask to go to a latrine, am pointed in the proper direction, and on the way pass a bulletin board which provides some insight to the humanitarian line.

"BIG PINE 2 NEWS FOR ALL THE TROOPS," says a notice. "Thursday's 'media day' was a roaring success. A few tough questions were asked of personnel during the media 'blitz' but they were handled in stride."

Evidently, the U.S. military learned from Vietnam the central importance of media coverage and has geared itself to trying to make sure that in the future an acceptable image is presented on the home front. Warfare has traditionally been accompanied by propaganda aided by censorship of the press, but in the new undeclared warfare of recent decades—"police" actions and covert war—new ways of image-projection are being devised. *This time* the U.S. military is going to be very careful about how it presents itself after public realization of the ramifications of U.S involvement in Vietnam ended that catastrophe.

So here, appropriately just before 1984, U.S. warriors are making it perfectly clear that their function is peace. An old public relations man once stressed to me, "PR has nothing to do with reality; it's an image you want to project." In these new, partly media wars, imagery is seen as essential.

*IN THE FIELD: An excitement among the GI's.*

We pile into some U.S. Army jeeps and drive around the base. There are more than soldiers from the 43rd Logistics Support Group here. U.S. Marines are busy setting up communications lines, I see a U.S. Army Ranger in camouflage uniform. "He's a Green Beret," a soldier in the 43rd says. "Most of the Green Berets are Rangers."

I am surprised by the number of women soldiers, and am told that about 20 percent of those at the camp are women. As a support unit the 43rd has a "large proportion" of women, a soldier explains. In the hot mess tent, the cooks are women soldiers and I see women, pounding away with hammers, involved in the construction of new tent platforms as well. Some of the jeeps that hurtle by are driven by women soldiers.

There is an excitement among the GI's. They seem exhilarated by having been sprung from Fort Carson and being in the field, doing what they have been trained to do: playing soldier and getting set for several months or more under canvas. "Doesn't bother me being in a tent," a 43rd sergeant says. "I was in a tent for three years in Nam." A decade later, the U.S. Army is again setting up camp in a far-off foreign land and one can sense that military pulses have quickened with the transition from stateside base boredom to overseas adventure.

A soldier arrives with a bag of mail. GI's scurry to see if there is anything in it for them. I walk over to one soldier lucky enough to get a letter but he is less than thrilled by it: it is a bill, mailed through the 43rd's APO forwarding box during its Central American mission—an address in Miami—for storage of some of the GI's property, in Colorado, while he is away.

A group of Honduran air cadets comes running down the road, seeming to have caught the excitement of the American soldiers—they're gung ho, flashing smiles, unlike the dour, menacing Honduran military I've come across so far.

The crew from KMGH-TV, a CBS affiliate, and I say thanks for the tour, and we return to the cab which took us from Tegucigalpa which had been waiting while we were shown around the camp.

Driving back through the poor Honduran countryside, passing people traveling with donkeys as they've done for centuries, seeing simple thatched cottages with little gardens outside from which subsistence is scratched, passing a group of vultures circling above, we finally arrive back at a Honduran police checkpoint near Tegucigalpa and then drive into this city of 170,000. On the sign over one of the main movie theatres in town, a multiple-screen movie in the U.S. mold, I notice that one of the films playing is *Apocolipsis Ahora* (Apocalypse Now).

That evening I go to a *barrio* or neighborhood of Tegucigalpa—the *barrio* of Pedregal—with members of the Federation of Honduran Women's Association. This is a group of well-educated women, many of them professionals: writers, lawyers, teachers. They look like members of any group of upper middle-class women, like the matrons of the East Hampton Garden Club, for example. But as I ride in a Volkswagen Rabbit with these ladies, I find that in this case appearances are deceiving.

The nicely-dressed, proper-looking women are speaking of the suppression of women in Honduras, the pervasive poverty, the further military domination of the nation caused by the increasing U.S. military presence.

One woman refers to the revolution in Nicaragua as "a complete and total revolution in which women had a major a part." She quickly asks that she and the other women not be identified by name because they fear reprisals.

"We have had to struggle step by step to be given the rights we have won," says one woman, speaking about female students finally getting into Honduran universities in any numbers in recent decades, and being allowed entry into professions. But, she says, there are great distances to go. In government, it is noted, there are extremely few women.

"There has to be change," says another. "But given the mentality existing here right now, such change is doubtful."

They speak of Pedregal and how they have worked to help this poor *barrio* organize itself by running leadership training, through educational programs, and with income-generating projects. But poverty is so awesome in Honduras, they say, that this is but a small dent against it. "These problems are deepening and getting worse under the present government," one woman says. "What they have done is just demagogy."

Of the U.S. military in the nation, another woman says: "With each day the intervention is greater. We consider ourselves an occupied country."

We arrive at Pedregal, a hundred shacks made of cement blocks and tin, spread alongside a brown river, the lights of downtown Tegucigalpa flickering in the distance. People from the *barrio* are waiting for the ladies to arrive and they greet them effusively—with hugs, kisses and many smiles. There are children, loads of children, with beautiful faces. A tour begins.

It is heartbreaking.

*IN THE* BARRIO

Families of ten and twelve are crammed into these little boxes called houses. There are the smells of poverty, the most awful poverty. Skinny dogs run amidst the rubble. There is virtually nothing in the shacks: pieces of cardboard for partitions, a few beds, little stoves. But the children smile and the mothers hold them warmly and the men strive for dignity under the circumstances.

Back at the Hotel Alameda later that night, a U.S. soldier in camouflage uniform is near the front desk with some men in civilian clothes who wear those tell-tale Vietnam boots.

Colonel McMonegal says he was originally from The Bronx in New York City but has been in the U.S. Army for many years. He states he is with the Army's Readiness Command and has been in Honduras for four months. "I came here to do site surveys." He is happy to converse with a New Yorker and comments about how difficult it is for the people of Honduras with their small incomes "to live. The prices here are no different than in the States," he notes. "I know. I try to buy from the local economy." He saw action in Vietnam but does not think there is a comparison. "This is not like walking into a temple. We share a Judeo-Christian ethic." Commenting on the Honduran military, he says it is "very professional. They just need equipment."

The next morning, I go to see another colonel—Colonel César Elvir Sierra, public relations chief of the Honduran armed forces. The foreign minister of Honduras from 1980 to 1982, he sits in his office at a former TV station, now the headquarters of the public relations division of the Honduran armed forces, on a hill overlooking Tegucigalpa. Before being allowed to enter, I wait outside and the home of the U.S. ambassador, on an opposite and equally high hill, is pointed out to me.

Colonel Sierra remains cool but nevertheless seems bothered by questions concerning charges of abuses by the Honduran military. The spokesman flatly denies any such abuses.

Of disappearances, he says "some people leave the country clandestinely." Such allegations "can be officially presented to the Supreme Court." Of claims of human rights abuses in general, he says: "We see it from a different perspective. We see it from a perspective of security."

He goes on to stress the growth of the military in neighboring Nicaragua. He claims that Nicaragua is building an armed force of 150,000 while Honduras has 17,000 in arms, 10,000 of them in the army. An assault by Nicaragua upon Honduras is "within the realm of possibility," says the colonel. As to Nicaraguan worries about an Honduran attack,

*COLONEL ELVIR SIERRA: "Some people leave the country clandestinely."*

"they are trying to use an external threat as a means to control their population.

"We now have the presence in the country of two subversive groups" with 200 people in them "in total." Some "deserters" from these groups "say they have been trained in Cuba." Since the Sandinistas took over in Nicaragua "we have had more kidnappings, hijackings, bank robberies" and "with all these acts there is complicity with the Sandinistas and the FMLN" *(Frente Farabundo Martí de Liberación Nacional,* the Farabundo Martí Front of National Liberation, the revolutionary movement in El Salvador. Augustín Farabundo Martí was an early revolutionary in El Salvador.)

"If El Salvador falls into the hands of the Communists," Colonel Sierra says "we'd have a serious survival problem."

Of brutality and "kidnapping" in the way Honduras conscripts its military, Sierra "wouldn't exactly call it kidnapping." It's just that some Honduran men "won't serve and in some cases they have to be made forcibly to serve."

As to the Honduran military's relationship with democracy, Sierra says that when civilian government was restored in 1981 after eighteen years of military rule, "those who backed the elections more than any part of the population was the army. They were very democratic elections."

Of Nicaraguan counterrevolutionaries or *contras* operating in Honduras: "No, that's not true. We have no knowledge." But, he adds, "We have knowledge of three Nicaraguan groups operating in Nicaraguan territory." Reports of *contra* camps in Honduras are "a result of international propaganda." Of course, "It's impossible to control the border."

As to U.S. Central Intelligence Agency support of the *contras,* Sierra who has a diploma from the U.S. National War College hanging on a wall behind his desk, says, "You shouldn't ask me. You should ask the government of the United States."

Of the increased U.S. military presence in Honduras: "I think the military maneuvers here have achieved" for Honduras "a tranquility."

Over lunch with Honduran reporters and a journalism professor, I find the PR line of the colonel has few obstacles from becoming the accepted reality in Honduras.

I ask them what would happen if a Honduran journalist began writing about the existence of *contra* camps in Honduras—something widely reported in the rest of the world. "You can't do that," says Juan Ramón Martinez of *La Tribuna.* "The official truth is that they are not."

"A lot of time we depend on people from the States. We don't have access to information here," says María Luisa Castellanos de Membreño of *Empresa Hondureaña de Prensa.*

"There is repression here," says Juan Ramón Duran, director of the School of Journalism at the National University and Honduran correspondent for the Inter Press Service. He illustrates the possible fate of a reporter writing about *contra* camps in Honduras by passing a finger across his throat, imitating the slash of a knife. "As long as you don't write anything against the state, you can write." He says the situation is "worse" in El Salvador and Guatemala, "better" in Costa Rica and excellent—"there is liberty"—in Belize. Why do journalists keep at it under such conditions? "They try within the limits to inform," he says, but he adds that "a lot have gone into voluntary exile."

Indeed, at the table is Vilma Gloria Rosales, a reporter for *El Tiempo,* who says she has been living in Spain and she doesn't "like what's been going on" with journalists in her country.

A press conference is scheduled at the U.S. Embassy in Honduras. It is a heavily guarded building. There is a tall chain-link fence surrounding the structure. Guards with shotguns check all automobiles going into its parking lot, opening and inspecting trunks and using some sort of electronic device on a stick to check undercarriages. Across the street from the embassy, Honduran soldiers in full battle dress—helmets, camouflage uniforms, automatic weapons, and the like—are posted. Soldiers in such gear are also on duty outside Honduran government buildings, in front of banks throughout Tegucigalpa and just along the streets, providing for very martial-looking street scenes.

To get into the embassy, you must walk through a metal detector and then have your body checked with the same sort of electronic device on a stick they use out front to check the undersides of cars. You then surrender your passport to a Marine in a booth.

I am pointed to a room upstairs. One side of the room is crammed with television equipment—commercial-level videotape playback recorders and numerous videotapes.

There are two posters on the wall, one for a 1967 Museum of Modern Art exhibit of works by Jackson Pollack, the other for Earth Day 1970. At a long conference table on the other side of the room, across from the TV equipment, is a panel from the embassy.

There is a discussion between the panel and the fifteen reporters who have come about "ground rules"—whether what the American government personnel say will be "attributed to U.S. officials, diplomatic sources or U.S. official sources." Most of the reporters here this day are not posted in Honduras and want comments "on the record" with those talking identified. I am particularly insistent on this point having long felt that "off the record" briefings by officials shield them from accountability and responsibility and compromise the principles of journalism. One senses that such an "on the record" press conference is somewhat unusual here. Reporters stationed in Honduras are not pressing for it. Such reporters are often dependent on embassies or government officials for tips and news—or think they are.

Chris Arcos, the embassy's public affairs officer, opens up by taking a question about America's perceived central role in Honduras. There is a "significant U.S. presence obviously" in Honduras, he says. "You look at the top firms in this country, four of five are American: Standard Fruit, United Brands, Texaco and Amax, a mining company out of New York. So I think when you look at that in a country that's got four million people, a Gross National Product of $2.8 million and a per capita income of $580, you can see our presence is seen as sort of standing out." Mr. Arcos says he has served under three U.S. ambassadors in the three years he has been in Honduras and "each one of them has been accused" of having a giant impact on the Honduran government, of being "a proconsul."

"Is it not true?" I ask him. "Is it not true that this particular role is highly important in the politics of this country?"

"I would say, yeah," he replies, "it's important in the sense of the way they see us because they trade with us." He asks the embassy's economics officer about the breakdown of how much Honduran trade is with the U.S.

Larry Cohen says it is over 60 percent. "When Ambassador Negroponte wants to speak to someone in the Honduran government," says Cohen, "he doesn't have a problem of getting an appointment. There are just so many things going on between the U.S. and Honduras, he seems to be always involved in some level of negotiations or discussions."

I speak of having been told "by the head of the Honduran human rights committee, by a member of Congress, by others, that this country is far less than a fledgling democracy. That there are disappearances, there is corruption in politics, and the suggestion is made that your leader in this embassy isn't ignorant of these issues."

Arcos declares that the ambassador—who he notes is in Colorado on a vacation leave—"acknowledges that there have been problems in human rights. We don't scream about it. We do let the Honduran government know in the most diplomatic way our concerns and that we'd like to see some action, and there has been action taken on several occasions, particularly when Americans are involved. And no one will deny," he continues, "that there have been police abuses in this country." But, he says, "the police in this country is a branch of the armed forces. Police is the one that they have the most problem with. It is the one that is the most ill-equipped. And remember, we do not train police by Congressional restrictions that go back twelve years. So we have not been able to do anything with police in terms of training. They are grossly underpaid. I think they are paid under $100 a month. The average education is about third grade—second or third grade . . . And even General Alvarez has admitted publicly that he's had a problem with police. And the president has also addressed himself to this . . . In terms of corruption, corruption indeed was a problem here particularly in the last regime, the military regime. By the time these guys came to power, the current government, the coffers were empty, the till was empty. I don't believe that you have the magnitude of corruption you had in previous governments. There isn't much to take. The Honduran government is really hurting in terms of funds. There have been indications of some abuses. This is not Norway by any means."

I go on that "there is an overlying charge that the military, in fact, dominates this country although they claim to have a façade of a civilian government and the ambassador is . . ."

"In league," says Arcos.

I suggest that this is akin to the situation presented in the film "Missing," of the U.S. embassy in league with repressive elements of society in Chile.

"No," says Arcos indignantly. "You can't compare the charges that were made in Chile—whether they are true or not—you cannot make them against Honduras. I think that is unacceptable!" he insists. "Now this is not to say, if you have a human rights abuse, we only had one here and you had a hundred next door. I don't buy it because I think morally both are reprehensible. And that's our position. But what I'm saying is if the military has been in power for eighteen years, has run this place for eighteen years, and now you got into a situation where they're trying to make a go of it civilian-wise, you still have the basic habits of how people see and perceive the military, that the colonels sort of arbitrate power here. Well, I think if you ask the president of this country what he thinks, and if you ask him in terms of the formulation of foreign policy—as the perfect example, the peace proposal, the six-point peace proposal [to Nicaragua] that was made back in March of '82, the military had nothing to say and, in fact, the rumors around this town were that the military was not very happy, but the president went with it. The foreign office continued dialogue up to November; in fact, the foreign minister went to Nicaragua and there was concern that the military didn't like it. Maybe they didn't, but he certainly went there and met with these people and has continued a dialogue in a very discreet manner . . . It is an important factor, the military here, in influence but they certainly do not run the show."

Albert Barr, the embassy's political officer, answers a question about the effect of the increased U.S. military support on the Honduran government and "whether it is strengthening the military and creating problems for those who want a true, civilian, democratic government in Honduras." He replies: "Someone who's been in Honduras a lot longer than I has said the military in Honduras can squash this government with ash trays if they wanted to. So they don't need increased U.S. military assistance to take over this government if that's what they wanted to do. I think that the increased American influence in Honduras is a factor which helps democracy, whether it's military or not."

I ask Colonel Jim Strachan, an Army Ranger with the U.S. Command in Panama and public affairs officer for Big Pine II, about whether "another Vietnam" could be in the making in Central America. I note the huge array of battle ribbons on his chest and say he must have been in Vietnam, so he would be in a position to make a comparison. He acknowledges he was in Vietnam. He goes on to give a lengthy and ultimately somewhat contradictory variation on the "humanitarian" theme.

"Certainly there is absolutely no intent that this exercise be provocative in any way, shape or form. And by the very nature of the troops that are here, for the Nicaraguans as well as anybody else who is here and has been through the area, there is no force constituted here than can be such a threat.

"For example, there are no combat units here during this exercise that are stationed in Honduras. The only combat force that is going to participate during the whole period is a Marine amphibious unit" of 3,000 which will "practice an amphibious landing with a Honduran batallion, and then they're going back to Camp LeJeune. The other 3,000 or so soldiers, sailors, airmen and Marines that we have here are in things like engineer batallions, aviation batallions, logistics support group, a combat support hospital, a radar detachment and one artillery batallion which we consider to be a combat support unit training with Honduran soldiers. It doesn't constitute a combat unit in that it doesn't have a mission to close with or kill or capture the enemy. It supports other forces. So in a very real sense we have no combat troops here that would constitute any kind of provocation.

He speaks of "the composition of our people. Most are things like truckdrivers and engineers and doctors, well-diggers, water engineering detachment for potable water and sewage sanitation and vector control of mosquitos—a whole host of things that are going to be assisting in national health projects. . . And our helicopter support obviously, which will even be flying food out to refugees. So we think overall the whole positive thrust to come out of this presence is going to be very favorably received by the Hondurans as a country as a whole. We hope to be able to make significant inroads in improving the national health picture in this country."

But when asked about the specifics of military units coming into Honduras he lists a 50-member headquarters unit, the 1,000-person 43rd Logistics Support Group, the 480-member 101st Aviation Batallion with 34 helicopters, the 46th Engineering Division with 600 construction engineers, 85 Seabees, twenty more Navy personnel to "work with the Honduran Navy," 300 Air Force personnel "involved in the deployment down and the re-deployment back," with another 100 Air Force people from the Tactical Air Command "with a couple of spotter planes who will be working with the Honduran Air Force improving their ability to make defensive air strikes," the field artillery unit, the Third Batallion 319th Field Artillery, composed "of 370 men . . . who will be working with Hondurans in fire coordination exercises," and 70 Special Forces Green berets "who will be working with four Honduran infantry batallions." The colonel goes on to say that Honduran military leaders "know that they have a lot of problems and they are asking us to help them solve them." The aim is to "give them better capabilities to deal with their national defense challenges." He says the U.S. involvement will mean "about 6,000 Honduran military personnel will in some way be touched by one phase or another of the exercise."

Barr, asked about the likelihood of U.S. actions setting off a "military spiral in a region that has not been terribly militarized," says the region "has become militarized. The

*AT THE U.S. EMBASSY BRIEFING: Colonel Strachan, press attaché Callahan.*

Soviet Union and Cuba have supplied more military equipment to Nicaragua than is possessed by all its neighbors together and that will represent an opportunity, wouldn't you think?—a Honduras that's increadibly weak next to a strong Nicaragua?" He continues that "U.S. policy is to provide a credible defense." Further, he says the "Hondurans complain they cannot afford to build up their defense forces. They don't have the money. They say that should be our burden." Honduras, he notes, has an annual military budget of $45 million. As to any defense arrangements between the U.S. and Honduras, Barr cites a 1954 "military cooperation treaty" and the Rio Treaty, but says it is questionable whether the U.S. has a treaty obligation to go to Honduras's defense if there would be an attack from Nicaragua. "I don't think we're bound together. The Rio Treaty is a bit difficult to invoke," he says, because it provides for a shared defense only when a signatory nation is threatened by an "extrahemispheric power . . . All we've said so far is we're a friend, an ally of Honduras, and if they came under attack, we suppose friends would stand with friends."

I ask him about what he thinks the likelihood is of a Nicaraguan attack. He says "very low" and adds that he bases his evaluation "on my perceptions of what the Nicaraguans ought to be thinking, and I think the Nicaraguans would be stupid to attack, a conventional attack coming across the border. Yet people do stupid things. The point is they do have tanks down at the border where the invasion route ought to be."

Barr and the embassy's press attaché, Robert Callahan, refuse to comment on any embassy involvement with the *contras* based in Honduras. "It's the policy of the government," says Callahan, "to withold comment on any questions of intelligence."

As the press conference nears an end, political expert Barr stresses that Honduras is "very new at" democracy. Still, he says, it is "a functioning democracy. It's not the United States. It's not England, but it's more than Nicaragua."

And Callahan makes a point of emphasizing that "there is almost a total absence of anti-Americanism in this country . . . Even in the democratic left, which often critizes American policy, there is none of that viceral anti-Americanism you often find in other countries in Latin America."

Outside the U.S. Embassy, a reporter stationed in Honduras points out to me where the embassy building was machine-gunned in 1980. The guards in front of the building are still busy. The Honduran troops in battle regalia still wait anxiously. *"Almost a total absence of anti-Americanism in this country,"* the American PR man had said. The U.S. soldiers going to Honduras are mostly *"things like truckdrivers and engineers and doctors, well-diggers"* and such, insisted the Ranger colonel, and they'd be *"assisting in national health projects"* and the U.S. helicopters would be *"flying food out to refugees."* But when it came to an accounting of units and a discussion of what the Honduras military brass had in mind, many of the U.S. military were from combat units. I wondered who were the bigger bullshit specialists? Was it Colonel Sierra, Honduran armed forces spokesman and the very picture of the modern banana republic colonel who simply denied everything, or these guys from my own country stretching points, slickly trying to manipulate the media-dominated homefront.

Ian Cherrett, I figured, would be a neutral amidst all this. For ten years, Cherrett, 37, had been living in Honduras working in Central America for a Dutch aid program, Humanistic Institute for Development Cooperation (HIVOS). He is English, an economist who is a specialist in rural development, and married to a Honduran.

First of all, he is saying, large amounts of U.S. financial support that has been going to Central America, "particularly in terms of loans . . . ends up in Southern Florida . . . That's where all the money, all the capital from Central America goes—to Miami, or into Panama and offshore banking centers."

This transfer of money "works in a number of ways, all sorts of ways," Cherrett explains, "from the most crass ways whereby the army officers' wives carry suitcases of dollars to Miami to people receiving loans for investment and, in fact, they invest say 50 percent of the money they receive; the other 50 percent is transferred abroad." In Central American governments, cuts are "always taken in programs. The level of corruption here is incredible. They've got a nice word for it in the local language here, which in English would be chip. They would say, 'Do you got your chip?' Which comes from wood chip because the term is the term of when you are cutting up wood to make firewood. So everybody gets his piece of the trunk.

"A lot of the officials" of the U.S. Agency for International Development, AID, "the professionals, know this. You have a lot of competent professionals. Unfortunately, your professionals in the foreign service, in AID, don't have much power. What I call the politicians do."

Further, there is "not a coherent aid program here. It changes. And the problem is that every time it changes, there's new personnel, new policies on what was begun. Any coherent aid program has to have a certain lifetime, it has to be followed through. But what happens is you bring in a number of vehicles, you bring in some expertise and you initiate a program. And you go to the ministry a year later and all the vehicles are lying there because there's not the follow-through, so there's not the maintenance of vehicles."

Massive aid is "not the answer. It might be an important answer, but it has to go with certain socio-economic structure. There was a large level of investment during the 70s in Central America and I consider one of the results of that is the level of instability that exists now, because it has been concentrated in a very few hands and has definitely disrupted the economy.

"In this part of the world," Cherrett continues, "I would say democracy has never really existed. You've had the type of politics which could be called clientele politics. The parties, traditionally, have been set up by large landowners. In their areas the landowners have control of a certain population. In return for giving allegience to them, they provide certain services to that population. They provide them with security in terms of land—they prevent other people from coming in and taking them off the land. In terms of disaster, drought, they would often provide food supplies. This is the kind of relationship which existed in most societies, for example, in western Europe in the Middle Ages. These large landowners have allied themselves in certain parties and the politics that they manage is based upon these particular individuals fighting each other for power." He says "a reflection of that" was the primary election just held for the Honduran Liberal Party. "The types of fraud carried out were so blatant: fifteen year olds taken to vote three times. A total fraud in the elections."

Asked whether the sort of revolution that happened in Nicaragua is inevitable under such conditions, Cherrett says: "Yes. I mean the only way to stop it, as far as I'm concerned, is to maintain a military apparatus which is going to maintain a level of control and repression." Such an example, he says, is Guatemala since 1954 when the Central Intelligence Agency engineered the overthrow of the democratic government of Jacobo Arbenz and a series of military governments took over. Now, in Guatemala, "every time the military apparatus relaxes, you have an explosion."

What about the claim that revolution is being exported into Central America by Cuba and Russia? "Obviously Castro, Russia, everybody is going to try to take some advantage. But it is not they who created the conditions. It's the chemistry of the area," he says.

As to the Reagan administration's "east-west theories, the domino theory, is there any legitimacy in any of that?"

"In the sense that it becomes a self-fulfilling prophecy," says Cherrett. "I personally don't see, I don't understand the thing about left and right. I see the United States and Russia involved in a power struggle. Now, to me, if the United States is concerned about insuring that Russia is not going to build up some strength to be able to overthrow the United States or something, the key issue to me is to create a network of commitment with societies so Russia is not going to be able to exploit them. Now, I don't see what that network of commitment has to do with particular ideologies of those governments. It seems to me that the United States has quite happily done a deal with China, has quite happily managed to incorporate Yugoslavia into the western system to the extent that Yugoslavia is now an important bulwark against Russia.

"You have to do an analysis of social processes. Look what's happened in Chile, or in Haiti. You may deal with people who are preventing change so the only way they can maintain themselves in power is by force. You've got to recognize as the economy changes, social structures change and there'll be changes in the power structure. To me, you have to promote and support those elements involved in change which are going to, at the end of the day, democratize. Democracy is a very fragile thing, and it's so easily crushed. And all I'm saying is that change is a fact of life. You either prevent change, and then it occurs in a violent and often a brutal way, or else you try to understand what's happening and relate to the change process, and therefore you can help influence it or moderate it and end up with it being democratic.

"You can stop what was happening. We'll say, 'We stopped the Communists from taking power.' But you've got to have something more than that. I mean there are reasons for what has happened. You've got to try to have some policies for going beyond that point; otherwise you are going to be stuck in maintaining and supporting highly repressive, bloodthirsty regimes forever. And the blood might flow this year and it might pacify the country. Then in the next generation the same thing is going to happen, which is what has happened in Guatemala since 1954. So all I'm saying is where do you go from here? It is a messy situation, it is a difficult situation, and I'm not denying that the United States has certain interests to preserve. And that requires a very delicate touch. And that is the last thing that I see coming out of Washington."

As with the aid program, there is also "a lack of coherency" in U.S. foreign policy," says Cherrett, an absence of "a perspective which sees foreign policy in a long-term perspective. Since I've been here, my impression has been more and more that U.S. foreign policy is a cheap ball game for domestic politics and people are more concerned with scoring goals against each other at the expense of other countries."

Particularly under the Reagan administration, foreign policy "has been handled by what I would call politicians, people who have nothing to do with the area, know nothing about the area, and have come in here to apply certain policies. The professionals in the foreign establishment who are highly competent, highly skilled people, although they may not tell it to you—I know they're totally embarrassed with what they're having to do. Their advice is ignored. And they're the people who I feel have some understanding of the area and some longer-term perspective. Now I would have thought, if you have a foreign office, the first thing you would do is promote people who know how to handle foreign relations, know how to relate to other countries. And they're the people, it seems to me, who don't get anywhere."

As to what U.S. policy toward Central America should be, he repeats it must be "coherent" and "long-term. In other words, even to negotiate—I think you can negotiate in Salvador—but to negotiate in Salvador amongst the guerilla groups you've got some very hard-line groups, some pretty heavy ones. You've got other people who are not. I mean, to me, you've got to have patience, and it means long-term negotiation with people. It's very delicate.

"The United States has one power in relation to Central America which forces even the most extreme Marxist-Leninists to think twice about installing an absolute pro-Russian regime. And that is: where in the hell would they get the money from to develop their economy? Russia is not going to provide it. The United States is the only country that

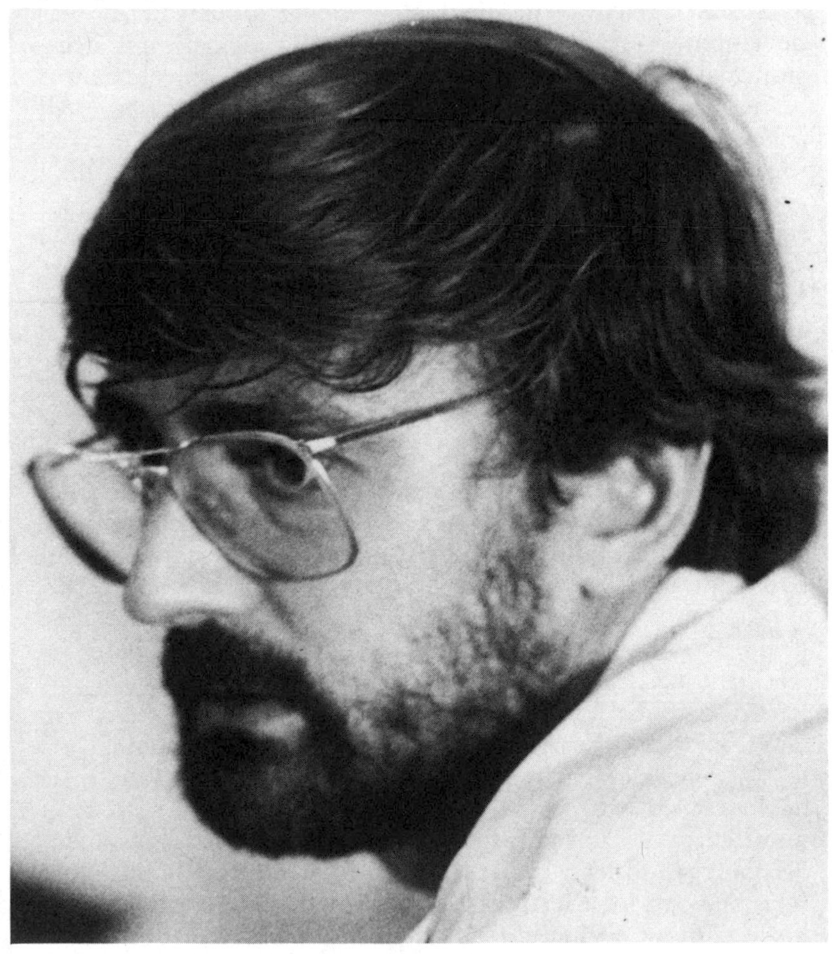

*CHERRETT: "Change is a fact of life."*

has the resources. And to me, that is her power." Also, America has the close-by markets. "The issue of development to me here is: it is not the amount of aid that the country receives, it's trade and it's price stability of the products that they have. To me those are the key issues."

As to U.S. troop presence in Honduras, Cherrett says: "Honduras was different from the other countries. It was developing its own process, one way or the other, with its weaknesses. There was agrarian reform, people were participating in the political process, people recognized that the peasants could have their own means of expression. It is that, as far as I'm concerned, which is being destroyed. It was development of the possibility of wider participation in decision-making. What I see happening is that only one element is being reinforced at the moment and that is the military. All other sectors of society are being weakened. This is seen in all the political parties at the moment; they are divided, falling apart. Even the governing party is divided. You see it in all sectors of society. In the peasant sector that I am working with, there is a weakening. The leadership is more-or-less falling apart. You know, a lot of money is being thrown around. I'm afraid you don't need much money to buy a peasant leader. And so I see the civil society here beginning to rot."

Of the Nicaraguan *contras,* "The operation is direct and very straightforward. There are large-scale operations in Nicaragua. Peole move back and forth. I remember one military officer I know who said to me, 'If it weren't for the *contras,* the [Honduran] national airline [Tan Sahsa] would go bankrupt.' "

Cherrett is especially worried that, because of the way political and economic dynamics are impacting on the environment in Central America, "if no real change occurs in this part of the world within the next twenty years, it will be too late." There is "the total destruction of the environment going on at an accelerated rate." If this is not stopped, "you'll be dealing with another set of Haitis. Haiti is a dead loss. I wouldn't work in Haiti because there's no possibility of development." But in Central America "there is still sufficient forest cover left, there is still a possibility that if changes are installed now, this could be stopped and a more rational system designed; otherwise, as far as I'm concerned, within twenty years it's going to be too late." One of the "direct results" of the forest cover being destroyed—in Honduras to make way for wealthy land-owners to set up cattle ranches—is that there is "increased vulnerability" to the "more extreme climactic variations" of the region. As a result, "this city"—the city of Tegucigalpa—"is drying out. This year, there were two or three weeks when there was no water." The destruction of forest lands has meant a "destruction of the watershed, so the water does not percolate into the subsoil, so you have a drying up of sub-soil water." Speaking of environmental issues further, he discusses the export into Central America of agricultural chemicals restricted or banned in the United States, such as DDT. "As a result" of the export of DDT into Honduras "the mosquito here is now immune to DDT. Malaria, which had been totally eliminated, is now back." DDT is being sprayed "even in the cities."

I ask Cherrett why he continues to knock himself out against such odds, amidst such grave troubles. He pauses, and says: "I have a lot of respect for the people here."

I go to pick up bags in my room at the Hotel Alameda. As I walk down the hall, I pass two Honduran soldiers in full battle dress wielding automatic weapons going through the hotel looking for something or somebody. I take my luggage to the lobby. A group of U.S. soldiers—again obvious by their Vietnam jungle boots—lounge on couches in the lobby.

I run into another neutral near the desk.

Douglas Laing, an Australian, is director of research for the Swiss government-funded Center for Interstate Agriculture Tropicale, CIAT, and works out of the group's facility in Colombia. He says he is running a conference at the Hotel Alameda of representatives of the governments of Honduras, Nicaragua, Guatemala, Salvador and Costa Rica about beans.

Beans, he explains, are the "number one source of protein" in these countries and "they have a problem: bean production is declining per capita."

Farmers "can't afford chemicals" to use on beans so what CIAT is doing, he says, is "breeding" new strains of beans "for resistance."

He comments that as we speak "upstairs you have around a table, working together, people from all these countries. The Honduran representative sits with the representative from Nicaragua and with the representative from Salvador and so on." He bemoans the usual divisions between the nations of the area. Indeed, notes Laing, also members of his group from the Central American and Caribbean region are countries including Panama, Cuba, Dominican Republic, Guatemala, Costa Rica, Mexico.

"They have so much in common," he comments, not only common problems but similar cultures and a common peoplehood. "They *could* work together."

We walk outside. A U.S.-built Honduran military helicopter is making a low swoop over Tegucigalpa. "You know," says Laing, watching it, "the whole operational budget for agricultural research for this country is $215,000 a year. They could finance their whole national program for ten years with the cost of that helicopter."

Driving to the airport, I again pass the movie theatre I had seen earlier. It is still playing "*Apocolpsis Ahora.*"

# "A REVOLUTION IS LIKE THE EMERGENCE OF A RELIGION"

The flight from Tegucigalpa to Managua, the capital of Nicaragua, takes a half-hour. Geographically, the distance is not great. As nations, however, even in just the way they appear, Honduras and Nicaragua are very different.

On the airplane, I spoke about Honduras to the person alongside. Colonies, I suggested, often provide a good picture, as a distillation, of the mother country. English colonies were mirrors of England, French colonies reflections of France, Spanish colonies versions of Spain. Is Honduras, although originally a Spanish colony but now for many decades carefully modeled and shaped by the United States, a reflection—perhaps in the extreme—of the U.S.? Is the two-party political system of Honduras which, in fact, is a sham, the purported free press which it turns out is not free, the control of the nation by a ruling class, the manipulation of Honduran institutions by those in power, a caricature, a picture in the extreme of America? How much does Honduras resemble its twentieth-century mother country with elements that might be hard for many of us to perceive back home?

The Tan Sahsa jet lands in Managua. Unlike the airport at Tegucigalpa—done in Central American decrepit and swarming with stern armed men—the Augusto César Sandino Airport is modern. Its terminal building features wide expanses of glass framed in stone. Security is laid back. (No doubt it is a little less laid back since I left because within two weeks the airport terminal was bombed in a *contra* air attack; indeed the room where I waited while my papers were processed was demolished.)

Banners of cloth emblazoned with Sandinista slogans drape

the exterior of the terminal building, one of the last edifices built by the Somoza family which ran Nicaragua as a personal fiefdom for decades, until 1979 and the triumph of the Sandinista revolution. The banners give the structure the air of a college take-over in America during the 1960s.

Above the entrance way to the terminal from the field is a rendition of Sandino, a lit-up portrait. It is certainly not your usual super-serious Marx, Lenin or Mao head-and-shoulders. In his ever-present hat—a super-sized Tom Mix cowboy hat—Sandino in this picture, and in the many hundreds I would later see, gives the impression of a spunky, energetic revolutionary, kind of a smaller version of Marlon Brando's Emiliano Zapata in "Viva Zapata!"

There is not a soldier to be seen. Indeed, in the whole airport upon arrival I see only one armed man, a slight, young guard with a sidearm standing at the terminal exit, smiling and talking with another man. (When I depart, at a busier time, there are about ten soldiers around, in the typical uniform of the Sandinista army: fatigues and sidearm, a contrast from the Honduran martial presence.)

Although there are no men bristling with weaponry and projecting intimidation—so common in Central America—to be experienced when one enters revolutionary Nicaragua, there is a level of bureaucracy that can be agitating.

Entry forms, it seems, have to be filled out perfectly. The representatives from Nicaraguan customs say I have invalidated my entry form by correcting a mistake. I had written my birthdate with the month first and then the day, then realized the somewhat difficult Spanish instructions wanted the day first and then the month, so I crossed out the first notation and added the new one. I am given another one of the lengthy forms to fill out. But this time I don't place the address where I'll be staying in the correct place. I am directed that I will have to do this one again, too.

I am given a third form and do what I usually do at places where bureaucrats are extremely particular about form—such as at the motor vehicle bureau: make a stink. I insist that if this form is not acceptable, I want to speak to whoever is making these decisions, get his or her name, "photograph the person," and further I will not fill out a fourth form, and if Nicaraguan customs doesn't like my penmanship or how I fill out forms, it can expel me from the country right then on those grounds. My loud protest seems to be working. I get the form back and an O.K. to pass, although I notice that it is not my third version of the entry form but a fourth, filled out for me. Having to hassle with such bureaucracy is a bad note on which to enter any country, but as angry as I am about the red tape, I laugh to myself that I am able to make such a fuss here. A half-hour by air away, in Honduras, such a stink might have caused an entirely different scene. That such a man-against-bureaucracy eruption is apparently allowable in Nicaragua, I think as I get onto a bus to the hotel, would seem like some measure of freedom.

The scenery of Managua is a marked change from Tegucigalpa. Surprisingly to me, there are still plenty of U.S. company names along the highway. Billboards for Diners Club, Black & Decker, Bank of America, pass by. There is an Esso gas station, a Chevron gas station, a Goodyear tire store. There are even golden arches—a McDonald's hamburger joint in revolutionary Nicaragua! But the billboards for the U.S. products and businesses seem more fitting here than in poverty-strewn Tegucigalpa. The highway is tree-lined, wide and in excellent shape; the buildings on both sides of the road are modern and neat. It feels like Los Angeles.

There is no mistaking that a major revolution is going on. Banners hang all over—it isn't just the airport terminal that looks like a college take-over. Managua is clothed in banners and loaded with posters and revolutionary billboards: *Sandino Ayer, Sandino Hoy, Sandino Siempre* (Sandino Yesterday, Sandino Today, Sandino Forever), *Luchamos Para Vencer* (We Struggle To Overcome), *Con La Revolución Socialista* (With The Socialist Revolution), *Entre Cristianismo Y Revolución No Hay Contradicción* (Between Christianity And Revolution There Is No Contradiction), *Todas Las Armas Al Pueblo Para Defender La Revolución!* (All Arms To The People To Defend The Revolution!), and *No Pasaran* (They Shall Not Pass). And everywhere are black and red flags with the letters FSLN on them—for *Frente Sandinista de Liberación Nacional* (Sandinista Front of National Liberation). They are the flags of the Sandinista movement. In huge white letters on a mountain overlooking the town—like the letters HOLLYWOOD in the hills above that city—are FSLN. The license plates say *Nicaragua Libre* (Free Nicaragua).

The bus, with its radio playing revolutionary songs about struggling and fighting for the revolution, heads into downtown Managua which is still a wounded place—not from the fighting during the revolution but from the earthquake that struck Managua over a decade before, in 1972, killing over 10,000 people and destroying much of the downtown area. The tallest structure left standing, and it is still there, is the Bank of America building, designed by California architects to withstand an earthquake. Much of the rest of downtown is now cleared lots, grass growing where buildings once were. Here and there a skeleton of a building remains. The huge amounts of emergency aid provided to Nicaragua by the U.S. to help it recover from the earthquake, to help downtown Managua businesses rebuild, were largely stolen by the Somoza dynasty. This realization was a key reason why much of the Nicaraguan business community—notably the business people of Managua—joined with the revolutionary movement in demanding Somoza's ouster. Meanwhile, the Sandinistas have been otherwise too preoccupied, the nation's limited funds going to many other things, to divert money to downtown Managua revitalization right now.

The Hotel Inter-Continental is another large structure downtown that made it through the earthquake. In the shape of a Mayan temple, it was partly owned by the Inter-Continental Hotels chain and partly by Somoza. The Inter-Continental chain's ownership continues but Somoza's share is now held by the Nicaraguan government.

One surely doesn't get the feeling walking into the posh hotel that we are behind some Latin Iron Curtain as the U.S. administration would have us believe. On a pillar next to the desk is a sign for Rotary International which lists the weekly meetings of the Managua Rotary at the Inter-Continental. There is not a soldier to be seen (and I never did see one in the Inter-Continental), quite a change from the Hotel Alameda. The newstand contains U.S. publications: *Newsweek*, *Time*. There are U.S. paperbacks—from a book about "Kojak" to one on gardening. There are texts of speeches and essays by Fidel Castro, and a collection of publications from all over Central America, including many from Nicaragua. I buy the current issue of *Patria Libre*, a Nicaraguan magazine, and while waiting to check in, thumb through it.

My attention is drawn to an extensive article sub-headlined: *Pruebas irrefutables contra la CIA y el ejército hondureño* (Irrefutable proof on the *contras,* the CIA and the Honduran exercise) and headlined: *Angiguilada "Operación Managua 83"* (Annihalation "Operation Managua '83").

The piece includes eight pages of photographs beginning with one showing, in front of a U.S.-made military helicopter, a group of *contra* leaders including Tomás Martínez Tito, "*ex-oficial de la guardia*" (a former Somozan National Guard leader) and an Argentine colonel identified as Santiago Villegas. On the next page is a photo showing a sign over an entrance way which declares: *COMMANDOS BIENVENIDOS ESCUELA DE COMMANDOS FDN* (Welcome Commandos, Commando School FDN) and on both sides of the sign are lines of armed FDN or *contra* soldiers. The photo caption reads: *La "Escuela de Comandos" que la CIA has instalado en suelo Hondureño* (The Commando School that the CIA has installed on Honduran soil). The piece goes on showing photos of U.S. pistols and automatic weapons, and plastic explosives with, it is noted, "Made in USA" on them. It includes photos of and interviews with two purported FDN deserters who describe how the U.S. Central Intelligence Agency has been directing the *contra* effort in Honduras. Much of the supervision comes from Tegucigalpa, they say. The article ends with a photo of a former Somoza National Guardsman, José Benito Bravo, a leader of the *contras* and who it says now goes by the name "Mack," armed and out in the field with Colonel Villegas, the Argentine, who the article says is *"el assessor de la CIA"* (advisor of the CIA) at the *contra* commando school in Honduras.

As I sign my name on the guest register, I think that it's too bad that this sort of information is not widely available back home—surely U.S. taxpayers would like to see where their money is going.

That night at the Inter-Continental, Commandante Tomás Borge Martínez, the sole survivor of the three founders of the FSLN in 1961—the others were killed during the nearly two-decade struggle—and a principal in the Sandinista government as minister of the interior in charge of the police and internal security, will be interviewed by American reporters.

The interview will be held at the Nicaraguan government's press office at the Inter-Continental which, interestingly, is the seventh floor suite that billionaire Howard Hughes lived in during the time he used the Inter-Continental as a hide-out. Hughes, the morning after the 1972 earthquake, jumped into a helicopter out front and departed Nicaragua never to return.

First, however, I have another hassle with Nicaraguan bureaucracy. I am advised at the press office that I need a government press card to function in Nicaragua, and the cost is $5. "We have a shortage of hard currency in this country," explains Leonor Rondón, the deputy press attaché with the *Ministerio del Exterior* or foreign ministry. I assure her that I "have a shortage of hard currency of my own" but the matter of having to pay for a press card is far secondary to being required to have a press card from the government. In the U.S., as a founder and president of a press organization, I raised protests about the practice of police departments deciding who is eligible for a press card. Such cards are not needed for reporting, as such, in the U.S. but are necessary to get through police lines, for security checks by the Secret Service, and so on. I was critical—and continue to be—of what authority exists in the U.S. for components of government, like police departments, to decide who is or who is not a proper journalist, considering our constitutional guarantee of freedom of the press. In some areas of the country, such challenges from journalists have been dealt with by the creation of committees of reporters and editors deciding who gets press cards, rather than police agencies. And, there are journalists and newspapers flatly refusing to obtain press cards where the practice exists of police departments issuing them.

So here I am in Howard Hughes' old suite, as Nicaraguan security men—very young like the Sandinista soldiers—are beginning to arrive for Borge's appearance, arguing with Señorita Rondón about my freedom of the press in revolutionary Nicaragua.

Señorita Rondón is, meanwhile, about the opposite of Colonel Sierra back in Honduras. She is very pretty, 26, a University of Denver graduate, has a warm smile and is far from the picture of hard authority. She is telling me how she returned from Colorado to help in the revolution, how she believes strongly in it, how her family is deeply split about it, and of her difficulties in dealing with the U.S. media. Reporters in Nicaragua seem to understand what is occurring in the country, she says, but after their dispatches go "through their main offices back in the States" their stories often end up terribly biased. She says that *Newsweek* is "very negative," yet the *Washington Post,* owned by the same company, "has been pretty good."

I talk about the theory that big press in the United States is very much allied with other big businesses and their interests. She speaks about what she considers the influence "of the transnationals on how the news about Nicaragua has been manipulated in the U.S. It has been very bad for us." She goes on about how the Sandinista revolution has so completely altered Nicaragua. "For the first time people have a say in what the government is doing."

As enchanted as I am with Señorita Rondón, I still persist in arguing about the required government press card. Meanwhile, the security men want to check my cameras in the suite's master bedroom. If Howard Hughes only knew what was going on in his old suite . . . I also object about being parted from my Nikons. The U.S. Secret Service, when you cover a presidential appearance, checks your cameras but they don't take them from you, I argue. The security men smile and an explanation is made about how they will be very careful, they are experts in this, the cameras will not be damaged in any way and that the situation in Nicaragua is such that extensive security precautions must be taken.

So, faced with good-natured folk and figuring I have made my points, I surrender my cameras for a check on Howard Hughes' old bed—it doesn't look much different than any hotel bed—and give Señorita Rondón $5 so I can get a press card. But, when I sit and have a Polaroid photo taken of myself for the press card, I make sure to scowl—just to show this press card business is being done under protest. When Borge doesn't show up for an hour, I ask for my $5 back.

But then he does show up, along with a couple of soldiers in fatigues and more security men, these with Israeli-made Uzi submachine guns, the preferred gun of the U.S. Secret Service and apparently the weapon of choice of security people in most countries.

Borge is a little bull of a man. He says he has "so many North American friends that I have decided to learn how to speak English" but doesn't know English yet. So Senorita Rondón will do the translating. "First of all," says Borge, who is in a military uniform, "I'd like to ask a question: are you interviewing me?" Yes is the reply. "Then I'm going to put on a face of a person about to be interviewed," he jokes, making a serious expression and then smiling again.

I had read a good deal about Borge earlier. Now 52, he had fought against the Somoza dictatorship from the time he was 13, ending up for many of the years between the 1950s and 1970s in jail—which included extensive periods of solitary confinement and torture by the Somoza National Guard. The National Guard, in the final days of the revolution, killed his wife after raping and torturing her.

*TOMAS BORGE: Sole survivor of the FSLN founders.*

But despite his personal ordeal, the horror he has seen, he is full of life, sitting there fielding hardball questions from American reporters, some highly critical of the revolution of which he is so much a central part.

Question: "Sir, there is a good deal of criticism in America because there has not been an election in this country. Don't you feel that it would be advantageous to your argument that the Sandinistas have public support to have an election?"

Borge: If we would have had elections two year ago, and we are now speaking more seriously than in jest, the pluralism in Nicaragua would not have existed because the Sandinistas would have been elected overwhelmingly and there would not have been one single representative in the Congress in the opposition. At this moment, the Sandinistas have the overwhelming support of the people. If we are to look at it strictly from an electoral point of view, it would be more convenient for us to hold elections now. We do not want to play electoral games. We want to resolve the fundamental problems this revolution has and, considering that, we have two things to solve: first of all, we have to create a legal instrument that would guarantee the elections, and second of all, by creating this instrument we would be more in harmony with the goal of the revolution. It's a public promise that we have made to the people of Nicaragua and we will keep it . . . We will have elections in 1985 and they will be free and open.

Question: How is it possible to have free elections in the sense that Americans think of free elections? Political opposition is harassed and the press is censored or suppressed.

Borge: All of you know we are facing an emergency situation . . . We are facing a state of undeclared war. There are thousands of men that are fighting on both borders. We have received information that within the next few weeks this war will increase, get worse, and this has taken us to impose a state of emergency, a legalized state of emergency and we have established a certain framework of control that enables controlling the press. It's legal, and its objective is to try to preserve the balance of the internal situation. There are twelve political parties in Nicaragua including the Sandinista, and we hope that when this emergency is over they will express their desires, their ideology, and their programs freely.

Question: Are you concerned about alienating people in Nicaragua who were formerly sympathetic to the revolution?

I, myself interviewed a woman, Geraldine Macias who is the wife of Edgard Macias, a former head of the Popular Social Christian Party. She told me how hopeful they had been for the revolution in 1979 and how they made bonds to support the Sandinistas and participated in activities with them, and yet how disillusioned they are now. Her husband had to take refuge in the Venezuelan Embassy and was allowed to leave Nicaragua after the president of Venezuela intervened.

Borge: Unfortunately, the United States, generally speaking, propagandizes in such a form that either everything is white or black. Now, we say we're going to hold elections in 1985 but they keep on asking us. It seems as if the year 1985 is the year 2000. They think that we are liars. They worry too much and they put it as a fundamental thing, as the elections being a fundamental thing. I have not seen the same concern in the North American government over Chile. In any case, I will repeat again: consider that a country facing war will hold elections. Of course, they will say that in El Salvador there were elections, but do you think that the people will take seriously that there were elections in El Salvador? . . . Even though we say we are going to hold elections, no, they still call us the totalitarians. She [the questioner] asked me of an isolated case . . . The problem is that this Señor Macias may have affiliated himself with the CIA . . . It's a very isolated case but there are some people out there (who are) discontent with the revolution. And there are many more content with the revolution. Over 90 percent are not only satisfied but they're supporting it with their own blood; they're giving their lives for the revolution. A revolution always produces great and deep contradictions. A revolution is like the emergence of a religion. When Christianity evolved or emerged, many contradictions came about. And a revolution always creates enormous social contradictions. Otherwise it would not be called a revolution.

I ask him why he thinks the U.S. government is against the Sandinista revolution and is trying to terminate it.

Borge: When has the North American government ever let any revolution alone? I will give you many examples. For instance there was a democratic government elected in Guatemala, the government of Arbenz. It was overthrown by the North American government [in 1954]. In the Dominican Republic, also a democratic government was elected, and again [in 1965] overthrown by the North American government. In Chile, again a democratic government was elected (and) the CIA [in 1973] helped to overthrow the government of Chile . . . Whenever serious changes are beginning to take place in Latin America—for instance, like in Brazil [in 1964]—the United States has intervened, to change that, not to accept it. It would seem very funny if the United States would be content with the Sandinista revolution.

Question: Commandante, the Honduran government feels that a Nicaraguan attack is imminent. The result is, they think they desperately need help from the United States which apparently the United States is only too happy to give. Do you think the Honduran fears are groundless?

Borge: Sometimes it's very hard for us to hold our equanimity when we hear so much cynicism. In the last six months about a thousand Nicaraguans have been killed by counterrevolutionary activities, by counterrevolutionaries who have their bases in Honduras. Some of these deaths have also been caused by the artillery attacks from the Honduran army. I think we have had infinite patience. What would you think if we organized counterrevolutionary bands against the United States in Canada? What would you think if we would begin to organize blacks, Chicanos and discontented people in the United States and organized them in Canada and they would begin to make armed attacks into the United States? What would you think, sir? And they would have in Canada airfields, helicopters, planes, supplies, etc. I know I've just drawn a pretty impossible situation for you, but that's just to show you how we feel when we see that military bases are being organized and armed in Honduras. And counterrevolutionaries have killed thousands of Nicaraguans. We are really the ones who are being destroyed. They are calling us now the aggressors. It would be as if I would walk into your house, kill your son, destroy the furniture inside and still accuse you of being the aggressor. We have no interest in making war on Honduras. If we had wanted to, we would have had so many pretexts to do so. Never has a Nicaraguan plane flown over Honduras. Never has a Honduran soldier been killed by a Nicaraguan. Then why are they saying that we are threatening them? So for a Nicaraguan to hear a very arrogant voice accusing us of those things, it's very hard for us to listen to that.

Question: Do you deny providing aid and support for the anti-government forces in El Salvador?

Borge: Beginning on the nineteenth of July of this year we have agreed not to deny or accept that charge but to bring this into negotiations.

Question: I'm going to ask if the commandante and the rest of the junta would willingly step down if, after an election, they lost?

Borge: If we lost elections, I would stop believing in the human race.

Question: That's not my question.

Borge: Yes, of course, the electoral law will allow the party with the most support to gain power, but we say that it is inconceivable that we will not receive that great majority . . . Nicaraguans are not idiots. They are a people who have a sense of history, and I consider this to be a historical impossibility that anybody else would gain power.

Question: Are you worried about the U.S. military maneuvers on the Honduran border?

Borge: I want to say that Nicaraguans are not afraid, but just concerned. We are concerned that it might facilitate a direct military intervention. I will make a dialectic analysis of the situation. The proximity of the [U.S.] fleet has staved off direct intervention because the American people have rallied against the politics of the government. And the American government for electoral reasons appreciates the opinion of its people. This has also, at the same time, provoked a world reaction against Reagan's politics. We can say that the proximity of the fleet has made a very strong reaction. When the United States can place 16,000 men along the Honduran border, this exacerbates the situation. An incident might occur that will provoke this intervention. Therefore, we think that there is a great possibility that intervention will take place. The North American presence in Honduras stimulates the Honduran army and it also stimulates the counter-revolutionaries. And they become more aggressive; therefore, we can say they become more provocative.

I ask him, "Isn't Nicaragua helpless if there'd be a direct U.S. intervention?"

Borge: We have seen this possibility. And what would develop here is a popular war. Thousands and thousands of people would take up arms. I think the war would make it very hard for the interventionist soldiers in Nicaragua. Against a people in arms, there are no techniques, there are no technical weapons and there will be a great world protest, even bigger than the one there is now. It's not easy.

A question is asked about the Sandinistas exporting revolution.

Borge: One million weapons could be sent to Mexico or the United States and we know that a revolution could not take place. Revolutions emerge over concrete and objective basis within each county. Why was there a revolution in Nicaragua and why will other revolutions take place in other Latin American countries? For every 1,000 children who were born in Nicaragua, 200 died. For each 100 Nicaraguans, 50 did not know how to read or write. The National Guard assassinated over 200,000 Nicaraguans. There was not even liberty to laugh. Therefore the revolution emerged from determined, objective reasons. The infant mortality rate before was so high. In comparison with that, less than half of those children die now. It was not very easy to reduce the illiteracy rate, to become one of the countries that has the least illiteracy. The dark situation that existed in Nicaragua still exists in Latin America, and how can you ask that there be no revolution? They blame us for the revolution in El Salvador. How can we be to blame that only thirty families in El Salvador control all the wealth of the country? Why should we be to blame that thousands of children die there? How can we be to blame for the enormous differences between the rich and the poor in that country? How can we be blamed for the assassinations that take place there? How can they blame us for the small percentage of rich people and the huge amount of poor? In that case, we can only be guilty because we represent an example. And as an example, we do influence other peoples.

Question: Do you think that eventually the United States will accept this revolution and reach some sort of rapprochement?

Borge: The American government doesn't have another alternative.

Question: In the meantime . . . is there a possibility that Soviet missiles could be placed in Nicaragua?

Borge: That's a fable that was invented in order to put fear into the North American people. The Soviet Union has never proposed to us installations of its missiles in Nicaragua.

Question: In a hypothetical situation, if they were to, what would the Nicaraguan government do?

Borge: We promise, along with other countries in Latin America, not to have missiles installed.

Question: Is there any hope for the Contadora Group to bring peace between the U.S. and Nicaragua?

Borge: We should have some hope.

Question: Do you have hope?

Borge: Yes.

A question is posed about Nicaragua becoming a "satellite" of Cuba and the Soviet Union. Borge speaks of "our great and magnificent relations with Mexico" and says "just as we maintain relations with Cuba and the Soviet Union, the U.S. maintains that we are a satellite of them. I don't think our relations" with these countries "are any better" than with Mexico. "Why don't they call us a satellite of Mexico when we have such good relations in Mexico? But you will see here that we don't have the face of a moon or of a satellite because if we wanted to be a satellite, we would be that of the United States to save ourselves many, many problems."

I ask about the charge made by two Jewish Nicaraguan expatriates who went to see President Reagan at The White House alleging that the Sandinista government is anti-Semitic.

Borge: What happened was that these two men had their lands confiscated because they had ties with the security apparatus of Somoza. They left Nicaragua. The minister of tourism here is a Jew, and there are also other Jews in the government.

He is asked about a building formerly used by the Jewish community of Managua reportedly confiscated by the Sandinistas, and whether the Jews in the Sandinista government are still "practicing Jews."

Borge: I really don't know who are the practicing Jews in this country. I must suppose there are a few, but I really don't know even as minister of the interior. It's true that this building belonging to a certain Jew was taken away from him by the government, but it was taken away because he was a Somozista. Nevertheless, I invited a high-ranking Jewish leader to come to Nicaragua and we are willing to give back this house that was taken.

I ask Borge about the relationship between the Sandinista government and the Palestine Liberation Organization.

Borge: We are friends of the PLO and we are enemies of the Zionists who commit genocides.

I ask him, "What about the Jewish people?"

Borge: We are enemies of the Zionist assassins and not of the Jewish people.

"What about the PLO?" I ask. "They're pretty nasty—they assassinate."

Borge: They are struggling for the liberation of a Palestinian homeland. We are with the weak. The Palestinian people have been victims. We broke relations with the State of Israel because of the Lebanese situation, and also the Israeli government gave arms to Somoza in order to kill the Nicaraguans. They have given arms to the Honduran government to kill the Nicaraguans, and we have no gratitude. But one thing is the people of Israel who are in opposition to the policy of its government, and another thing is the government of Israel. The same goes for the North American government. We're not against the people of North America. We think that our warmest friends are the North Americans. And you will see it here for yourself. Our people, the *pueblo,* have a great love for the Americans because our people can distinguish the politics. The North American people are victims because . . . it's very sad to be hungry, to be poor, but it's even sadder to be duped.

Borge looks at his watch. It is 11:30 p.m. but he says he would still like us to accompany him to a *barrio* of Managua to "get a taste of the people of Nicaragua." Still full of energy, he strides out of the Howard Hughes' suite with the security men behind. We all jam into elevators, go to the front of the Inter-Continental and pile into a bus with Borge. A security man drives the bus; there are cars full of security men in front and behind it as it proceeds through Managua.

I am on the bus near a soldier named Daniel, 29—who doesn't want to give his last name. A Latino version of a young Tony Curtis, he had assisted in the translation up in the hotel suite. He explains that he knows English well because before he came back to Nicaragua to fight in the revolution, he was in college in London and at the University of California at San Diego. Of the revolution, he says: "I think it's great. I believe in it." Why? "Because it gives us dignity and liberty for the first time, and we cease to be slaves of a foreign bourgeoisie."

Borge is, meanwhile, conducting a running commentary with reporters in the back of the bus. After twenty minutes we arrive at the *barrio,* called Nuevo Libia.

Borge is welcomed as a hero. This *barrio* is in sharp contrast to the Honduran *barrio* I had visited. The people look similar, the soft brown eyes and wide smiles of the children are the same, but here the mood is jubilant, joyous. Sandinista posters are abundant. A hundred of the *barrio* residents march arm and arm with Borge chanting, "*Alerta. Alerta. La revolucion esta caminando a traves de America Latina*" (Be Alert. Be Alert. The revolution is walking through Latin America) *and "Patria libre o morir*" (Free country or death).

Borge breaks to go from house to house, shaking hands, hugging babies. The crew from KMGH-TV in Denver films away under a brilliant portable light, flashbulbs pop, and this old guerrilla, a hardened veteran of jungle warfare, carries on in a way that would make a media luminary such as New

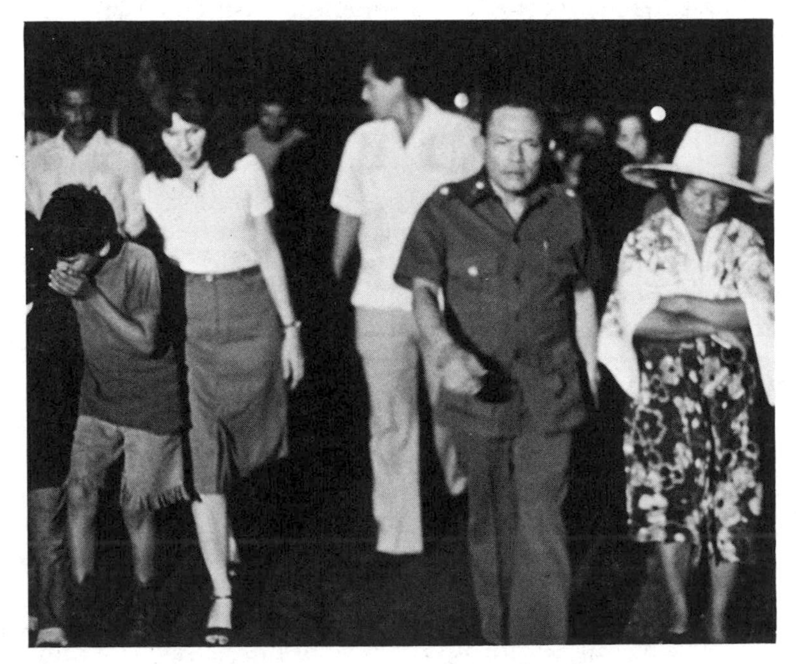

*BORGE IN THE* BARRIO: *Welcomed as hero.*

York City Mayor Edward Koch envious. But here, the realization comes back, the political stakes are very high. In one house is the widow of a member of the militia, his mother and the little boy he left. The soldier was killed several months before on the Honduran border by *contras*. His photograph and a citation from the government hangs on a wall. Borge speaks quietly to the family. He is feeling what he says.

He goes outside and now, to about 150 people, begins a speech discussing diarrhea—which might seem an odd subject but it is a major cause of infant mortality in Central America.

He speaks of the need for hygiene. "Mothers have to wash their hands after they take care of their necessities," he says. "They must clean their nails and not breast-feed their children when their hands are dirty. As soon as you see a child dehydrated, you must take the child to a clinic."

He thunders against "pushers" of medicine that simply "take the pain away." He says "commercial propaganda is used to fool you" and urges people to buy generic medicines. "Pain killers are a lot more expensive than simple aspirin."

He tells of how, with clinics now set up all over the country and a nationwide program of vaccination, "polio has disappeared from Nicaragua, malaria has diminished."

He talks about the "Literacy Crusade" in Nicaragua. He asks for a show of hands of people who "don't know how to read or write." A few raise their hands. Then he asks for the hands of those "if you learned to read or write in the Literacy Crusade." About a third of the group raise their hands.

After his little speech, he continues going house to house until shortly after 1 a.m. when we all go back on the bus.

He is still seeking questions. He is asked about the archbishop of Managua, Miguel Obando y Bravo, a staunch critic of Somoza but now a critic of the Sandinistas. Borge says, "We have no objections to him as an archbishop, but we have an objection to him as a reactionary political leader."

He speaks about elections in Honduras as "an electoral farce. The poor man who is president in Honduras has less power than the porter in this hotel. The person with most power in Honduras is General Alvarez."

We are back at the Inter-Continental, at 1:30 a.m., and in front of the hotel the show goes on. Borge is fielding a question about "a fear on the part of Americans that Nicaragua will suffer the same unfortunate fate that has befallen other small nations that have tried to accept aid from the Soviet Union and have become 'satellitized.' "

Borge: I think the American people are scared. We will never be a satellite of anyone. What sense does it make to have a revolution to become a satellite? So much blood is sacrificed to then become a satellite?

He cautions about our plan to travel to Jalapa. "There is a new offensive that is developing at the border. There are forces that are concentrated on the Honduran side." But, he adds, "journalists have an adventuresome spirit" and "the most beautiful thing in the world is to have a certain fear and then to overcome it."

# REVOLUTIONARY WAR . . . AND "PEACE AND LOVE"

I wake up early the next morning and take a walk from the Inter-Continental through the area where the earthquake struck and come to a monument several blocks from the hotel. It marks an event which was a catalyst in the final victory of the revolution, that triggered riots and strikes. Eighteen months later the Somoza regime was toppled.

Here a circle of sculpted stone slabs, including a tall piece pointing towards the sky, and a sculpture of a head on a column, commemorate the assassination of Pedro Joaquín Chamorro on January 10, 1978. Chamorro, 53, was the popular editor of the largest-circulation Nicaraguan newspaper, *La Prensa,* and a tough and consistent foe of the Somoza dynasty who spent time in jail for his opposition. At the time he was slain, he was regarded as the most likely head of a center-left government to replace Somoza. His murder by a group of gunmen connected to the Somoza regime, while he was driving alone to work at *La Prensa,* set off weeks of disorder. The day after the killing, 30,000 people marched through the streets of Managua, taking Chamorro's body to *La Prensa,* shouting anti-Somoza slogans. Some went on to attack and set fire to Somoza-owned industries and businesses seen as linked to the dictatorship.

The violence continued the following day with the setting fire to more businesses including the Managua office of the First National City Bank of New York. On the third day after the murder, 50,000 people assembled for the funeral; there were more anti-government protests and the intervention of the National Guard.

A national strike organized by the middle class followed to

try to force Somoza's resignation. Then came a step-up in the FSLN's armed struggle which, by the middle of the following year, culminated in the revolution's triumph.

I walk on, in the direction of Lake Managua—a huge lake on which the city of 750,000 lies—towards the *Plaza de la Revolución.* The plaza, the frequent setting of rallies involving tens of thousands, is empty on this beginning of a new day. Two Sandinista soldiers are posted at the entrance of the national palace, a seat of Nicaraguan government. *Palacio Nacional* and *Republica De Nicaragua* are carved in the stone

*Monument to Pedro Joaquín Chamorro.*

of the old building. A man is mopping the front steps. On twin Grecian pillars on each side of the entrance are large portraits of Sandino and Carlos Fonseca Amador who, with Borge and Silvio Mayorga, founded the FSLN. Along a series of pillars hangs a banner: *La Lucha Es El Mas Alto De Los Cantos* (The Struggle Is The Highest Of The Songs).

I walk further in the plaza this quiet morning going up to the Cathedral of Managua, its interior and roof destroyed in the earthquake of 1972, but its shell—its stone exterior and steeples—left standing. Draped across its front is a giant banner depicting Sandino against the Sandinista colors of red and black.

I walk across the plaza from the cathedral to where there is a memorial to Fonseca. It is Fonseca's grave. An eternal flame burns, making the monument resemble the John F. Kennedy grave in Arlington National Cemetery. *Jefe De La Revolución* (Leader Of The Revolution) is carved in the stone

*Grave of Carlos Fonseca Amador.*

of the monument. *Commandante Carlos Fonseca Amador,* it continues. *Nicaragua Entera Te Dice Presente* (Nicaragua Tells You You're With Us). *Carlos Es De Los Muertos Due Nuncan Mueren* (Carlos Is Of The Dead Who Never Die).

Before going to sleep the night before, I had read an article by Fonseca, written in 1968, regarded as the first major political analysis by the FSLN and on which the future strategy of the revolution was based.

Entitled "Nicaragua: Zero Hour," in it Fonseca railed at how "the people of Nicaragua have been suffering under the yoke of a reactionary clique imposed by Yankee imperialism." He spoke of Anatasio Somoza Garcia being installed as "commander in chief of the so-called National Guard, a post that had previously been filled by Yankee officials. This clique has reduced Nicaragua to a neocolony—exploited by the Yankee monopolies and the local capitalist class."

The article told of the "economic crisis" of Nicaragua. "The exploitation of minerals such as gold and copper, which is directly in the hands of foreign investors, pays ridiculously small sums to the national treasury through taxes. Parallel with this, the handing over of the national riches to the Yankee monopolies has continued to increase. In 1967, for example, a law went into effect that gave Magnavox, a company specializing in the exploitation of forests, absolute ownership of a million hectares of national territory. At the same time, the ruling clique handles the funds of the state banks as if they were personal funds, while fraud and smuggling reach staggering dimensions. The Somoza family, which had very limited economic resources when it took power, has obtained a vast fiefdom, whose domains go beyond Nicaragua's borders and extend into other countries of Central America."

The article went on to complain about hunger in Nicaragua and "numerous deaths through hunger" and various diseases. Infant mortality "reaches dreadful levels in Nicaragua. More than 50 percent of the deaths in the country occur among persons under fourteen years of age. Out of every 1,000 children born, 102 die. Six out of every ten deaths are caused by infectious—meaning curable—diseases."

Fonsesca hit at illiteracy. "Only 1.1 percent of the Nicaraguan population has completed primary school. Fifty percent of the population has no schooling whatsoever."

The article spoke of "a tradition of rebellion" in Nicaragua.

Indeed, walking alone in that *Plaza de la Revolución* that morning, I think of the more than a century of conflict in Nicaragua and of Nicaragua being—through all that time—the continual subject of a very heavy hand by American interests and the U.S. government: before Sandino, before Somoza, before Fonseca, before the Reagan administration's orchestration of the *contras*.

This plaza that I walk on, I muse, and the *Palacio Nacional* overlooking it have borne witness to much of this strife, these invasions and interventions.

Importantly, most Americans are not aware of this history—although Americans and America were principal participants.

I had brought two books covering the history of Nicaragua with me to Nicaragua. One, *Triumph of the People: The Sandinista Revolution in Nicaragua* by George Black, published in 1981 in England, is sympathetic to the Sandinista revolution. The other, *Nicaragua: A Country Study*, published by the U.S. Army in 1982, is not.

But both, interestingly, tell about the same historical tale.

"From the time of its independence from Spanish colonial rule in the early nineteenth century," noted the U.S. Army book, "Nicaragua has been ruled by and for a socioeconomic elite consisting of, perhaps five percent of the population . . . The state has rarely, if ever, operated in Nicaragua as an instrument working for and responsible to the mass of the population. Instead, it has served a variety of interests, both foreign and domestic, devoting the largest part of its energies to perpetuating the rule of whatever faction was currently in power. As a result, Nicaraguan history is replete with tragedy and frustration, leaving a heritage of national cynicism concerning government and deep distrust of foreign influences and intentions. As the dominant external influence in Nicaragua for the past 130 years, the United States is the focus of much of this suspicion."

Nicaragua's potential as the site of an Atlantic-to-Pacific crossing long served to cause foreign interest in the country.

The navigable Rio San Juan connects the Atlantic to Lake Nicaragua. That leaves "only a narrow strip of territory on the Costa Rican border to be excavated" as a canal to the Pacific, and this had "already appealed to the Spanish colonial engineers," *Triumph of the People* pointed out.

"Foreign interest in Nicaragua as a potential canal or isthmanian transit route grew steadily during the early years of independence," related the U.S. Army account. "Great Britain and the United States had the most direct interest, but even France tried to negotiate a canal treaty." In 1850, the two major rivals, the U.S. and England—without Nicaragua even being consulted—made a deal: they signed the Clayton-Bulwer Treaty in which each nation agreed that neither would have exclusive control over any canal in Nicaragua.

Meanwhile, a U.S. business called Accessory Transit Company headed by Cornelius Vanderbilt had already begun using steamers on the Rio San Juan and Lake Nicaragua and coaches on the thirteen-mile overland strip along the Costa Rican border to transport large numbers of Americans heading to California during the Gold Rush. In 1853, however, "control over the company was acquired, by somewhat devi-

ous means, by rivals of Vanderbilt," noted the Army study. "The situation led to an intense business struggle that had serious consequences for Nicaragua."

Indeed, the Army book continued, "events in the 1850s led Nicaraguans to question the relative advantage of their new connections with the United States. In 1853 United States Marines were landed at Greytown [on the Nicaraguan Atlantic Coast] to protect Accessory Transit Company property. The following year a series of incidents, culminating in an attack upon the United States minister in Nicaragua, took place in Greytown. The minister, who had made no secret of his desire to see the United States annex Nicaragua, used the incident to demonstrate United States power in the area. The sloop *Cyane* was dispatched to the port with demands for an apology and payment of an indemnity. When this was not forthcoming, the vessel shelled the town and landed Marines who burned the remaining buildings."

But that was nothing compared to what happened in 1855 when American William Walker and a group he called the "American Phalanx of Immortals"—men who were what was then called filibusters (irregular military adventurers or freebooters)—hit Nicaragua. Walker ended up grabbing the Nicaraguan presidency for himself, making English the official language and declaring slavery in Nicaragua legal.

Walker, a Tennessean and supporter of the U.S. slave states, intended to take over Nicaragua and then the rest of Central America and make the five Central American nations a white-run slave republic to be annexed to the U.S. South, to bolster it against the abolitionists of the North.

He was invited to Nicaragua and partly funded by leaders of the country's Liberal Party who were unaware of his true aim but thought they could use his armed assistance in battling the Conservatives. Walker, in 1853, had led a band of filibusters in an invasion of Mexico.

The Liberal Party of Nicaragua hardly reflected what the term liberal signifies in the U.S. Small landowners and artisans, its members were champions of free trade more than civil rights and freedoms. The personal dictatorships they established through the years were no less severe than those of the Conservatives. The Liberal Party became Somoza's political vehicle. The Conservative Party right up to the Sandinista revolution was the party of oligarchs: aristocratic landowners, cattle ranchers and large merchants. The Liberals and Conservatives fought each other for 150 years in civil wars very much like feudal wars between rival nobles.

Walker, whose activities also "received powerful backing from the Southern slave states," according to *Triumph of the People,* routed Conservative troops with ease, and then turned on his Liberal hosts to take over the country. His government was recognized at once by the president of the United States, Franklin Pierce.

Walker "also allied himself with Vanderbilt's rivals in the contest for control of the transit route, hoping that this would provide both funds and transportation for future recruits," said the U.S. Army account. "His tactics, however, backfired." Both the Liberals and Conservatives were against him, "Vanderbilt was determined to destroy him, and the rest of Central America feared that if he were not brought down he would try to extend his rule in their direction." Walker's goal was clearly enunciated by the motto on his army's flag: "Five or None!"

The English government was upset by Walker, too. It was still trying to counter the Monroe Doctrine of 1823 which claimed the Western hemisphere as solely in the U.S. sphere of influence, and was dominating much of the Caribbean and, in Central America, British Honduras (now Belize) and eastern parts of Honduras and Nicaragua. A British superintendent presided in the Nicaraguan Atlantic port town of Bluefields. The British held sway on the Nicaraguan Atlantic Coast even while the Spanish ran Nicaragua, and as a result English has been—and still is—widely spoken there. The Atlantic Coast population is mainly composed of Miskito Indians and Creole blacks.

"The struggle to expel Walker and his army from Nicaragua was long and costly," noted the U.S. Army book. "In the process, the colonial city of Granada was burned, and thousands of Central Americans lost their lives. But Vanderbilt's funds, the opposition of the British Navy, and the combined forces of all of Central America eventually proved too much for the filibusters."

A final scene came in 1857 when the joint force of Central American soldiers stood ready to defeat Walker's troops in the town of Rivas. "At this point Commander Charles H. Davis of the United States Navy, whose ship had been sent to Nicaragua's Pacific coast to protect American interests, arranged a truce. On May 1, 1857, Walker and his remaining followers, escorted by a force of Marines, evacuated Rivas, marched down to the coast, and took ships back to the United States." In 1860 Walker was back in Central America in an attempt to regain the Nicaraguan presidency. He led a force that took the Honduran town of Trujillo but he was captured by the British Navy "which promptly turned him over to Honduran authorities. On September 12, 1860, a Honduran firing squad put a permanent end to his efforts to take over Central America."

The Walker episode, because it so discredited the Liberals, was followed by thirty-six years of uninterrupted Conservative rule in which "the economy stagnated further and the peasant majority were kept in misery by repressive legislation or forced to fight for landowners in useless, unending civil wars," said *Triumph of the People.*

A series of revolts led, in 1893, to the rise to the presidency of Liberal José Santos Zelaya who for sixteen years ran the nation in an authoritarian manner. He stayed in power by conducting what *Triumph of the People* described as "farcial" elections to sustain what was essentially a dictatorship. But he did improve the economy, mainly for the benefit of the new "agroexporting bourgeoisie" of the Liberal Party. He modernized Nicaragua by building roads, railways and port facilities oriented towards these interests.

Zelaya was a nationalist, taking on the British on the Atlantic Coast and causing them to leave after Royal Marines, landing in Bluefields and sent up the Rio San Juan, were defeated by Zelaya's troops.

He bothered the United States government by pushing for a new Central American Federation. The U.S. government annoyed him by opting for a Panama site for a cross-Central American canal in 1903, a year after the U.S. House of Representatives passed a bill appropriating funds for a Nicaraguan canal. Zelaya had been counting on an inter-ocean water route through Nicaragua to further boost his country's economic development.

Zelaya finally infuriated the U.S. government by, first, contracting a large loan from an English financial syndicate to construct a railway rather than getting a loan from American bankers, and then by opening negotiations with Japan and

Germany for the construction of a canal which would rival the American one.

"By mid-1909," noted the U.S. Army account, "the United States was quite willing to give its support to any effort to bring down Zelaya." It got its pretext that year when the Zelaya government captured and executed two Americans hired by Conservatives to sabotage Nicaraguan government ships during a Conservative uprising in Bluefields.

"That gave Secretary of State Philander C. Knox an excuse to break relations with Nicaragua and issue a blistering statement condemning Zelaya," related the Army study.

Some 400 U.S. Marines then invaded Nicaragua to "protect American lives and property," an intervention partly financed with $1 million from American businessmen "including substantial contributions from the U.S.-owned Rosario and Light Mines Company, for whom Secretary of State Knox—curiously enough—was legal counsel," noted *Triumph of the People.* Aldolfo Díaz, a Conservative and an accountant at Rosario and Light Mines Company, was thereafter installed as the Nicaraguan president.

Díaz had great difficulty, however, controlling Liberal and nationalistic opposition and in 1911 he advised the United States: "The serious dangers which beset us can only be destroyed by skillful and efficient aid from the United States, like that which produced such good results in Cuba. For this reason it is my intention, through a treaty with the American government, to modify or enlarge the Constitution . . . permitting the United States to intervene in our internal affairs in order to maintain peace."

The following year, when a Liberal force under General Benjamin Zeledón, formerly a minister of Zelaya's cabinet, led a rebellion against Díaz, a contingent of 2,700 U.S. Marines moved into Nicaragua. Zeladón's army was the first manifestation of truly popular resistance: it was largely composed of peasants and poor artisans. For this reason, years later, the FSLN would use the name of Zeledon for its southern front during the offensive against Somoza. The Zeledón troops controlled several major Nicaraguan towns and held siege to Managua. The end came, noted the U.S. Army book when "United States forces supported by Nicaraguan government troops stormed the Liberal position on Coyotepe Hill [in Masaya], scattering the army and capturing Zeledón, who was promptly shot." Peace, enforced by American bayonets, returned to Nicaragua. From that year, 1912, until 1933 "with the exception of a brief nine-month period in 1925–26, the United States maintained troops in Nicaragua."

Racism was also a factor in the U.S. "big stick" and post-"big stick" periods. As President William Howard Taft declared in 1912: "The day is not far distant when three Stars and Stripes at three equidistant points will mark our territory: one at the North Pole, another at the Panama Canal, and the third at the South Pole. The whole hemisphere will be ours in fact as, by virtue of our superiority of race, it already is ours morally."

Even by 1914 "foreign investments were small" in Nicaragua. The nation's "principal asset in the eyes of the rest of the world remained its location as a potential canal site," related the U.S. Army account. "Since the canal through Panama was about to open, the United States had no interest in constructing a Nicaraguan canal—but it was interested in making sure that no other nation did so."

So in 1916, as Conservative Emiliano Chamorro became president of Nicaragua, the Bryan-Chamorro Treaty was ratified by the U.S. Senate. It gave the U.S., among other things, exclusive rights in perpetuity to construct a canal on Nicaraguan territory. "The Bryan-Chamorro Treaty helped transform Nicaragua into a virtual protectorate of the United States," declared the U.S. Army study.

During Chamorro's tenure, a three-member commission composed of the Nicaraguan minister of finance and two Americans, one a State Department nominee, the other a U.S. banker, was set up to have financial control of Nicaragua.

In the 1920s, a major corporate presence in Central America, the American Standard Fruit Company came into the country. "The United Fruit Company [now United Brands] had been exporting small quantities of bananas from Nicaragua since the start of the century, but Standard's activities soon outstripped its rival," related the Army study, and by the late 1920s "became the largest single private employer and the largest source of foreign investment in the nation."

But there was political conflict again. When Chamorro showed some political ambitions by attempting to bypass a Constitutional provision and having himself elected to a second presidential term in 1920, it annoyed the U.S. His plans were vetoed by the U.S. State Department which sent a Princeton University professor to redraft Nicaragua's electoral laws. But an unstable coalition of dissident Conservatives and Liberals came to power in 1925—Conservative Carlos Solórzano as president, Liberal Juan Bautista Sacasa as vice president.

Soon afterwards that year, Emiliano Chamorro and his supporters staged an uprising forcing the ouster of the Liberal members of the governmental coalition. Solórzano gave up the presidency to Chamorro in 1926, but the Liberals fought back. "As usual United States cruisers were rushed to the area and landing parties sent ashore to establish neutral areas," noted the U.S. Army account, "but this time the tactic had little effect" because the fighting "had virtually bankrupted the Chamorro regime which was steadily losing ground to the insurgents." The U.S. imposed a solution: it brought back former President Díaz, the Rosario and Light Mines Company accountant, to replace Chamorro.

"At the urging of the American legation, [the Nicaraguan] Congress proceeded to select Adolfo Díaz as president," the U.S. Army book related. "The United States promptly recognized his government. The Liberals refused to accept this arrangement. Instead Sacasa returned from exile and established his own government, which was recognized by Mexico. Fighting resumed, and the Díaz regime had no more success in defeating the Liberals than had Chamorro. United States forces were landed in increasing numbers, ostensibly to protect foreign lives and property, but their presence did nothing to deter the insurgents. A hurried loan of $1.3 million from New York banking interests staved off bankruptcy for the Díaz government but was ineffective in enabling it to deal with the uprising . . . By the spring of 1927 it was obvious that only direct United States intervention could prevent a Liberal victory."

President Calvin Coolidge then sent a former war secretary, Henry L. Stimson, to Nicaragua—backed by 5,000 U.S. troops in Nicaragua—to see if a settlement could be imposed by the U.S. Díaz was most willing as long as the Liberals did not gain control. Sacasa's political representatives were hesitant. Stimson "confessed that he found military men easier to understand than politicians and declared that Nicaraguan politicians were no longer capable of running their country," according to *Triumph of the People* and, noted the army account, "decided to confer directly with the Liberal's military commander, General José Maria Moncada, rather than with Sacasa's representatives. . . . Combining conciliation with the threat of direct intervention, Stimson secured Moncada's agreement to a complex peace plan."

It was called the Pact of Espino Negro and "although the Somoza regime was still nine years away" it "signified the establishment of a military dictatorship with no social basis. Moncada was the man who prepared the ground for *Somocismo*," declared *Triumph of the People.*

Under the pact, Díaz would remain president through 1928, the U.S. would supervise elections in 1928 and 1932, there would be a ceasefire and disarmament by both sides and the handing over of weapons to the U.S. Marines, and future order would be kept by the new *Guardia Nacional* or National Guard to be under the supervision of U.S. military officers.

One Liberal general, Augusto César Sandino, refused to accept the arrangement. He "opposed United States domination of his nation and the virtual occupation of Nicaragua by the Marines," said the U.S. Army study. "Instead of laying down his arms he moved into the mountains in the department of Nueva Segovia and prepared to continue the conflict."

It was Sandino's view that at the heart of Nicaragua's problems was U.S. imperialism. He had experience working for American companies: on a banana plantation run by United Fruit in Guatemala and at an oilfield run by the South Pennsylvania Oil Company in Mexico.

Under his leadership, a guerrilla-style war began in Nicaragua, a popular revolt which, although on a smaller scale, shared many characteristics of America's subsequent Vietnam conflict.

As the U.S. Army account phrased it: "For the Marines this ongoing campaign became a source of endless frustrations. Massive sweeps proved ineffective, and aggressive small unit patrols, while effective, were costly and exhausting. Increasingly the United States sought to turn over combat operations to Nicaragua's National Guard."

With his *Ejercito Defensor de la Soberania Nacional de*

*Nicaragua* (Army in Defense of the National Sovereignty of Nicaragua), Sandino first set up a base on the cloud-shrouded mountain peak of El Chipote along the Honduran border. From there he conducted attacks on the U.S. Marines and the National Guard. An early major offensive was in 1927 in Ocotal during which the U.S. conducted aerial bombing against Sandino's soldiers. Subsequently, massive air strikes were launched against El Chipote, it was surrounded by Marines and National Guardsmen, but when the summit was reached "they found nothing but a ring of straw dummies wearing the red and black kerchieves" of Sandino's army. "His ability to escape with his entire army and supplies from El Chipote," related *Triumph of the People,* "showed that the Americans would never defeat him in a guerrilla war fought on his own territory. The FSLN later took the lesson profoundly to heart: never fight the enemy on their own terms."

Through the years until 1933, Sandino's forces moved around the country attacking U.S. troops and the National Guard. As in Vietnam, there was no victory for the U.S. against the guerrillas despite the use by the U.S. of modern military equipment including considerable air power.

United States intervention in Nicaragua shared "many of the characteristics of the later war in Vietnam," *Triumph of the People* stressed. "Enormous destruction was wrought on a small country by sophisticated military technology and counter-insurgency operations, and most of this was borne by the peasant population. Most important, the U.S.A. suffered defeat—and again sought to justify it as 'withdrawal with honor'—at the hands of nationalism, mass popular opposition, a highly intelligent guerrilla movement rooted in the people, and the unpopularity of the war at home."

During the Sandino period, "the cruelty of both the U.S. Marines and the new National Guard became notorious," according to *Triumph of the People.* "The uncompromising methods of the Marines were consciously used by the U.S.A. as a propaganda weapon, epitomized by the widely circulated photograph of a Marine lieutenant holding the severed head of a Sandinista combatant. The most classic form of 'Vietnamization' was a program to create what might later have been called 'strategic hamlets' . . . Farms were burned down, crops and animals destroyed, and peasants transferred to concentration camps . . . Anyone left in the target zones was

*AUGUSTO CÉSAR SANDINO: As guerrilla fighter.*
*of view" revolution is "absolutely fantastic."* Haskell Wexler

treated as an enemy."

Meanwhile, a large anti-war movement was growing in the U.S. and Sandino was becoming a romantic hero in America and around the world. Cecil B. DeMille wanted to make a movie about him. The loss of American lives was bemoaned, there were protests during the Depression about such cost in the defense of Wall Street interests, a spotlight was put on the situation by several muckraking journalists, there was open conflict about it in the U.S. Congress, strong opposition by Democrats (the 1928 Democratic election platform took a stand against intervention), and a split among Republicans.

"We are not soldiers. We are the people. We are armed citizens," Sandino said during the struggle. Indeed, like the Sandinista army thirty and forty years later, most of Sandino's soldiers were young and many were women.

"I am not prepared to surrender my weapons even if everybody else does," Sandino said. "I would rather be killed along with the few who accompany me, because it is better to die as rebels under fire than to live as slaves."

He wrote: "I said to my friends that if there were a hundred men in Nicaragua who loved their country as much as I, we would redeem its sovereignty, now endangered by the Yankee empire. My friends replied that there might be that many men, or even more, but the problem would lie in our finding each other."

And Sandino declared: "The present lies with the peoples of Hispanic America to whom I speak. When a government does not represent the aspirations of its citizens, these people—who gave that government its power—have the right to be represented by virile men and women and by ideas of an effective democracy, and not be useless puppets without moral value or patriotism who shame the pride of our race. We are ninety million Hispanic Americans and we only need reflect on our unification to understand that Yankee imperialism is the most brutal enemy that threatens us and the only one which is determined to end through conquest our racial honor and the freedom of our peoples. Tyrants do not represent nations, and liberty is not won with flowers."

On January 1, 1933, U.S. forces withdrew from Nicaragua, unable to win a military victory and facing rising political hostility at home. On February 2, Sandino accepted a ceasefire. His terms for peace were an end to U.S. management of the National Guard, the calling of a Pan-American conference to revoke the Chamorro-Bryan canal treaty, an end to political and economic dependency by Nicaragua on the U.S., redistribution of land in the interests of the peasantry, and the establishment of a region of Nicaragua to be controlled by his soldiers where forms of cooperative social organization begun in Sandinista-run areas during the war would be put into effect.

At the height of the war, Sandino's army of twenty-one columns and 6,000 soldiers held a large area of Nicaragua and in these zones organized agricultural production through cooperatives, ran a communications network with telephone and radio equipment captured from U.S. troops, circulated money and conducted literacy classes for peasants and soldiers.

Meanwhile, Somoza had been installed as *jefe director* of the National Guard. The U.S. Army account reported that "Somoza was born in Nicaragua in 1896. He later attended school in Philadelphia where he gained a good command of English and met his future wife, a member of the influential Debayle family. He played a brief role in the 1926 civil conflict and later helped translate for the Stimson mission. He carefully cultivated the friendship of the Marines and the United States minister while serving in a variety of cabinet and subcabinet posts for Moncada."

Peace negotiations were held with Sandino in Managua in 1934. Somoza at one point posed with Sandino in an embrace of friendship in a now-famous photograph. "After several meetings, some of the issues were apparently resolved," noted the U.S. Army, "but as Sandino and his chief aides were leaving a farewell dinner at the presidential palace on February 21 they were seized by a Guard contingent acting under Somoza's orders, taken to the airfield, executed, and secretly buried." Some accounts say the slaying was cleared by the U.S. ambassador to Nicaragua. The National Guard then began a slaughter of Sandino's supporters. Somoza, who subsequently staged a coup d'etat and thus began what was to become the longest dictatorship in Latin American history, banned the name of Sandino in Nicaragua and did all he could to wipe out his movement.

Somoza flirted with the fascists in the 1930s. He formed a group of storm troopers called the *Camisas Azules*

(Blueshirts) armed by the National Guard and organized on the Nazi and Italian fascist models. They were used to intimidate political enemies.

But he kept in step with his principal patron, the U.S. government, declaring war on the Axis powers in December 1941 when the U.S. did, allowing the U.S. to install naval and air force bases inside Nicaragua during the war and receiving arms for his National Guard in return. He used the war, too, as an excuse to declare a state of siege and suspend constitutional guarantees.

He also utilized the war to appropriate German-owned properties in Nicaragua—for himself. By 1944, Somoza, whose family owned only a broken-down coffee plantation when he took control of the National Guard in 1933, owned 51 cattle ranches, 46 coffee plantations, and eight sugar plantations—making him the country's leading producer of sugar and associated products. During the war, in addition, he cornered the gambling rackets, brothels and illegal alcohol production and began monopoly control over granting import and export licenses. After the war, he moved on to mines and expanded into the industrial sector taking over the country's only cement factory, textile plants and establishing control over the processing of milk. Further, he took over the Nicaraguan merchant shipping line, the national airline and port installations at what was then called Port Somoza (now Port Sandino) on the Pacific.

He used "his position to make himself the wealthiest individual in Nicaragua if not in all of Central America," said the U.S. Army account. Meanwhile, "the dictator was grooming his sons to succeed him. Both had been sent to the United States for education; the younger, Anastasio Somoza Debayle, graduated from the United States Military Academy at West Point. They had been installed in key government posts, further expanding the family's power."

In 1956, Somoza was assassinated by Nicaraguan poet Rigoberto López Pérez. With the assistance of the U.S. ambassador to Nicaragua, leadership was transferred to the eldest Somoza son, Luis Somoza Debayle. Anastasio was already in command of the National Guard. And the strong support of the Somozas by the U.S. continued unabated.

In turn, Nicaragua aided the U.S. government. The Bay of Pigs invasion of Cuba was launched from Puerto Cabezas on the Nicaraguan Atlantic Coast. The relationship between the Somoza dynasty and U.S. officialdom was well-exemplified by the printing of a Nicaraguan 20 cordoba bill with a picture on it of the U.S. ambassador to Nicaragua during the Richard Nixon presidency, Turner Shelton.

In 1967, Luis died of a heart attack and Anastasio took control. "Lacking his father's or brother's political skills, Anastasio Somoza relied increasingly on force, corruption and personal loyalties to maintain the system," related the Army study. Meanwhile, under Anastasio "the size of the elite" ruling Nicaragua "was further constricted" and "using family inheritances and business dealings made possible by his dictatorial control of the governmental apparatus, Somoza accumulated a fortune worth hundreds of millions of dollars." By the mid-1970s as much as one-quarter of Nicaragua's total assets were owned by Somoza." (When he fled to Miami after the Sandinista triumph in 1979, Somoza's worth was put by U.S. government sources in a *New York Times* account at $900 million.)

The road to the Sandinista victory began in July 1961 with the founding, in Tegucigalpa, of the *Frente Sandinista Liberación de Nacional* by Fonseca, Borge and Mayorga. They fought to resurrect the ideas of Sandino. The Cuban revolution was a major influence on the three men who had all originally been members of the Nicaraguan Socialist Party.

Wrote Fonseca in "Nicaragua: Zero Hour": "The principal characteristic of the period from the assassination of Sandino in 1934 until the triumph of the Cuban revolution in 1959 was the interruption of the traditional armed struggle as a systematic tactic to fight the ruling regime.

"The Sandinista National Liberation Front understands how hard the guerrilla road is. But it is not prepared to retreat. We know that we are confronting a bloody, reactionary armed force like the National Guard, the ferocious GN [*Guardia Nacional*], which maintains intact the practices of cruelty that were inculcated in it by its creator, the U.S. Marines. Bombardment of villages, cutting of children's throats, violation of women, burning huts with peasants inside them, mutilation as torture—these were the study courses that the U.S. professors of civilization taught the GN during the period of guerrilla resistance led by Augusto César Sandino.

"The frustration that followed the period of the Sandinista resistance does not have to be repeated today," Fonseca continued. "Now the times are different. The current days are not like those in which Sandino and his guerrilla brothers battled alone against the Yankee empire. Today revolutionaries of all the subjugated countries are rising up or preparing to go into the battle against the empire of the dollar. At the apex of this battle is indominatable Vietnam, which with its example of heroism is repulsing the aggression of the blond beasts."

Fonseca concluded "Nicaraga: Zero Hour" with: "Before the image of Augusto César Sandino and Ernesto Ché Guevara; before the memory of the heroes and martyrs of Nicaragua, Latin America, and humanity as a whole; before history; I place my hand on the black and red flag that signifies 'Free Homeland or Death,' and I swear to defend the national honor with arms in hand and to fight for the redemption of the oppressed and exploited in Nicaragua and the world. If I fulfill this oath, the freedom of Nicaragua and all the peoples will be the reward; if I betray this oath, death in disgrace and dishonor will be my punishment."

Armed actions by the FSLN against the Somoza regime began in the 1960s from Honduras. In 1963, the FSLN gathered in Honduras 60 combatants including Fonseca and Santos Lopez, a veteran of Sandino's army, and thus two generations of fighters under the banner of Sandino were united. By 1967, FSLN guerrillas moved into an area around the mountain of Pancasán in Nicaragua and launched attacks from there. They were, in turn, attacked and in one assault by the National Guard on FSLN guerrillas that year, Mayorga was killed along with other senior FSLN leaders. Sandinista workers and students groups were forming inside Nicaragua and the FSLN put an emphasis, too, on urban organization and actions. A key event occurred in 1974 when thirteen FSLN guerrillas burst into a reception in the Las Robles area of Managua being given by José Maria "Chema" Castillo Quant, formerly associated with Somoza's Office of Security and a minister of agriculture and a close confidante of the dictator. High Somoza government officials and several Somoza relatives were in attendance. The reception was being given for U.S. Ambassador Shelton who left just minutes before the thirteen FSLN guerrillas—including three women—barged in with the declaration: "This is a political operation. Hands on your heads and against the wall. This is the Sandinista National Liberation Front. Viva Sandino." The guests were held for $2 million ransom, freedom for a number of FSLN prisoners including Daniel Ortega Saavedra (now coordinator of the ruling junta in Nicaragua) and demands that communiqués be published in Nicaraguan newspapers and broadcast on radio and television. The guerrillas flew to Cuba after the 60-hour siege and were applauded along the airport road, according to *Triumph of the People*, by a crowd shouting "Viva el Frente!" and "Viva Sandino!" Somoza then imposed a state of siege, martial law, press censorship and a dusk-to-dawn curfew for thirty-three months.

Guerrilla action in rural areas continued. In 1976, a National Guard counter-insurgency patrol mounted a night ambush on an FSLN band in the mountains near Zinica. One of those killed that night was Carlos Fonseca Amador.

A division in tactics then began in the FSLN. There were those believing a protracted struggle involving rural guerrilla warfare was ahead, the *Guerra Popular Prolongada* or Prolonged Popular War grouping. There were those thinking an upsurge in working class militancy and a mass Marxist party was ahead, *Tendencia Proletaria* or Proletarian Tendency. And there were those feeling opposition to the Somoza regime by many segments of society—including the middle class and those involved in the church—meant that the revolution could be won in the short term by explosive insurrectional actions and broad class alliances combined in the *Tendencia Insurreccional* or Insurrectional Tendency.

Each segment fought in its own way.

The Chamorro assassination, meanwhile, brought Nicaragua to a boiling point. And it was followed in August of 1978 by a guerrilla assault on the National Palace. Involving twenty-six FSLN members, it was led by Edén Pastora Gómez, *Commandante Cero* or Commander Zero of the Sandinista revolution. The FSLN guerrillas had their hair shaved in the style of the National Guard, were carrying weapons captured from the Guard and wearing uniforms of the elite unit of the Guard which usually accompanied Somoza. They drove up to the heavily-defended palace in Guard trucks. As Pastora screamed, "The boss is coming," crowds in the National Palace melted away and in short order the FSLN guerrillas were deep inside taking 1,500 prisoners including virtually the entire Congress and, as in the "Chema" Castillo attack, close associates and relatives of Somoza. Some 58 FSLN prisoners, including Borge, were released from jail as part of the demands made during this 45-hour siege. Aircraft was sent by Carlos Andrés Pérez, president of Venezuela, and Omar Torrijos, president of Panama, both now allies of the Sandinista cause, to fly out the guerrillas and the freed prisoners.

New strikes were called that month and by September a full-scale insurrection was at hand. The Somoza regime replied with brutal air and artillery strikes against densely populated towns. The fighting was fierce and widespread throughout Nicaragua. The Somoza regime turned back the revolution, but not for long. By 1979, it was war on all fronts. Insurrection, strikes, and armed attacks continued. Towns fell to the FSLN. Thousands were killed and injured. The U.S. moved for a settlement—Somoza's resignation but continuation of the National Guard—which was scored as "*Somocismo* without Somoza" by the FSLN.

There was consideration of direct U.S. military intervention with Zbigniew Brzezinski, chairman of Jimmy Carter's National Security Council, his assistant Robert Pastor, and U.S. Defense Secretary Harold Brown reportedly favoring it.

But another killing of a journalist occurred, this time outraging the American public. ABC-TV reporter Bill Stewart was murdered in cold blood by National Guardsman in Managua, a slaying documented by his cameraman from some distance away. The film of the slaying was smuggled out of Nicaragua and shown throughout the United States within hours. A plan for a U.S. invasion of Nicaragua had been prepared, but Stewart's murder, most high U.S. officials concluded, left insufficient domestic support for direct intervention to save either Somoza or the National Guard.

A principal U.S. government operative involved in the situation was Assistant Secretary of State for Inter-American Affairs William Bowdler, a former member of the National Security Council and the State Department Office of Intelligence, someone with long and close ties to the CIA. He tried to arrange a government dominated by non-FSLN figures and, failing that, supported a junta which included non-FSLN members.

Somoza, on July 17, 1979, took his wife and family, his mistress, some close political allies and senior military officers and flew to Miami. (In 1980, he was assassinated in Bolivia.)

Still, intense fighting went on but the Guard was beginning to "disintegrate," said the U.S. Army study. "Members of the air force took all available planes and flew them to neighboring nations. Other units began to march toward the Honduran and Costa Rican borders seeking asylum."

FSLN columns were entering Managua on July 19, 1979. From all over the country, said *Triumph of the People*, "thousands of armed Sandinistas drove into the streets of Managua . . . Red and black flags appeared everywhere. But even before the guerrilla forces arrived, the people of Managua had taken the city" and "it seemed that the whole population of the city was armed and firing volleys into the air from their liberated weapons. For the whole next day the streets were filled with family reunions after years of clandestinity and combat."

Said Sergio Ramírez Mercardo, who went from being a novelist and university dean to a principle figure in the Sandinista government: "When the motley columns of guerrilla fighters entered Managua on July 19, 1979, when thousands of fighters entered Managua on July 19, 1979, when thousands of victorious combatants raised their liberating rifles high, there had been two decades of mortal combat on our continent; of doubts and dissension, of theoretical recrimination, of watching and waiting through a long revolutionary night. And then the light of history shone upon a new praxis, for a wise, heroic vanguard had joined together all the elements required to construct the circumstances of victory according to a new model. They led a people's war to break the hard, dead shell of a ruling system that had endured half a century of pressures, and then they smashed it completely, leaving only a trace of all the repressive, criminal, and ultimately genocidal violence."

Noted the U.S. Army account: "The struggle against Somoza was not strictly a class-based revolution; virtually all sectors of Nicaraguan society had joined in the effort to oust the dictator. In 1978 and 1979 a sizable portion of poor and working-class Nicaraguans were organized, in their neighborhoods and workplaces, into militias and various other organizations that supported the struggle spearheaded by the

FSLN guerrilla units. Businessmen, professionals, the Roman Catholic Church, and the traditionally compliant opposition parties also cooperated with the Sandinistas and led the successful effort to rally international opinion behind the effort to oust Somoza.

"The victory had come at a high cost," continued the study which calculated that "30,000 to 50,000 Nicaraguans had been killed during the civil conflict, a figure equal to about one percent of the population, and some 100,000 had been injured. An estimated 150,000 had been left homeless." The "economy had been devastated: commerce and agriculture were almost completely disrupted." The Army book noted that a United Nations report placed the amount of "material damages alone from the 1978–79 fighting" at $500 million. "Destruction of the industrial base represented 23 percent of its total value. . . . In addition, Somoza had left an empty government treasury and some $1.6 billion in outstanding foreign debts."

Subsequently, I visit a museum devoted to the Nicaraguan revolution, two miles from the *Plaza de la Revolución,* next to the main bus station in Managua.

In front of the Museum of the Revolution are piles of bricks—street stones produced by Somoza's cement factory which were turned into barricades during the revolution. A few of the primitive armored vehicles used by the Sandinistas are also out front. The simple museum is administered in a very protective fashion. You are asked to leave anything you are carrying with a guard to be checked at the entrance.

Inside the museum, in glass display cases, are historical items: Sandino's rifles, portable typewriters used by FSLN guerrilla leaders to type various communiqués during the years of war and copies of some of those communiqués, weapons of the guerrilla leaders, a poster demanding freedom for a jailed Tómas Borge, a collection of newspaper stories from the times of Sandino through the subsequent Sandinista revolution. There is a Nicaraguan newspaper photo of U.S. President Franklin Delano Roosevelt with Anastasio Somoza Garcia and the caption beneath it is that of Roosevelt saying of Somoza: "He may be a son of a bitch but he's our son of a bitch." Also on display are Anastasio Somoza Debayle's helmet and uniform. I never saw as many medals on one uniform.

People are moving slowly from display case to display case, studying the artifacts of their culture, relics of the revolution. Standing by the display of Sandino's guns, two Springfield rifles, I ask a young man looking with me at the rifles, Fernando Hernandez Sanchez, 21, an engineering student from Managua, how he feels about what he is seeing. "We had to have change," he says.

Many of the artifacts are not just of the Nicaraguan culture, but are American such as newspaper clips; one exhibit includes a *Los Angeles Times* cartoon-photo montage of U.S. Marines in battle against Sandino's army.

I walk out of the museum with three boys who were with me at the last display case, the one with Somoza's uniform. They had gazed wide-eyed at the display. I had asked the boys what they thought of Somoza. One declared, "*Bruto!*" (Brute!).

Outside, I ask the three to pose for a photograph in front of one of the Sandinista armored vehicles. They do, all immediately holding up two fingers in V-signs.

*OUTSIDE MUSEUM OF THE REVOLUTION: Reynaldo Jesus Castillo Saravia, Carlos Vilchez Guido, Noxollys Almedarez.*

Considering all the years of violence in Nicaragua and the fact that I am an American, I am surprised when they explain the sign stands for "peace and love."

Later, I go to interview Carlos Fernando Chamorro, at 27 the youngest son of Pedro Joaquín Chamorro, and the editor of his own newspaper, *Barricada*, the paper of the FSLN. It was founded a week after the revolution's triumph. The masthead includes an illustration of an FSLN guerrilla at a barricade made from the Somoza bricks—where *Barricada* gets its name. In front of the *Barricada* offices is a symbolic barricade, made from the bricks.

Carlos, educated at McGill University in Canada, speaks about his father, a man who "had full respect, was honest and ready to give," and of the day "my father was assassinated." He says he is continuing in the journalistic tradition of his father and pursuing his father's quest for equity in Nicaragua. He says as an editor his philosophy is to be "critical of the revolution but not to destroy the revolution."

His older brother, named Pedro Joaquín Chamorro after their father, remains as editor of *La Prensa*, but *La Prensa*, says Carlos, "is capitalizing on the prestige my father had" and is against the revolution. Nearly all of the reporters at *La Prensa* "never worked with my father," says Carlos. As *La Prensa* began taking an opposition stance towards the Sandinista revolution, most of its reporters joined an uncle, Xavier, a brother of his father, and left *La Prensa* to begin a new newspaper, *Nuevo Diario*. Carlos charges that there is "no possibility" now for any expression of a view backing the revolution at *La Prensa*.

Since March 1982 there has been press censorship in Nicaragua, Carlos notes. *La Prensa* has been the main target of the censor. "We feel uncomfortable with censorship but feel it is necessary . . . We are not living in a normal situation." The forces of counterrevolution led by the United States are eager to use the Nicaraguan press to undermine the revolution, he says. He cites the situation in Chile in which the CIA poured money into the newspaper *El Mercurio* and used it to destabilize the socialist government of President Salvador Allende Gossens before the Allende government was overthrown—with CIA help.

It is a sensitive time in Nicaraguan history, says Carlos, a period during which the FSLN is trying to "institutionalize democratic processes" in Nicaragua, something new for the country.

Carlos is an ardent supporter of the revolution. He notes one of the Sandinista slogans—*Todos Las Armas Al Pueblo* (All The Arms To The People)—and says almost there is

*CARLOS FERNANDO CHAMORRO: Optimistic about revolution.*

no other country in Latin America in which the government could "give people arms" and have the people defend the nation with the weapons rather than use them against those in power.

He speaks of the American press as "following stereotypes in responding to what Reagan says." He complains that because so much of the world—including Latin America—is dependent for overseas news on the two U.S. wire services, Associated Press and United Press International, it gets a warped account of the situation in Nicaragua.

He talks of the *contras* and says essentially all their "high command are former members of the National Guard," despite "the CIA's attempts to give *Somocismo* a new face" to make it appear otherwise.

Carlos is optimistic about the future of the revolution—as long as "we can pass this critical situation of aggression."

# PROBLEMS WITHIN

"They've waged a strong campaign against this newspaper," Carlos' brother, Pedro Joaquín Chamorro, is saying at *La Prensa*. "We have all the imagined types of harassment." The newspaper has been "closed down five different times." Sandinista "mobs" have attacked *La Prensa* "throwing stones."

Pedro, 32, also educated at McGill University, takes an opposite view from his younger brother towards the Sandinista revolution.

Principal problems with the revolution, Pedro says, include a lack of "separation between the party," the FSLN, "and the state." The party, he says, is the government and the military; there is a "party army, a party air force." Further, there is political "indoctrination of youth," he complains. And, he says, a "lack of pluralism" exists in government policies and this is especially evident in a non-questioning stance toward the Soviet Union. "They do not criticize the invasion of Afghanistan, they did not criticize suppression of the Solidarity workers, they did not criticize Russian maneuvers near Poland." In addition, Pedro protests, there is press censorship, of a stupid variety, and press intimidation. "Our reporters have been threatened. Our reporters have been beaten by mobs, in front of the police."

The comments of Pedro Chamorro and other critics and opponents of the Sandinista government I interview in Nicaragua suggest the Sandinista revolution has faults.

Some of the problems in revolutionary Nicaragua are perhaps inevitable given the turbulence of revolutionary change in a land where there has never really been democracy, in a region where democracy is exceedingly rare. Some of the problems are clearly an outgrowth of the war being waged from outside against the nation: a siege leads to a siege mentality and, often in history, losses of freedom. But as the opponents see it, the faults also involve the Sandinista government being intolerant of dissent as it, in their view, propels the nation toward socialism.

The Sandinista government, complains Pedro Chamorro, in a room at *La Prensa* containing an impressionist painting of street demonstrators marching with a poster of his father, "allows the existence of pluralism but not the actuality." A "main criteria" of the revolution which "is not fulfilled is freedom of the press, unlimited, unrestricted freedom of the press."

Ever since censorship was imposed in Nicaragua under the 1982 Decree of National Emergency, stories prepared for *La Prensa* and other publications must be passed on by the censor who operates out of Borge's Ministry of the Interior. The censor's rulings are often ridiculous, says Chamorro. For example, "they don't allow in the paper the word zero" because of Edén Pastora having been known as Commander Zero and

*PEDRO JOAQUÍN CHAMORRO: Scores Sandinista government.*

his now being in exile and fighting the Sandinista government. "But zero means zero number," Pedro argues. The name of Alexis Arguello, a Nicaraguan boxer with an international reputation, cannot be mentioned, he goes on, because he left the country and is a critic of the Sandinista government. *La Prensa* had wanted to print two stories about a rematch Arguello was to have the following week in Las Vegas to try to regain the World Boxing Association junior welterweight title, but the censor killed both pieces. The stories hang on a bulletin board outside, next to the entrance of *La Prensa.* Although the government censors articles in Nicaraguan publications, it allows the censored articles to be posted if the publication so desires. The bulletin board has a sign: "Censored in *La Prensa.*"

Beyond petty censorship, any criticism or negative comments about the government are deleted by the censor. This "destroys the soul of the newspaper," Pedro declares. The censorship process also delays the publication of what is supposed to be an afternoon paper. "Yesterday, we began printing at 4:30 when we should have started at 1:30."

Says Jaime Chamorro, Pedro's uncle, another brother of his father, and general manager of *La Prensa:* "They would like *La Prensa* to close. They are trying to get us to go broke. They are making us weaker."

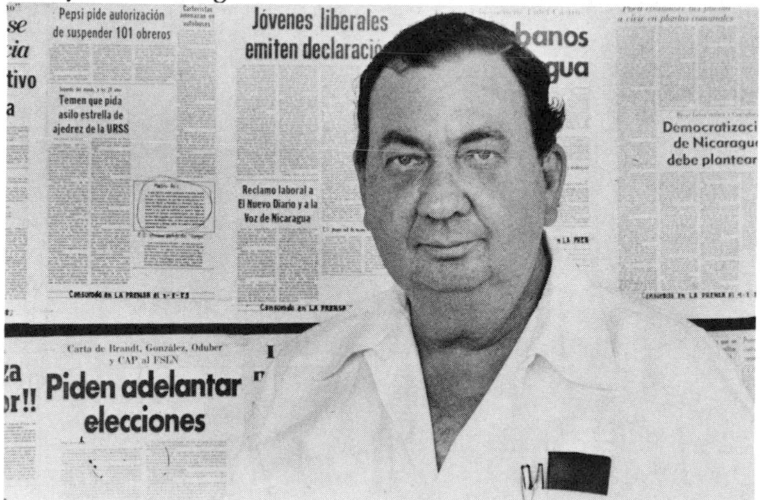


*Jaime Chamorro at bulletin board with censored* La Prensa *stories.*

Pedro goes on about how the FSLN's "verbal rhetoric against the U.S. is far too high" while there is "never any criticism of the Soviet Union" or nations such as Vietnam and North Korea. The government would have Nicaragua have "friends so far away," he comments.

Pedro complains about a new first grade text being used in Nicaragua entitled *Carlito,* about Carlos Fonseca Amador. Pedro says the book glorifies Fonseca and the Sandinista revolution with propaganda. "It says, 'This is Carlos, This is a gun' . . . Should children six years old be subject to this?"

Pedro says that if the FSLN was in power when his father was alive, "they would have censored my father."

Jaime estimates that only twenty percent of the Nicaraguan population supports the FSLN and Pedro agrees.

Pedro is cynical about there being a true election in 1985. "They may have an election but not a free election."

Of his brother Carlos, Pedro says: "I think he is doing something he believes in, no matter how wrong he is. He is a true revolutionary" and "within the limits of censorship, I think he is doing a good job, too."

In a small political office in Managua sits Adán Fletes, the leader of the Social Christian Party in Nicaragua. "The Sandinista government has already failed. It needs to be replaced. The mechanism to replace it should be shared," he is saying at his party's headquarters which "has been attacked by mobs . . . under the nose of the police, with the acquiescence and knowledge of the government."

Since the Sandinistas took office, "members of my party have suffered imprisonment; some have been assassinated," says Fletes, 38, who had been an economics professor at the National University of Nicaragua in Managua until "I was kicked out" in late 1979. "I was opposed to teaching orthodox Marxist-Leninist economics" so, according to him, along with other professors who would not adhere to a Marxist line, he was dismissed. In other areas of the educational system of Nicaragua, he asserts, those who are not Marxists have been purged.

"The Nicaraguan people struggled against Somoza in order to have freedom of expression, freedom to organize trade unions, political parties, to have elections. This has not come about. The people of Nicaragua suffer scarcity of many goods, are subject to a system of rationing. Beliefs have been disrespected due to government policy on religion."

Fletes pauses and says: "When one says these things one does it overcoming fear."

He speaks of "threats, death threats" against him. "The Sandinista Front doesn't accept dissidents," he continues. And it wants only an "official news media."

He says he does not support the *contras* because "as a matter of principle, we are opposed to any foreign intervention in the affairs of Nicaragua." Still, he goes on, there are "many Nicaraguans who are disillusioned with government policy and they have taken the option of looking for violence."

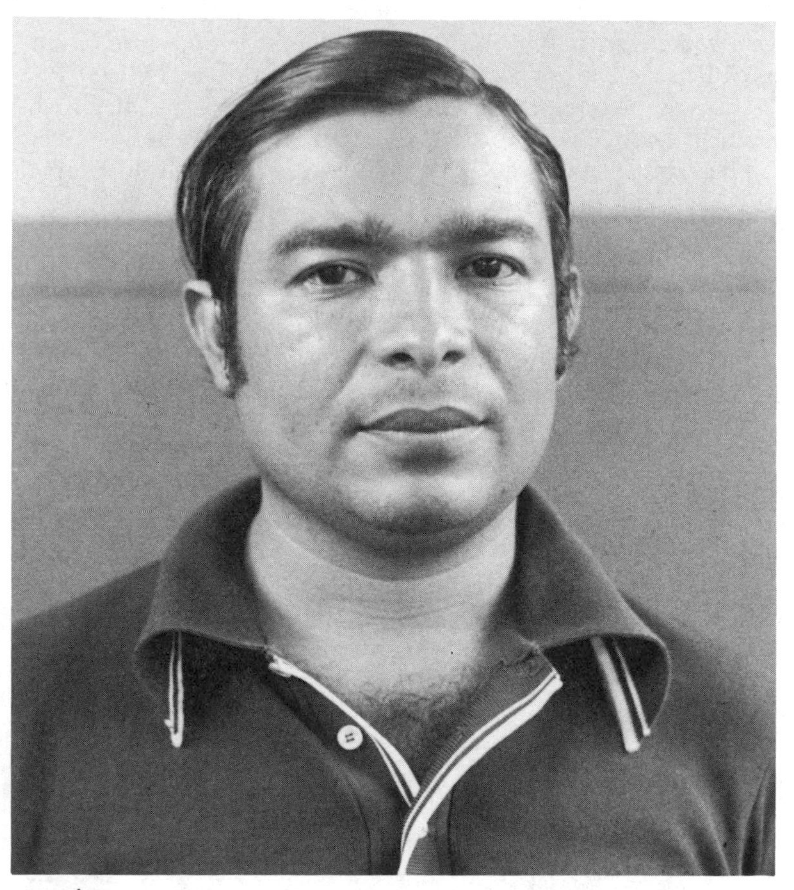

*ADÁN FLETES: "The Sandinista government has already failed."*

Fletes estimates that not more than thirty percent of the Nicaraguan population supports the Sandinistas. "The country still has an opportunity to come up with a regime which is socially advanced and democratic." Fletes questions "whether the Sandinistas will hold free elections" and says if elections are held he would like to see the Sandinistas provide an "international guarantee that the results of the elections will be respected."

He says his party is for "nonalignment in international affairs" and complains that the FSLN is an "orthodox Marxist-Leninist organization" which is moving Nicaragua towards the Soviet Union.

Enrique Bolaños Geyer is one of the presidents of *Consejo Superior Empreas Privada de Nicaragua,* the Supreme Council of Private Enterprise of Nicaragua, acronymed COSEP.

"How's business?" he is asked as the interview begins at COSEP's office in Managua. "Very bad," he replies.

The Sandinistas are "Marxist-Leninist in their ideology" and are "taking more control over the economy," says Bolaños, one of Nicaragua's major rice growers. Now 55 percent of the nation's economy is "in private hands," but the government is "confiscating whatever it can. The state controls all banks, all exports, nearly all imports, industrial enterprises from cement to mattress factories, owns cotton and coffee plantations and cattle farms and even disco places and ice cream parlors."

The revolution involved "true national unity," says Bolaños, "of all political parties, labor unions, a lot of leading citizens. The strategy was to overthrow Somoza and the top echelon of the National Guard."

But "the history of this country is that whoever holds the weapons holds the shots" and it was an FSLN army that came with the revolution, not a "mixed army . . . If we had an army with such composition we wouldn't be in the sorrowful condition we are in today."

He speaks of the economy as being in a shambles. "Cotton production, corn, milk, sorghum is half . . . most everything is half," he says. "The "public debt" is $4.2 billion.

Bolaños tells of personally feeling the bite of the Sandinistas. In October 1981, he was jailed for six days after COSEP leaders wrote a letter "complaining about the language used by the minister of defense [Humberto Ortega] when he said that when aggression comes, those who do not aid the revolution will be the first to be hung on the trees along the roads of the nation. We said that was no way for the minister of defense to talk—and we received a brutal response."

Bolaños, 55, says he was placed in a "vault"-like cell in a jail "behind the Inter-Continental. It had no bars, no windows. There was a little hole in the ceiling, eight inches by three inches wide, and a chimney connected to it through which I could get a little air."

At the same time, three other COSEP presidents were also jailed—for four months each. One COSEP president took refuge for the four months in the Venezuelan Embassy and two were out of the country and "stayed out."

In July 1982, Bolaños was put in jail again, for twenty-four hours, and never knew why. He was freed, he relates, because of a special request by the president of Venezuela who was coming to visit Nicaragua.

As to the level of support for the Sandinistas in Nicaragua, he says, "If people talk without fear and could search their consciences, I don't think you could find twenty percent."

*ENRIQUE BOLAÑOS GEYER: Jailed by the Sandinistas.*

Someone might say, I tell Bolaños, that the complaints he and other business people would have against the Sandinistas stem from their being the Nicaraguan bourgeoisie while the Sandinistas are committed primarily to the working class.

"We, the bourgeoisie," declares Bolaños, "supported the revolution. We played a very important part in the overthrow of Somoza." There are many entrepreneurs in Nicaragua, he continues. "There are 800,000 people who are employed; 260,000 of these are self-employed. . . . The private sector in this country after the revolution secured funds for the government." Bolaños insists the Nicaraguan middle class does not represent the "typical bourgeoisie, like in El Salvador."

He asserts: "We understand changes have to be made in Nicaragua. We want to rescue the revolution."

Another major post-revolutionary issue concerns the Miskito Indians, long separated from the mainstream of Nicaraguan life and many of them alienated from the revolution, too.

Ethnically, culturally, linguistically, in geography and in religion, the Miskitos—indeed most residents of the Atlantic Coast of Nicaragua—have been apart from the large majority of Nicaraguans. Spain was unable to crush Miskito Indian resistance as it colonized Nicaragua in the 1500s. Britain entered the Atlantic Coast in the 1600s, started trade relations with the Miskitos and used them as surrogates in battles with the Spanish. Also in the 1600s, blacks, who became known as Creoles, arrived as slaves or escapees from slavery. English and the Miskito language have been the principal tongues of the Atlantic Coast; the English encouraged a hatred for those who spoke Spanish. Geographically, the area has been separate from the Pacific side of Nicaragua. To reach Atlantic Coast communities from the west, the only means has been—and is—taking a road to a river and then traveling by water. The Sandinistas have embarked on building a major west-east road but the burdens of war have slowed that project. The religion of most Atlantic Coast residents (who comprise about ten percent of the population of Nicaragua) is not Catholic but Moravian. The residents were proselytized beginning in 1849 by missionaries, initially Germans and then Americans, of the Moravian Church, a pre-reformation church which began in Czechoslavakia.

The Moravian Church "became the church of the Indians

of eastern Nicaragua," Norman Bent, a Moravian minister is explaining in an interview. He is half-Miskito, half-Jamaican. Jamaican blacks migrated to the region to work for foreign companies, mainly American ones, which arrived at the turn of this century as the British withdrew. The companies exploited—indeed over-exploited—the area's gold, bananas, rubber, sea life (notably turtles) and forests. The massive cutting of forests so eroded the land that it became prone to severe flooding. By the 1950s, many natural resources had been exhausted and these companies were pulling out, leaving a population to deal with hunger and malnutrition. Some people migrated in search of work, others relied on traditional substinence (slash-and-burn) farming, fishing and hunting.

The Somoza dynasty ignored the Atlantic Coast other than cutting itself in for a piece of the exploitation and, with the revolution in Cuba, directing a major anti-Communist propaganda campaign at the region, warning of an imminent invasion of the Atlantic Coast by Cuba. The Miskitos were already conservative from the years under the Moravian Church which, in the absence of governmental authority, functioned as a political apparatus. Moravian leaders "introduced a conservative political ideology that was strongly anti-Communist and anti-revolution," noted *Nicaragua: A Country Study,* the U.S. Army Nicaraguan history. "Their position, to which Miskito lay pastors were exposed as part of their training, advocated tolerance of the Somoza regime as protection against a perceived greater 'Communist' evil." The Somoza regime's anti-Cuba campaign climaxed with the 1961 launching by the U.S. of the Bay of Pigs invasion of Cuba from Puerto Cabezas on the Atlantic Coast.

The Sandinista struggle against Somoza barely touched the Atlantic Coast. And thus the revolution passed by the Atlantic Coast—in locale and in politics.

The Sandinistas, upon the revolution's victory, looked upon the peoples of the Atlantic Coast eagerly. They viewed them as the poorest, the most exploited and most alienated of Nicaragua's residents and thought that with communication they would want to fully participate in the revolution. "The revolutionary government of Nicaragua has evidenced seemingly exceptional interest in the Atlantic Coast region," said the U.S. Army analysis, "given its small population and undeveloped economic condition. It made a major effort to adopt the literacy campaign to the special needs and interests of coastal peoples, particularly the Miskito and Creole, and has evidenced considerable interest in trying to develop a working relationship with local and indigenous leaders."

Some Atlantic Coast residents embraced the revolution. Many did not. Some of the problems are due to Sandinista "mistakes," says Rev. Bent. "Conflict with the government has been because of cultural conflict," a result of "a lack of experience" of the government "with the people there," he relates. This was evident in the first moves of the Sandinistas. The new government sent Cuban doctors and teachers to the Atlantic Coast not understanding, the minister explains, "the anti-Cuban sentiment" of the inhabitants because of Somoza's anti-Cuban propaganda. It would "have been better," says Rev. Bent, "if the government had sent Americans, Canadians, Europeans" who supported the revolution to work on the Atlantic Coast. Of the Sandinista soldiers sent, almost none spoke English or Miskito, they had little comprehension of the Atlantic Coast culture and consequently there was mutual suspicion, a series of confrontations and bloody incidents leaving Sandinista soldiers and Miskitos dead.

A major break between the Sandinista government and many Miskitos came with the arrest in 1981 of Steadman Fagoth Mueller, the head of a group called MISURASATA, and other leaders of the organization. The Sandinista government helped form MISURASATA to expand commercial opportunities for Indians and others of the Atlantic Coast. It is the acronym for *Miskito, Sumo, Rama, Sandinista, Asla Takanka* (Miskito, Sumo, Rama, Sandinista, All Together). Fagoth, who had attended the National University in Managua, was also a representative—the only Miskito representative—on the Nicaraguan Council of State. The MISURASATA leaders were charged with planning armed actions to foment a separatist uprising. All were released after a short time except for Fagoth who was held for two-and-a-half months causing many Miskitos to leave for Honduras in protest and out of fear.

Fagoth was released on the condition that he leave Nicaragua to study abroad, but instead he went to Honduras and began working with the counterrevolutionaries there.

In that year, 1981, *contra* raids from Honduras against the Atlantic Coast greatly increased. By late 1981 and early 1982 the raids became an almost daily occurrence. In one December attack, thirty-five people were tortured and killed by *contras*. In February 1982, the Sandinistas arrested 160 people on the Atlantic Coast, among them a former Moravian minister, and said they had broken up a plot called "Red Christmas" to set off a general uprising in the region aimed at forming a separate state.

Meanwhile, the Sandinista government began moving people from Miskito villages along the Rio Coco—which separates Nicaragua from Honduras—to five settlements thirty to thirty-five miles inland to, it said, protect them from *contra* attacks. Some 8,500 Miskitos were relocated while others crossed the Rio Coco into Honduras rather than be moved by the government.

The Miskito villages and crops were burned by the Sandinistas after the villagers left, in order, said the government, to deny the *contras* encampments and food on the Nicaraguan side of the border.

The Reagan administration began charging that the Sandinistas were setting up "concentration camps" for Indians and that a major repression was going on.

Rev. Bent says this was not the case. "The fight is basically a struggle between the oppressed and the oppressed," he says, adding that there have been mistakes "on both sides and both sides could have corrected the mistakes."

From a military perspective, he understands why the relocation was necessary but "from an anthropological and Christian perspective, it really hurts when you take a people away from where they have lived for hundreds of years. So there are mixed feelings about it. I do support a move for military defense, for protection. On the other hand, it is very sad."

Seriously exacerbating the situation, he says, are CIA activities using Miskitos who have lived in Honduras (the U.S. Army analysis estimated their number at 75,000, the same total as for the Miskitos in Nicaragua) and Nicaraguan Miskitos who fled to Honduras, to attack the Miskitos who remain in Nicaragua. The CIA, he says, is "using the Miskito people . . . arming them to come and kill their own Nicaraguan brothers and sisters." This had made a "situation" that is "very complicated and it is getting worse now that the CIA is involved. Unless the CIA pulls out of this situation, the Indian people will continue to suffer."

Rev. Bent believes that the Sandinista government seeks a "reconciliation" with the Miskitos. He says government leaders "admit their mistakes and want to know what they can do to overcome them." He says he is impressed by a "total freedom of religion under the government here" and thinks an "approach of reconciliation" can succeed.

He warns, however, that "we are living a little internal colonialism" in Nicaragua and, specifically, the people of the Atlantic Coast do not have adequate representation in the Sandinista government.

He urges that the Sandinistas release the roughly 400 Miskitos they have jailed for counterrevolutionary activity. If that happened "the [Miskito] people would rejoice and reconciliation would be possible."

Later, I take a trip to a prison for Miskitos about an hour outside of Managua. It is called the "Open Farm" and living there are some 80 Miskitos. Security is relaxed; there are no

*REV. NORMAN BENT: Mistakes "on both sides."*

jail cells. The men are working in a tobacco field. I ask to speak to them beyond hearing distance of guards. The guards step away.

"We've been falsely denounced," protests one prisoner who says "they accused me of being a counter-revolutionary." He relates that he has "been here for two years" and "the treatment here is good, the food is not good."

*"OPEN FARM" for Miskito Indian prisoners.*

Says another: "We don't like being prisoners. We don't see our families. We talk about our sadness."

Says another: "There has been a lot of *contra* activity on the Atlantic Coast, but most of the counterrevolutionaries went into Honduras." He tells of how Sandinista soldiers came "to my house to take me. They said I was a *contra.* I am not."

A fourth Miskito speaks of the "poor economic conditions" on the Atlantic Coast and how "we had a lot of problems through the years under Somoza, and there was no reason, we felt, that things were to be different under the Sandinistas."

The men live in a large, rustic building. In front of it is a sign: *Somos Sandinistas. Siempre fuertes en el combate y generosos en la victoria* (We are the Sandinistas. Always implaccable in combat and generous in victory).

An official at the "Open Farm" says that "we're reeducators here" and that the Miskitos at the facility are regarded as people who took part in anti-revolutionary activity because they were "misled. They didn't do it on their own." After they are taught about the revolution, he says, they will be allowed "to go back home."

An earful about problems in Nicaragua can be received at the U.S. Embassy there. The embassy in Managua is slightly less conspicuously protected than its counterpart in Tegucigalpa.

Chain-link fencing topped by razor wire surrounds its sides and rear, but the front view is more conventional: an expanse of lawn behind black estate-style iron gates.

Ambassador Anthony Quainton has agreed to be interviewed by a group of U.S. reporters. But after we arrive, are passed through a metal detector and led into the lobby of the embassy, we are told that no photographs will be allowed: all cameras must be left with guards in the lobby.

We are taken down a long hall decorated with Norman Rockwell prints, past office doors each with double locks. Next to a door marked "Defense Attaché Office" is the spacious office of the ambassador. Large photographic portraits of President Ronald Reagan, Vice President George Bush and Secretary of State George Shultz are hung behind the ambassador's desk. He directs us to sit on a couch, in front of a coffee table on which lays a book entitled *Terrorism, Legitimacy and Power.* According to a biography the embassy's public affairs officer hands us, Quainton, a foreign service officer since 1959 and posted through the years in Africa, Europe and Asia was the director of the State Department's Office for Combatting Terrorism from 1978 until he became U.S. ambassador to Nicaragua in 1982.

He begins the interview by directing that he cannot be quoted by name. "You can refer to me as a western diplomat," says Quainton.

The western diplomat then launches into a discussion of the Sandinista government. In his year-and-a-half in Nicaragua, says the western diplomat, "it is clear to me that the Sandinistas have lost popularity."

He does not defend the Somoza regime. He says an overthrow of the Somoza dynasty was "inevitable . . . A radical transformation had to take place in this country." The U.S., he says, "put together a mediation effort and former Assistant Secretary of State Bowdler tried to convince Somoza to get out" and to arrange for a "moderate government to come in. Considerable efforts were put into that."

He says there "would not have been a revolution without Somoza" in Nicaragua, that it was not caused by an outside force. The Carter administration "saw this as a popular revolt" containing "a lot of elements we could work with." The hope was that a "moderate democratic government" could be established. He places the Nicaraguan revolution in the context of Latin America. "Fundamental social grievances exist in Central and South America. Dissatisfaction growing out of those conditions exist."

The Nicaraguan revolution has coalesced politically into one organization becoming a "national institution." He describes the Sandinista Front as an "extraordinary organization which covers the whole country." He says "opportunities for dissent are repressed in the society as it now exists." He says the U.S. wants to see elections in Nicaragua because "our concern is that people have a chance in some institutional way to decide their future."

The Sandinista government has made "significant achievements in literacy and public health particularly," he says, but he notes serious economic problems. The nation has "100,000 new mouths to feed a year, one of the highest growth rates of Latin America." The economic difficulties have left people "not better off."

He raises the questions of Nicaragua's role in "exporting revolution to other countries in Central America" and "how far" the Sandinista government "has been exploited by outsiders."

The western diplomat speaks of "the 2,000 Cubans here" and says they are working with the Nicaraguan government and its military and are also engaged in construction work.

*U.S. AMBASSADOR TO NICARAGUA: Anthony Quainton.*

He says the "Soviet presence is quite small; there are 150 to 200 Russians including embassy personel."

The United States' "position" is that it is "not prepared to hold bilateral talks" with the Nicaraguan government on its differences but wants such discussions "dealt with on a regional basis."

On the *contras,* he describes the FDN, the main *contra* group, as an organization which is "strongly anti-Communist and believes in the defense of political democracy." Of U.S. government support for the *contras,* he says, "We never comment on aid or what we are giving or might be giving."

As to the possibility of "another Vietnam" involving Nicaragua, he says there are "some distant parallels" between Southeast Asia in the 1960s and Central America in the 1980s. The "danger of war in Central America has obviously grown because of the high levels of tension between Honduras and Nicaragua." But, he insists, "I think the Vietnam comparison is overblown."

In relating to foreign nations, under the Reagan administration "human rights is not the only criteria" of U.S. policy but that "our economic, political and strategic interests" come very much into play. Nevertheless, before we leave, the western diplomat has the embassy's public information officer give us a copy of a "1983 Human Rights Report" on Nicaragua.

The document begins by saying that "a group of nine Marxist revolutionary leaders who took control in July 1979 holds political power in Nicaragua" and "although" the government "maintains that it is committed to pluralism and a mixed economy, the FSLN has progressively consolidated its power and restricted civil liberties."

The document speaks of the Miskito Indian situation. It charges that the Sandinista government "forcibly moved thousands of Miskito Indians from their traditional homes along the river boundary with Honduras to camps in the interior, claiming that it had done so in reaction to an outbreak of anti-government armed violence. Between 11,000 and 14,000 Indians fled to Honduras. Many villages were burned and animals belonging to the Indians slaughtered. Miskito leaders have documented incidents of forced marches, tortures, and executions of Indians by government forces."

It relates how the government, "claiming an imminent threat of invasion," declared a State of Emergency which "suspended many civil liberties guaranteed in the Statute of Rights and Guarantees, the basic law guaranteeing personal and civil liberties decreed by the revolutionary government in August 1979. . . . Under the State of Emergency, the government has instituted prior censorship of all media, imposed extensive restrictions on political party activities and detained without due process many Nicaraguans on charges of 'counterrevolutionary' activities."

The report continues, "While the government claims to favor a mixed economy, it has adopted discriminatory policies against the Nicaraguan private sector."

The document speaks of "political prisoners" and says "the government currently holds about 7,000 prisoners, about 3,000 of these can be considered political prisoners, most of whom are ex-members of the National Guard who were convicted by special tribunals. Overcrowding and substandard conditions remain serious problems which the government acknowledges and attributes to its limited resources."

The embassy report says that "torture is not widely practiced by the government" but it says there have been a few "cases. . . . State security regularly uses sophisticated methods of psychological interrogation. There are credible reports of prisoners under interrogation being forced to remain nude, threatened with the death of members of their family and subjected to other types of psychological abuse. In some instances, the prisoners have been beaten."

The report claims that there is also "credible evidence that security forces have been responsible for the death of a number of detained persons." It alleges that there are also a few cases of "disappearances under circumstances which indicated security forces were involved."

Under "invasion of the home," the embassy report says "the legal requirement for a search warrant was suspended under the State of Emergency" and "there have been numerous instances of the police arbitrarily entering and searching private residences. The government taps a number of private telephones. There are substantiated reports that the government is violating the privacy of the mail."

Of education, the report states that "the 'Curriculum Rationalization and Coordination' imposed on "the National

University and the other Nicaraguan university, the University of Central America, a Catholic institution also in Managua, "is a government measure which has limited the universities' autonomy in developing the curriculum and has circumscribed university freedom. Moreover, . . . texts with a high ideological content are used. Nevertheless, the universities retain a significant degree of independence in naming their faculties."

On religion: the State of Emergency did not suspend any rights; "nevertheless" there have been "numerous Sandinista-sponsored attacks on individual churches and churchmen. Catholicism is the predominant religion but other churches are legal and operate freely. Conversion from one religion to another is permitted and members of minority religions generally have not been discriminated against or persecuted because of their affiliation." Still, the report continues, the government has "accused certain religious sects of engaging in anti-Sandinista activities, including, in some cases, calls for non-participation in the military, and orchestrated a campaign against these groups. Pro-Sandinista groups took over churches belonging to the Seventh Day Adventists, Mormons and Jehovah's Witnesses. Government leaders, however, later described the confiscation of the churches as excessive and discouraged further takeovers. Some, but not all, of the churches have been returned to their original owners. Government officials also accused Moravian pastors of supporting anti-Sandinista activities on the East Coast. As a result, some have been arrested and sentenced to lengthy jail terms."

"One of the most visible attacks on the church," the U.S. report goes on, "involved a plot to entrap the head of the Catholic radio station. The priest, who was lunching with a female parishioner, was forced to disrobe by an intruder and then led off naked by the police who detained him for six hours. Pictures of the naked priest shown on Sandinista TV and published in pro-government newspapers deeply shocked the populace."

As to the "government attitude" concerning "alleged violations of human rights," the report says "the goverment has welcomed the interest of the international community in human rights observance in Nicaragua and claims that it has a human rights record of which it is proud."

As negative as Quainton and the U.S. Embassy under him

in Nicaragua are, however, about the Sandinista revolution, it is not negative enough for the Reagan administration. As 1984 dawned, *The New York Times* reported that Quainton "is expected to be recalled from his post in Managua soon for re-assignment" and "State Department officials say Mr. Quainton's imminent recall is a result of his incurring the wrath of Henry A. Kissinger." *The Times,* attributing its information to these officials, said Kissinger—chairman of a twelve-member commission appointed by Reagan to study Central America—"told the White House that Mr. Quainton . . . had undercut some of the commission's findings by reporting that, among other things, the Sandinista government in Nicaragua was performing fairly well in such areas as education. Mr. Kissinger's feelings were then relayed to the State Department." The impending action against Quainton was said to be "upsetting some senior Foreign Service officers" *The Times* noted that Quainton is a "career Foreign service officer."

"There have been some mistakes," Amando Lopez, dean of students at the University of Central America and a member of the twelve-member National Commission for the Protection and Promotion of Human Rights established by the Sandinista government in 1980, is saying in an interview. But "the real question," he continues, is whether the Sandinista government "respects human rights." The answer, he declares, is "basically yes."

He and his colleagues—"priests, evangelical pastors, professors and lawyers, housewives"—were "invited by the government to form a commission which would have power over the police and the Council of State."

The government, he says, has taken seriously the criticisms made by the commission and moved to correct errors.

Lopez, 47, a Spaniard, says he has been in Nicaragua since 1974 and before that lived in other countries in Central America, a region of "very corrupt societies, with corruption in every sphere." This was the condition, too, he says, in prerevolutionary Nicaragua. He speaks of living in El Salvador where "a radio patrol car followed me for two years, everywhere I went" and death squads preyed on the population, murdering people he knew. "Human rights is an absolute thing. It is not a question of comparison," he adds, but revolutionary Nicaragua's human rights records should be considered against this dark Central American backdrop and tradition.

He says the way the Sandinistas dealt after their victory with over 8,000 captured National Guardsmen and other functionaries of the Somoza dynasty was an important indication of how they intended to fundamentally change the way human rights were handled in Nicaragua.

They instituted a policy of "mercy," says Lopez, eliminated capital punishment, and "freed" the majority of these prisoners creating, in fact, a tremendous problem for themselves because, he notes, many later became *contras.*

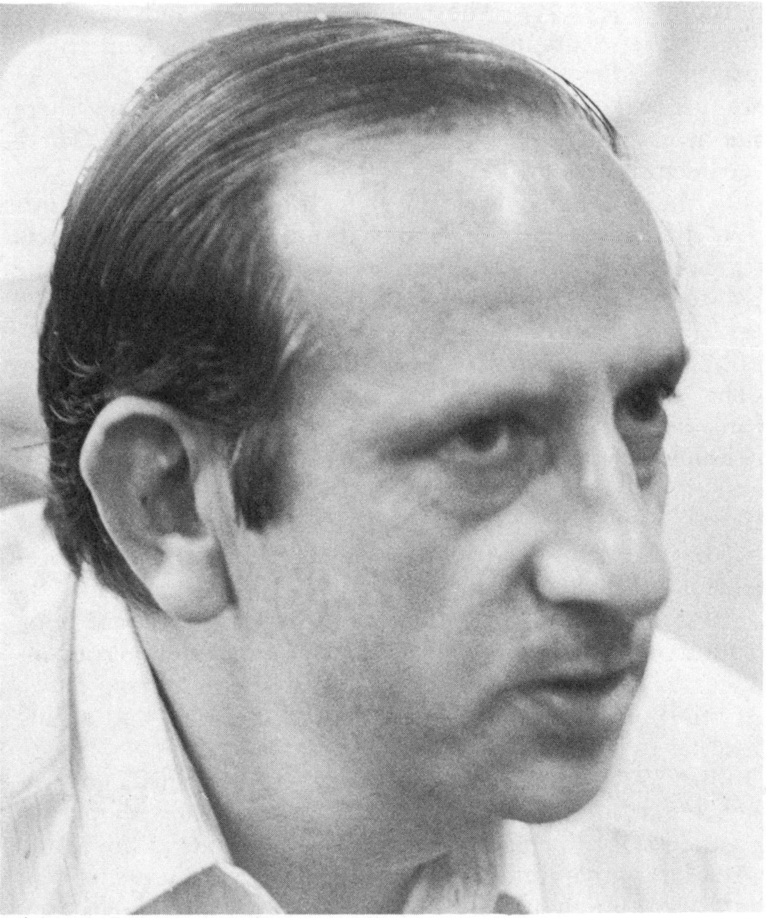

*AMANDO LOPEZ: Sandinista government "basically . . . respects human rights."*

Of censorship now in Nicaragua, he acknowledges that there is, indeed, a "limitation of expression" and it is "very badly done. . . . In charge of censorship" is a person in her early twenties. He sees censorship as a result of anxieties generated in a "society being attacked from outside."

Similarly, the maintenance of political diversity is "very badly done. This is not to say there's no political expression," but it is not what it should be. Again, he attributes this to external pressure, siege-caused fears. "This is a country in a state of war."

In some cases government action has been precipitous and unjust," Lopez says. The jailing of Bolaños and the other COSEP presidents in 1981 and the jailing, at the same time, of seven leaders of the Nicaraguan Communist Party were "not justified," he declares. Further, in prison situations there have been "individual cases of torture." He repeats: "There have been some mistakes."

On the Atlantic Coast, the government "wanted to improve the situation of the people. It didn't understand aspects of the minority. The situation got very confused" and some Miskito Indians "got abused." The government, maintains Lopez, is attempting to "correct its mistakes" with the Miskitos.

The "judicial system is not well-developed. There are many problems." It is hard to find lawyers in Nicaragua—"not to say honest lawyers"—and there is "not money to put together a judicial system," particularly in light of "other priorities: defense, education, health, food. Everything is a priority." But, he declares, "I would say that overall the law is respected" by the government.

As for "atrocities" in Nicaragua, Lopez says these are being committed regularly by the *contras.* He relates numerous instances of *contras* torturing Nicaraguans, committing rapes, castrating prisoners and amputating their limbs, and killing "in order to sow terror."

In late 1983, after I left the country, the Sandinista government undertook a series of major actions to deal with matters identified as problems by critics and opponents at home and by the U.S. government. These included: greatly easing censorship; outlining an "election process" for a 1985 election; conducting dialogues—with critics in the middle class (particularly Bolaños and the COSEP leadership), in opposition parties (including the Social Christian Party of Fletes), and in the Catholic church; granting amnesty for Miskito Indians involved in "acts of insurgency;" and granting amnesty to other Nicaraguans engaged in counterrevolution, inviting them back into the country and agreeing to return to them agricultural lands they may have abandoned or to make compensation for the land. Further, the Sandinistas sent home over 1,000 Cubans, many of them military advisers. And it ordered several Salvadoran rebel leaders to leave the country.

The Sandinista government also offered to order all foreign military advisors out of Nicaragua and to stop buying weapons if other Central American nations would do the same.

"We have decided to discuss all the problems that worry the United States," said Daniel Ortega, coordinator of the Governing Junta of National Reconstruction. "By doing so, we are testing the will of the United States to achieve a lasting peace in Central America."

Said his brother, Humberto Ortega, the defense minister: "We are seeking the reconciliation of the great Nicaraguan family, particularly those political and social sectors which, for various reasons, have not been in complete agreement with us. In the interests of national reconstruction, it is our duty to find a common ground with these sectors that will permit our differences to be resolved in a constructive way."

Many of the actions were in the form of governmental decrees. The one "Regulating the Elections of 1985" declared that "in January 1984 the electoral process must be initiated by means of which Nicaraguans must choose the government that shall continue constructing the new Nicaragua . . . Despite the difficult circumstances through which the nation is passing as a consequence of imperialistic aggression, it is the will of the Sandinista Front" that the Council of State be "called into extraordinary session" and begin to "function uninterruptedly" . . . to the end of concluding the discussion and approval of the electoral law and other laws and regulations that form the judicial framework of the electoral process." That would be followed by "proselytizing activities of electoral character"—political campaigns—and the 1985 national balloting. Subsequently, the elections were pushed up to November 1984.

The decree concerning "Amnesty for Nicaraguans of Miskito origin . . . involved in certain aggressions" began with the Sandinista government maintaining it has had a "commitment to struggle for the true recovery of ethnic minority rights" of Miskitos that "incorporates them into the statute on the rights and guarantees of Nicaraguans." The people of "the indigenous communities of the Atlantic Coast" have "traditionally been exploited, oppressed and submitted to savage colonialism." In recent times "the government of the United States has fomented counterrevolutionary activity developing a campaign to impede the government of Nicaragua, together with authentic indigenous representatives, from advancing the solution to the difficult and complex problems inherited from the past." It continued: "The level of counterrevolutionary activity to which the zone has been submitted, together with the secular undevelopment and exploitation and lack of progress of the communities, has made them open victims to the manipulation, deception and terror of the counterrevolutionary bands. Taking into the account the special circumstances under which the Miskitos have lived and considering that it has been deception and coercion that has led them to commit crimes, the National Commission for the Protection and Promotion of Human Rights has recommended revolutionary generosity to the junta." Thus, the decree went on, "amnesty is granted to Nicaraguan citizens of Miskito origin who have committed crimes against public safety and order and any other related crimes . . . and who currently are . . . under detention, whether already sentenced, pending sentence, pending trial (or) at large, either inside or outside national territory."

The decree providing amnesty for other Nicaraguans involved in counterrevolutionary activity declared that "the present North American administration is promoting a cunning campaign of armed actions carried out principally by the genocidal former Somoza Guards directed against the Sandinista popular revolution and its will to assure internal democracy and pluralism. . . . Despite these actions, the revolutionary government wishes to create the necessary conditions that will permit the participation of the greatest possible number of Nicaraguans in the electoral process. . . . Citizens who may have left the country on any date subsequent to July 19, 1979, and who may have been involved in illegal activities contrary to public order, even those of an armed nature, shall have all the guarantees that this decree confers in order to return to the country and incorporate themselves into civic life and the electoral process, with full right to elect and be elected . . . The citizens who may have been involved in the activities of counterrevolutionary bands organized from abroad, upon laying down their arms, shall have, in addition to their respective safe conducts, the option of being incorporated into land distribution programs of agrarian reform." Further, declared the decree, "in the case of agricultural proprietors who may have abandoned their lands, and which later may have been occupied, their lands shall be restored to them or adequate compensation made . . . Excepted from the benefits and guarantees referred to (are) officers of the extinct National Guard and members of the Somoza security force involved in repressive acts who have not surrendered to the tribunals of justice . . . Those who have been condemned by judical processes for acts against public security and order . . . Those who, acting as counterrevolutionary chiefs or ringleaders, have publicly or privately requested the intervention of a foreign power in Nicaragua and the provision of funds by this same foreign power to finance counterrevolutionary actions in Nicaragua" and those who "have directed or planned terrorist attacks to cause damage to the Nicaraguan population or the economic resources of the country."

The Sandinista government presented its program in a full-page advertisement in *The New York Times* in December 1983 headed, "Message to the People of the United States from the People of Nicaragua," and declaring: "Realizing that war among brother nations is a real possibility at this moment in Central America, Nicaragua wants the American public to understand its position and not be misled by the confusion of reports or the campaign of misinformation directed against a nation that truly wants peace. Nicaragua is a small country of only three million people. We are struggling to build democratic structures and to restore an economy devastated by 40 years of Somoza dictatorship. We want the right to freely determine our own future in peace and security. We do not want or admit interference or direction from *any* foreign power. As your neighbors on this continent we seek a relationship of mutual respect and cooperation with the United States. But for the past two years our citizens have been subjected to acts of sabotage and terrorism, including aerial bombings. A covert war is being waged against the people of Nicaragua. Our people are united against this 'covert war' and unflinchingly defend Nicaragua's sovereignty, independence and territorial integrity. Foreign backed mercenaries have not been able to capture and hold a single village in our country. Thus, our generous amnesty decrees and offers of demilitarization among Central American nations are not a sign of weakness, but of strength. With tensions increasing and the threat of a wider war all too real, the people of Nicaragua are addressing the American people. It is our hope that you will seek ways to make your government understand that military solutions are not the path to peace. It also is our hope that the Reagan administration understands that a war in Central America will have no winners and that not only our people but also the people of the United States will suffer the consequences."

Reaction from Sandinista foes is skeptical—yet hopeful. Bolaños is critical of the Sandinista plan to return agricultural land saying "there is no restitution or compensation for industrialists, businessmen, many landowners, or factory owners . . . In truth, nothing or almost nothing will be reinstated." He describes the actions as aimed at "influencing international public opinion." Still, he says, "We are ready to listen, but we also have some points of our own to make." He says he intends to test the Sandinistas' new emphasis on dialogue by arranging for COSEP to sponsor a program to be broadcast daily on radio and weekly on television which would cover political and economic topics.

*La Prensa,* taking full advantage of the substantial relaxation of censorship, has run Bolaños' criticisms in full. Indeed, for weeks *La Prensa* published a series of strong statements by opposition leaders blasting the Sandinistas, accusing them of repressing freedom, of deceit, of turning the country over to Cuban advisers "who"—in the words of one Sandinista foe—"take food out of the mouths of Nicaraguan children." Pedro Joaquín Chamorro says of the reduction in censorship: "The government is going in the right direction, but it is still not enough."

# RELIGION AND REVOLUTION

"This is returning to the very source of the Bible," Father Antonio Castro, a Catholic priest in Nicaragua, is saying. He is in front of the altar and pulpit—both made from Somoza bricks—at his *Iglesia de la Merced* (Church of Mercy) in the neighborhood of La Reynaga in Managua. "We are Christians working through the revolutionary process," he says. "To us, prayer has no value if it does not bring you to a real commitment in daily life."

"Our support of the revolution," declares the priest, "comes from our Christian faith."

Father Castro is typical of a large number of Catholic priests and nuns in Nicaragua who—in the wake of major changes in recent decades in the Catholic Church's philosophy toward social change and having experienced, some as victims, the inhumanity of the Somoza regime—embarked on a theology of "liberation."

"The authentic nature of religion is the liberation of people," Father Castro is saying.

He describes the Sandinista revolution as fully complementary with the teachings of Christ; indeed he regards it to a large degree as a product of Christian theology.

"Now, religion is a problem that worries people because it is returning to the roots, the soul of the people," says Father Castro. God didn't found religion, men did. Jesus did not come to found a religion but to teach us about the road to justice, faith and love." In Nicaragua "we are building a new society," says the priest, and working to make these Christian ideals "an actuality."

He speaks of the life of Christ embodying the spirit he sees the Sandinista revolution pursuing. "Jesus invited the

Pharisees to change their ways, to not keep exploiting the poor people. He said to the rich people, 'If you want to find salvation, then divide your riches among the poor and follow me.' " Some people confuse religion with their own "self-interest," he says. But the "Kingdom of God," he says, involves a "transformation of society" to one in which "we are all brothers and sisters. Then we can say the Kingdom of God is near."

Humility and sharing are at the heart of Christianity, says the priest, in blue jeans and an open-collared shirt. "God says

*FATHER CASTRO: "Support of the revolution . . . comes from our Christian faith."*

if you want to be the first, be the server, lower yourself."

I ask Father Castro about the pronouncement of Karl Marx—whose theories, I note, also form a major part of Sandinista thought—that religion is but "the opiate of the masses."

"That was true in the 19th Century but not so now," he answers. He refers to the changes the Catholic Church went through with the Second Vatican Council, convened in 1962 under Pope John XXIII, and by the Latin American Bishops Conference at Medellín, Colombia in 1968. He speaks of how they both set a strong, new mission for the Catholic Church of identifying with and assisting in the struggles of the poor. The "tradition" of the Catholic Church of regularly siding in history with the rich and powerful in societies, including Nicaragua, was "broken by these events."

For many of the Catholic clergy of Nicaragua, the new institutional direction of their church was further brought home by their exposure to the repression of the Somoza regime: the killings and disappearances and other human rights violations; the forcing by Somoza, after the 1972 earthquake, of all relief supplies coming through international church channels into his political organization for ostensible distribution but, in fact, largely to keep; and the brutal aerial bombings, torture and murder by the National Guard during the revolution. With Father Castro are members of his parish talking about how it was in La Reynaga and at the *Iglesia de la Merced* during the revolution.

"This neighborhood especially suffered because there was a station of the National Guard here," says Felipa Obando Jarquin, 41, who now makes and sells baked goods. She speaks of when the National Guard for "no reason" gunned down a young man in the neighborhood in 1978. "On the very day we were returning from the funeral, the National Guard killed a second man," she says. "Then on the return from the second funeral, the Guard killed a third. That was the day the whole village took up arms. From that day on, day and night, all you could hear were bombs and fire."

Rosa Pereira, 65, a retired teacher recalls: "By December of that year we had organized the civil defense committees. We were organized and ready at any moment because we already had heard the news that the insurrection was coming."

Nicaraguan churches, including the *Iglesia de la Merced,*

became sanctuaries during the revolution, they say, for Sandinistas. Mrs. Pereira remembers the night National Guardsmen held a gun on Father Castro as they came to search for people suspected of taking part in the revolution. "I was here with him when he stepped outside of the church and they put a rifle to his neck," she says. "He told me to leave . . . He didn't want me to be hurt. I said, 'Why should I leave?' " She pauses. "In the end, they didn't take him. They saw that everyone in his parish supported him."

"On June 10, 1979, that's when the insurrection began in this town," says Mrs. Jarguin. "That's when we ripped out the bricks from the streets and made barricades. But the Guards broke them anyway. They came and killed three boys in front of their mother. They took the bodies away—and to this day she doesn't know where they are buried. Those were the Garcia boys."

Now, says Mrs. Pereira, "the revolution has given many benefits to the people—the Literacy Campaign, agrarian reform. There are no abuses, no discrimination. Everybody has food." The Sandinista government is "doing what the Bible says," she declares. "The Bible says the lands are here to feed the people—all the people."

I ask Father Castro how he squares revolutionary violence with Christian teachings. "When people have exhausted all peaceful means, they have the right to defense," he answers.

More on that point has been written by Father Gaspar Garcia Laviana, a priest of the Sacred Heart Order who died in combat with the Sandinistas in 1978. "I'd seen perhaps the most humiliated, the most miserable, the most oppressed of Nicaragua," he related. "I tried to respond in a Christian way, peacefully, promoting social and human development, looking for ways to help these people live better by their own means and with government resources. But I realized that it was all a lie, all deceit. . . . I became discouraged to see that so much work had meant nothing, that so many hopes were left in the air. The people continued living the same. . . . And so I joined the armed struggle, knowing that nothing peaceful was possible . . . any other way would have been dishonest to my people and myself."

Father Ernesto Cardenal, now the minister of culture in the Sandinista government who also joined the FSLN in the belief that nonviolent struggle was hopeless in Nicaragua, has said:

"Every authentic revolutionary prefers nonviolence to violence, but he does not always have the freedom to choose."

In the mid-1960s, Father Cardenal, a Jesuit, founded on an archipelago in Lake Nicaragua a religious community called *Solentiname* which studied Christianity in the context of revolution. Many of its members were involved in a 1977 attack on a National Guard post in San Carlos. Father Cardenal wrote afterwards: "Why did they do it? For one reason only: their love for the Kingdom of God. When the moment came, they fought with great bravery. But they also fought in a Christian way. That dawn in San Carlos, they tried repeatedly to reason with the Guard by loudhailer, so that they could avoid shooting. But the Guard replied with machine gun fire, and very reluctantly they, too, had to shoot. Alejandro Guevara, one of my community, entered the barracks when there was nobody left but dead and wounded soldiers. He was going to set fire to the barracks, so that there would be no doubt of the success of the attack, but refrained from doing so out of consideration of the wounded Guardsmen."

The amalgam of a socialist revolution and religious ideals in Nicaragua—a unique phenomenon historically—was not something that happened immediately.

"In the beginning," wrote Father Miquel D'Escoto, a Maryknoll priest and the foreign minister of the Sandinista government, the Sandinista Front "was Marxist and anticlerical, perhaps because a process of Christianization had not yet begun in the Nicaraguan Catholic Church, and it was identified with the interests of the privileged class. But with our evangelical radicalization, placing ourselves on the side of the poor and oppressed . . . the Front opened itself to Christians because they believed the Church an important factor in the struggle for liberation and because they realized they were wrong in believing that only a Marxist could be revolutionary. Thus the Front acquired maturity and it became authentically Sandinista."

Father D'Escoto declared that although the Sandinista movement has "been very much aided by Marxist thought to understand some great problems . . . we have been equally or more influenced by Christian thought."

He gave, in the American Catholic magazine *Sojourners*, this history: "A process of renewal in the Catholic Church began after Vatican II permeated our reality through the historic meeting of Latin American bishops in Medellín. It filtered down and reached Catholic schools where they began to have qualms of conscience that they were educating only the elite and helping them to live in a bubble separate from the rest of their brothers and sisters. The schools began to foment the idea that young students should voluntarily help out in the poor *barrios* with parish priests who were working with the poor. That's how the students discovered the plight of their brothers and sisters and began to search for what to do. From there they went to the mountains and joined the Sandinista Front. Many of these students who are in high government positions today are very young because all this happened in the early '70s. The great growth in the Sandinista Front occurred when the church began this process of renewal in Nicaragua and consciences began to open. Commandante Daniel Ortega publicly has said that he went to the revolutionary struggle because he understood that was what was demanded if he was to be faithful to Christ."

"God made us co-creators," Father D'Escoto concluded, "wanting us to participate and share in the canvas. God initiated a process and in a great love for humankind decided not to do it all. Having been given that orientation, we cannot accept being reduced to the level of simple spectatorship in a game in which only a few play. We have a built-in need to actively participate with our God-given rights in the common task of searching for a more human and just society."

There is division, however, within the Catholic Church of Nicaragua with a grouping of clergy led by the archbishop of Managua, Miguel Obando y Bravo, who are opponents of the Sandinistas.

Archbishop Obando was also a critic of Somoza. Among his early acts upon becoming archbishop was refusing to take a Mercedes-Benz Somoza sent him as a gift. (Somoza controlled the Mercedes dealership in Nicaragua.) For refusing to become indebted to the dictator, the archbishop was threatened and his house was ransacked by security agents.

He was for the ouster of Somoza but feared a Sandinista victory. He was opposed to violence; nevertheless, in one important speech during the revolution he declared: "A situation of violence is crushing the masses. I make a clear distinction between basic or institutional violence rooted in socioeconomic structures, and the violence of the oppressed which it engenders." One of the first public celebrations of victory after the Sandinistas won was a mass officiated by Archbishop Obando.

But as the revolutionary government took form, he became more and more critical of it. "We want a system that is more just, more human, that does away with the enormous gaps between rich and poor," Archbishop Obando said, "but we believe that Christianity is enough to change the conscience of man and the conscience of society without the need to resort to Marxism-Leninism."

At a Sunday morning mass in a middle-class Managua church, however, the archbishop was more concerned this day about a year-old incident involving his press secretary and top deputy, Monsignor Bismark Carballo who is also director of the Catholic radio station in Nicaragua, *Radio Catolica*.

It is a wild story: one of several incidents which left me regarding aspects of the situation in Central America as somewhere between *Heart of Darkness* and Woody Allen's *Bananas*.

Monsignor Carballo was photographed running naked in the street by TV and print photographers in the Managua suburb of Las Colinas. The photographers were there to cover a demonstration when shots rang out and dashing past them and the demonstrators came a naked man—later identified as the monsignor—with a dressed man in pursuit. Police took both away. Press accounts later reported that Monsignor Carballo had been caught at the home of his mistress by her angry husband. Interviews with the woman indicated a lengthy romantic involvement with the monsignor. Monsignor Carballo denied that story and claimed, at a press conference at *La Prensa*, that he was having lunch with one of his "faithful" when an armed man entered the house, forced him and the woman to undress and then chased him toward the front door. The police, he maintained, then entered the house, dragged him outside and past the passing demonstrators and photographers. It was a government setup to discredit him and the church, said Monsignor Carballo. This is how the "1983 Human Rights Report" on Nicaragua distributed at the U.S. Embassy also described the incident.

In his sermon this morning, Archbishop Obando is railing at a magazine of cartoons which has just been published which treats the episode. The cartoons "go against morality," the archbishop tells the congregation and are "insulting to Catholic belief."

After the service, he remains upset. "There is no doubt the triumph of the revolution was a result of the participation of the population," says the archbishop, "but there are certain attitudes that bother the faithful, for instance comics and television programs that mock the priests. And unfortunately, the laws of emergency leave a lot to be desired in the respect for human dignity. So the church has to remain critical."

In *La Prensa*, Archbishop Obando has scored those behind a "People's Church." He wrote: "Basically they present the following point of view: the Christian's first responsibility is to support the revolution, loyalty to it must be absolute and prior to any other consideration whatsoever, Christianity and

*ARCHBISHOP MIGUEL OBANDO Y BRAVO: "Attitudes that bother the faithful."*

Marxism are not only compatible but the latter represents the only way of embodying the former and making it effective. For them, two churches exist, the revolutionary church identified with the Marxists and the traditional or reactionary church which has to be replaced. Their principal activities consist in the broad dissemination of their opinions, in training militant cadre, and in systematically attacking the church hierarchy, whom they continually accuse of identifying with the rich and being counterrevolutionary." This is a move, he charged, "not only to divide" the Nicaraguan Catholic Church "but to create another church upon the ruins of the constitutional church."

This division in the Catholic Church over the revolution was at the center of the furor that arose with the visit in early 1983 of Pope John Paul II to Nicaragua.

William Callahan and Dolores Pomerleau of the *National Catholic Reporter,* who covered that visit, have noted how "the world press trumpeted Nicaraguan disrespect for the pope as one more sign of the 'Marxist-Leninist' government's hostility to religion. Those reports, we believe, are false. They are a fundamental misinterpretation of what took place." The U.S. Catholic journalists wrote that when the pope came to Nicaragua he "refused to speak of the peace and justice he preached in other Central American nations" on his tour. Rather, before 500,000 people at a mass in Managua, he stressed how Catholics "must live in solidarity with their bishops," taken by the crowd as support for Archbishop Obando "who heads the effort to distance the church from the revolution." He "would not address a single sympathetic word to the sufferings of Nicaragua" including refusing to acknowledge the death of seventeen university students killed by *contras* and buried the day before. "The crowd polarized," they wrote. "Some chanted '*El Papa*' and '*Obando*' . . . But the cry '*Queremos la paz!*' (We want peace!) quickly overrode all other chants."

The pope demanded "*Silencio*" (Silence) several times, but "the crowd would not be still. While the mothers of the young dead people held up pictures of their children directly in front of the pope and fruitlessly sought his blessing, the chant for peace continued until the pope left the plaza" and "a weary and saddened people began the long journey home."

The American journalists observed "that although he may

not have realized it, the pope was delivering a highly charged political homily. Insisting on unity with the current bishops of Nicaragua, especially with Archbishop Obando, is a political code for opposing the Nicaraguan government, the revolutionary process and the Christian base communities that have strongly supported the revolution. These communities see the revolution as a social effort to act out Christ's command to feed, clothe, heal and empower the poor. . . . The people came overwhelmingly ready to welcome him. Had he uttered even a few pastoral sentences recognizing the 'hopes and joys, sufferings and sorrows' of the people, the pope could—at any time—have recaptured their hearts and stilled the chanting. When the pope adamantly refused their pleas, a vulnerable and deeply disappointed people cried out their frustration in a great chant for peace. They had asked their father for bread and had received a stone."

* * *

Knowing the Baptist Church to be greatly conservative in the U.S., it was a surprise meeting Nicaraguan Baptist minister Gustavo Parajón, who is also a Harvard-educated physician, and listening to him extol the Sandinista revolution—and its linkage with religion. Dr. Parajón, co-pastor of Managua's First Baptist Church, is also the founder and president of the *Comité Evangelico Pro-Ayuda al Desarrollo* (Evangelical Committee for Aid and Development) or CEPAD. It is a social service umbrella group to which the majority of Protestant denominations (some 61) in Nicaragua belong.

"My support of the revolution is based on religious faith," says Dr. Parajón—speaking very much like Father Castro and the "liberation" Catholic clergy. "It's founded on the biblical idea that God is in favor of the poor and the oppressed. Our revolution is a sign of hope for the Nicaraguan people."

He continues, "Christians have played an important part in this revolution. In Cuba, for example, the Communist Party admits only atheists. But here, Christians have a vital role to play." He stresses, "It is clear that in Latin America for a revolution to triumph, it has to have the participation of Christians."

Dr. Parajón, as well as receiving a degree in public health from Harvard, completed his undergraduate studies at Denison University in Ohio (and met his wife, Joan, an American, there) and earned his M.D. from Western Reserve in Ohio. He declares that "it is difficult" to communicate with Americans about revolution "because of the fantasies they have about Communism and Marxism. It's easier to talk to Europeans who are more knowledgeable, I guess. What I would explain to Americans is that the problems we have in Central America and Latin America have to do with social injustice and the exploitation of a great many people—and the influence of the U.S. government, its long history of imperialism in this area.

"Our history is one of North American imperialism, and every Nicaraguan has been affected by that history."

He describes the succession of interventions in Nicaragua, the occupation of the country by the U.S. Marines, the many decades in which "everybody and his cousin knew that if they wanted something done you went down the street to where the American flag was flying and you'd get something done." This is a pattern—"of U.S. imperialism"—followed all through Latin America, one that is in total conflict with what the American revolution was about. He takes out a copy of a 1927 letter sent to Sandino by the American Friends Service Committee which reads: "The democratic principles of Jefferson and Washington are irreconciliable with what is being said in Washington." The same is true today, he says. "From 1898 on, all of the governments in Nicaragua have been appointed in Washington. This is why Mr. Reagan is feeding his lies. Nicaragua has declared its independence from Washington. And that's very dangerous."

The Cuban revolution was an "important landmark for all Latin Americans," Dr. Parajón continues, and something from which "a lot of lessons were learned." The way the Cuban revolution separated itself from religion is something not being repeated in Nicaragua. He refers to a "Statement on Religion" by the FSLN in 1980 in which, he notes, Christian involvement in the Sandinista revolution was acknowledged and Christian participation in the revolutionary government welcomed. This religion/revolution connection might be unusual but "this is not a Cuban, Russian, a Czechoslavakian revolution. It's a Nicaraguan revolution."

He speaks of how "impressed I am by what the government has been able to accomplish despite the aggression." He talks of the elimination of measles and polio. "To have no polio now is very significant to me because I had polio when I was three-and-a-half years old." Dr. Parajón, 47, who walks with a limp, cites, too, the marked reduction in malaria and goes on to speak of the reduction in illiteracy and the improvements in education and housing.

The Sandinista government has made mistakes, says Dr. Parajón. But, he maintains, it is more than willing to concede and correct them. "We have no fear with this government." He compares his meetings with Sandinista officials with a visit he and a delegation made to Somoza. "We had a well-documented series of 24 cases of murder by the National Guard. We were all shaking in our boots when we went to see him, prepared to go to jail. With this government there is openness. They have the readiness to admit mistakes, to amend them.

"We have had no problem working in this country with this government. We have had all the freedom we've wanted since the revolution." CEPAD began in the days following the 1972 earthquake as a relief program for those displaced, and quicky expanded to become a social service and development agency operating throughout Nicaragua.

Dr. Parajón hopes for negotiations to settle the problems the U.S. has with the Nicaraguan government. "All our government is asking is to sit down and talk," he says. He describes as the "saddest thing the number of dead we have and the families we have grieving" for those killed by the U.S.-supported *contras.* "My congregation has sent six young people to fight on the border, all volunteers. Every time one of them goes, we wonder if he will come back." Dr. Parajón fears an escalation in the U.S. campaign against Nicaragua, an invasion, and hopes "the American people will play a key role"—as they did in the days of Sandino—to moderate U.S. policy. "If our government can't defend us against the might of the American government," he asks, "who else can?"

* * *

As a Jew, my first concern about religion in revolutionary Nicaragua involved how Jews were being dealt with. I was concerned about media reports in the U.S. on charges of anti-Semitism by the Sandinista government and then, upon coming, bothered by Borge's hostility to Israel. I wondered if this was a reflection of the alleged anti-Semitism. Anti-Semitism is, of course, a personal concern, but I also view it in a wider context: as a pretty good barometer, historically, of a nation's tolerance level. Generally, when Jews fall under attack, others who are also different often end up under the gun as well. Jews have often been the first scapegoats as a society turns totalitarian.

Thus, it is with great interest that soon after arriving in Nicaragua, going for a restaurant breakfast, I come upon an elderly man wearing a yarmulke talking over coffee and croissants to a younger man who is also apparently Jewish.

I walk over to them. The old man, it turns out, is Rabbi Heszel Klepfisz, rabbi of the Ashkenazi Jewish community in Panama. His background is fascinating: originally from Poland, he escaped from the Nazis during World War II and was the Jewish chaplain of the Polish Army-in-exile. He accompanied Polish troops from England in the D-Day invasion, landing with them in Normandy and moving with them eastward. After the war, he "got a call," he recounts, to be a rabbi in Costa Rica, served there and subsequently in Panama, and has traveled extensively in Central America. The man he is talking to is Gary Ruchwarger, an American Jew

*Gary Ruchwarger and Rabbi Heszel Klepfisz*

from Berkeley, California who has been teaching English in Nicaragua.

"We are seeing history in the making," says the rabbi smiling. He is in Nicaragua, he explains, on an invitation to lecture on "social justice in the Bible" at the University of Central America, the Catholic university in Managua.

I ask: are the Sandinistas anti-Semitic?

"No, not anti-Semitic. Anti-Israel, yes," replies the rabbi saying this is a result of Israel having been a main supplier of weapons to the Somoza government. Israel continued, indeed increased, its arms sales to the Somoza regime after the Carter administration cut off U.S. aid and stopped selling weapons to the Somoza regime because of its human rights violations. Nearly all of Nicaragua's supply of weapons, at that point, came from Israel. Rabbi Klepfisz comments that if a Labor government had been in power in Israel it would not have done the same. But the Likud government of Menachem Begin sold a large amount of weaponry, including sophisticated aircraft, to Somoza until the very end, and now Israel is very lowly-regarded in Nicaragua. Nicaraguans are keenly aware, he says, of how many were "killed here by Israeli weapons."

As to the claim made a few weeks before by the Anti-Defamation League (ADL) of the B'nai B'rith in the U.S., and widely reported, that the Sandinista government has been bigoted toward the small community of 50 Jews that had been in Nicaragua, the rabbi says he met the day before with members of two of Nicaragua's remaining Jewish families and found this not to be true.

The ADL, in a press release, charged that "the Sandinista government has forced the country's entire Jewish community into exile, confiscating Jewish-owned property and taking over the synogogue in Managua."

There was an attitude among some of the Jewish families who lived in Nicaragua during the time of Somoza that "they were living here so they had to be with the regime," says the rabbi. This was particularly true, he was told by those from the Jewish families which had stayed, of Abraham Gorn and his brother-in-law, Isaac Stavisky, both cited by the ADL as victims of Sandinista anti-Semitism. Gorn and Stavisky subsequently went to the White House and met with President Reagan who gave further airing to the ADL accusation.

Reagan declared that "the entire Jewish community of Nicaragua has been frightened into exile" and it means that there was "not only loss of political freedom but of religious freedom as well" in Nicaragua.

The rabbi says the Nicaraguan Jews told him that Gorn and Stavisky had their property confiscated in 1980, after they left the country, because of Sandinista decrees allowing the government to confiscate property from people with ties to Somoza, not because they were Jews.

The synogogue in Managua, destroyed in the 1972 earthquake, rebuilt in 1976 and abandoned in 1979, was in Gorn's name. It was taken over in 1980 by the government for use by the Sandinista Children's Association. The Nicaraguan Jews who he had met with, says the rabbi, said the government has offered to "return" the synogogue.

Ruchwarger, 34, says he thinks the Reagan administration is using the issue of anti-Semitism in "trying to build up public support for the war" it is involved in against the Sandinista government and to alienate the American Jewish community from the Sandinista revolution "because the Jewish community is important and influential" in the U.S.

"As a Jew," says Ruchwarger, "I find the Jewish values I grew up with confirmed in many ways here. They are trying to live up to many of the ideals of the prophets. Indeed, they speak the words of the prophets. They really, conscientiously, want to create a society with righteousness and justice."

There is "grammatical confusion," says Ruchwarger, concerning the Spanish words for Israeli and Jew and they are sometimes interchanged in Nicaraguan newspapers, so when Israel has been criticized—and this happened frequently during Israel's invasion of Lebanon—it appeared that Jews as a group were being scored. Ruchwarger says he "complained" to Sandinista officials that the invasion of Lebanon was "something that was done by the government of Israel, and many Jewish people did not support what the government of Israel did." He said he argued that Nicaraguans "are specific when they speak of the Reagan administration's policies, not blaming them on all Americans, and they should do the same when speaking about Israel and Jews.

"Nicaraguans have great affection for the Jewish people. Nicaraguans love the Star of David. It is something Nicaraguan boys sometimes give their girlfriends." (Indeed, subsequently I saw a few Nicaraguan girls with the Star of David on chains around their necks.)

Later, I meet one of Ruchwarger's students, Sergio Espinosa, 18, and ask him his feelings about having a Jewish teacher. "It is good," says Espinosa. "People here are against Israel, not against Jews."

Rabbi Klepfisz says that some of his congregation in Panama "told me, 'Don't go to Nicaragua. You'll be put in prison.' I'm glad I came. It's different than people think from the outside."

One of the Nicaraguan Jews the rabbi met with, Jaimie Levy, who came to Nicaragua from France shortly before World War II and set up a textile and garment import business, declares: "What do you want to say? That I was persecuted? It is absolutely untrue."

Subsequently, I obtain a copy of a report by the National Commission for the Protection and Promotion of Human Rights on the ADL charges which also maintained that the Nicaraguan Jews who had property confiscated were treated this way because of their ties to Somoza, not because they were Jews. The report spoke of a telegram in 1979 from Honduras directing Gorn to pick up "merchandise labeled 'SUPPLIES, NATIONAL GUARD' arriving on SAHSA Airlines." It alleged that National Guard officers "visited Gorn's factory with frequency, including José Somoza," the dictator's half brother and inspector general of the National Guard. It told of workers at Gorn's factory staging a strike in 1971 at which time "Gorn called the National Guard. They arrived immediately, went into the factory and attacked with tear gas."

I also pick up a copy of a report entitled "The Controversy Over Nicaraguan Jews" by the Central American Historical Institute at Georgetown University which concluded: "While consistently anti-Zionist, the Nicaraguan government does not have a policy of anti-Semitism. It is important for the ADL to denounce anti-Semitism in whatever political circumstances it occurs, and history has given reason for the international community to respond strongly to such accusations. However, the ADL report does not seem to be based on sufficient investigation . . . The debate triggered by the ADL report exemplifies the growing gap between what is actually happening in Nacaragua and what forms the basis of discussion on Nicaragua internationally."

"Given the role that Israel has played in arming right-wing Latin American regimes," said the report, "including that of Somoza, anti-Israeli feelings have developed among many of those who oppose military rule. In addition, a strong affinity for the PLO has gone hand in hand with a Nicaraguan government policy of anti Zionism, expressed most dramatically with Nicaragua's breaking diplomatic relations with Israel after the bombing of Beirut. In Nicaragua, as we have seen in other parts of the world, there is the potential for anti-Semitism to grow from anti-Zionism. However, the cases of Gorn and Stavisky raised by the ADL do not warrant this conclusion."

Later, on the way to Jalapa, I pass through the town of Estelí and there go to a little museum set up to commemorate the revolution. Photos of those from Estelí killed in the revolution line its walls, there are other mementoes of the Sandinista cause, and on a table is a collection of weaponry and uniforms of the Somoza National Guard. I pick up a helmet

*A bullet-riddled building in Estelí.*

and look inside wondering where it's from. The lettering is in Hebrew.

Taking a deep breath, I walk out onto a balcony of the museum and take a photograph of an especially bullet-riddled building in this town left heavily scarred by the struggle. I think about what I have just picked up and Israel's continued role as a leading supplier of arms in Central America: to Guatemala, Honduras, El Salvador.

There are other countries, of course, which will sell weapons of destruction to anybody. France comes to mind. But Israel is a nation created out of the Holocaust largely by refugees from Nazi murderers in Europe. It was to be a country where a high moral tone would be struck. What is it doing as a merchant of weaponry to authoritarian forces in Central America? I know that the Somoza regime was one of the few consistent supporters of Israel from its very beginning, but was this sufficient justification?

I am a believer in the State of Israel and, on that balcony overlooking this Central American town pockmarked partly by Israeli shells no doubt, I think of how Israel has been—and is—playing with the devil in this region, and how that partnership inevitably carries a price.

# AMERICANS IN NICARAGUA

There are several hundred Americans living and working in Nicaragua including those helping the Sandinista government in areas such as foreign policy and agriculture, those serving in various private assistance programs, and priests and nuns.

* * *

Kay Stubbs looks like and has the background of the idealized All-American girl. Sunny, effervescent, upbeat, she's from Middletown, Ohio—in an area of southwestern Ohio sometimes referred to as the "buckle of the Bible belt." She was brought up a Baptist. Indeed, that's how she first came to Nicaragua, as a teenager in a Baptist youth group which went to the country to paint churches and hospitals. She describes her father as a "Bob Taft Republican, a conservative on most issues." Her brother, when we spoke, was running on the Republican ticket for municipal judge in Middletown. Kay Stubbs is a true believer in the Sandinista revolution.

Her first husband was killed by the Somoza National Guard in the last days of the revolution. At 31, Kay is one of the highest ranking Americans working with the Sandinista government. She is a consultant to the North American section of the foreign ministry.

She spent the summers of 1968, 1969 and 1970 in Nicaragua as a Baptist youth group member. And then, in 1973, after graduation from the University of Tennessee as a social work major, she returned to assist after the earthquake. "I got more politicized during that," she explains. She served, for a time, as a liason between the University of Tennessee's School of

Architecture and the Somoza government. "They had a project where they sent fifth-year architecture students down who had been trained in a number of earthquake-resistant construction methods. They were designing low-cost housing and things. Nothing that they designed ever got built. It turned out . . . nothing got built because we didn't take into consideration the fact that it had to be built with construction materials manufactured by Somoza. So that opened my eyes a lot."

She returned to Washington, D.C. to attend Antioch University's School of Law there and work at the Washington Office on Latin America.

It was in Washington that she met, in 1974, Enoc Ortez, a Nicaraguan who had been studying in Chile and just left Chile having been imprisoned and "brutally tortured" there. He came to the U.S. to study politics.

They formed the Nicaragua Solidarity Committee, fell in love and got married in 1977 when Kay finished law school. The next year, Enoc left for Nicaragua, to fight with the FSLN. "It was hard. We were very close. I understood why he had to go." Enoc had wanted to go back earlier "but it got worse as the fighting increased. He felt that he had no right to be outside of Nicaragua. . . . He felt so frustrated seeing young men killed and said . . . what could he say to his kids when his countrymen were dying and he hadn't done anything? . . . And so he came back to fight."

She speaks of how her father, an Ohio attorney, knowing Enoc as a "gentle man," was moved by his decision to "take up arms."

Enoc was sent by the FSLN to the north, where he was raised. (Indeed, I later passed his home while traveling on the dirt road to Jalapa and also passed where Enoc fell, outside of Estelí.)

Enoc had very little military training "but he was strong and could walk as long as any *campesino* (peasant)," Kay says. He fought with a group of "friends from his childhood."

Kay saw him a number of times. "Because he was in northern Nicaragua, sometimes he could be advised by radio that I was coming" and they would meet at the border. "The last time we were together was in the middle of June of '79. About ten days after I left he was killed, on June 30," just nineteen days before the Sandinistas won. She got the news in a phone call to Washington on July 10. "I came back on July 26 and went directly to the place where he had been killed and talked to the peasants, to make sure it was really him, because I was still hoping that it wasn't. They told me the circumstances of his death, that they'd buried him," she says softly, sadly.

"My family was all close to him and they knew how good he was to me. His death was a heavy blow to them as well. It's true that if a family member dies in an accident, or a loved one dies in an accident or whatever, you say, 'It's unfair, it's unfair.' But even more it affected them because he died in a war in which the National Guard had been trained and financed and armed by the United States."

Enoc was at the "head of a column which was ambushed by the National Guard. He stayed behind to cover the retreat." He was shot and rendered unconscious by a National Guard bullet. The next morning a boy from the village found him, as he awoke wounded in a field. However, the National Guard was "coming back" and Enoc told the boy to leave, Kay says the villagers told her. Then the National Guard came upon Enoc "and killed him."

She went back to Nicaragua to stay because "we had always planned on coming back. This had been our dream: to work in Nicaragua without Somoza."

After the revolution's victory she worked with the Ministry of Agriculture. There she met Reynaldo Diaz, an agronomist, a combat veteran of the FSLN whom she married in 1981. They have two infant sons. As we spoke, Diaz was on the southern border to assist in crop production in an area under attack from *contra* bands there.

"It's very scary," says Kay. "It's frightening. You worry when the phone rings at night. It's very difficult. But a lot of Nicaraguan families live like this."

As a consultant to the foreign ministry, Kay helps "with an analysis of U.S. policy in Central America." She says she expected that after the revolution the U.S. would have good relations with the Sandinista government. "Because I know a lot of the top leadership here, and I've been used as a translator at some sensitive meetings as well, I know that at the time of the triumph Nicaragua's intention was to have cordial relationships with the United States. It seemed at first under the Carter administration that was going to be possible. However, in the Congress there were some very powerful persons who saw Nicaragua as a threat from the beginning and didn't want any aid to go to Nicaragua that was 'going to help the Commies.' And they didn't believe it was to go to build a road—'it's going to indoctrinate the kids'—that kind of stuff."

Under Reagan, it's become war and, says Kay, "I think that it is a very erroneous policy the Reagan administration is embarked on.

*KAY STUBBS: Nicaragua has wanted "to have cordial relations with the United States."*

"Nicaragua is not Communist, viewed by the economy or by politics," she says. The major part of the economy—60 percent—is in private hands. "It's a mixed economy." In foreign policy, the "leaders of Nicaragua are struggling very, very hard to guarantee its independence." She is worried about constraints in the political process and the press, but feels these are in response to U.S. moves to overthrow the government and that the Sandinista leadership wants "political pluralism" and a free press.

As for the U.S. press, she is amazed at how often it tries to warp the story of the Nicaraguan revolution. She describes a recent visit by a photographer from *LIFE* Magazine who asked that she locate a Sandinista Army uniform in which she could be photographed. "He wanted a photo of Kay Stubbs with an AK-47 looking up at the MIGs flying overhead," says the young woman from Ohio smiling.

* * *

Peggy Healy has been a Maryknoll sister for fifteen years and has been working in Nicaragua since 1975. From Massapequa on Long Island, New York, Sister Peggy, 34, is a nurse-practitioner in pediatrics. She has worked in poor *barrios* in Managua and in the Nicaraguan countryside. She is a woman of angelic beauty.

I remark that "by and large, Marxist-Leninist revolutions are incompatible with religion" and ask "why should this revolution be compatible with your faith?"

"Well, I think first of all you have to define what the revolution is in Nicaragua," she replies, "and I think a lot of people think of it as a Marxist-Leninist revolution purely in the strict sense, in the kind of dogmatic sense. My experience with this revolution, and I have lived quite closely to it as it happened here—and our sisters did all over this country—is that it is not a revolution inspired by Marxism and Leninism, in that sense, but a revolution that arose especially from the social and economic differences that existed in this country. Like most of the countries of Central America, Nicaragua is a country where the majority of the people had very little access to any of the economic benefits of the country, political freedoms, and so on." It was that way "certainly under the Somoza regime for forty-three years," and before Somoza there was also only "a very small minority" ruling.

"The revolution was largely a product of that popular discontent and finally disgust with that reality and an intention to overthrow it. The *Frente Sandinista de Liberación Nacional,* which is the predominant political group in the country, and certainly the predominant political power in the revolution, is an organization that has a strong influence of Marxism-Leninism, in fact, but also within the Sandinista movement and its whole theoretical framework has been a large Christian influence. The people of Central America, by far and away, have a Christian heritage and background, and here in Nicaragua not just ordained members of the church but people who are Christian community members—people belonging to the Catholic church and the Protestant churches—have participated wholeheartedly, have been very supportive of the revolution, fought in the revolution, participated in humanitarian ways, whatever ways possible for this change to occur.

"Also, there's a strong degree of nationalism in the theoretical framework of the Sandinista revolution, a very clear desire that Nicaragua should be a sovereign country and should have its future in terms of being a Nicaraguan future, not anybody else's future. And I would say a fairly strong dose of pragmatism has been demonstrated by the leadership of the revolution. So there's many elements that enter into the revolution, and the special kind of revolution that it is. So I wouldn't define it specifically as Marxist-Leninist in its totality. Definitely, I think within the revolution there has been a coming together of different points of view on a pragmatic and practical level where people are working for people's welfare and benefit and are willing to come together and work together for these things."

She notes the Catholic priests who are leaders of the Sandinista government, Father D'Escoto, Father Ernesto Cardenal and his brother, Father Fernando Cardenal, head of the Literacy Crusade which "lowered the illiteracy rate from 50 percent down to thirteen percent. And there are many other priests and religious people working within the government, and many practicing Catholics and Christians. There's been a very close association between Christians—Protestant churches, Catholic churches and people from those churches—and this revolution."

I point out the long tradition of the Catholic Church being

a conservative influence in Latin America and ask what accounts for the sudden and dramatic change?

"You could probably see the change coming for a long time, but certainly over the last twenty years, since the Vatican II conference and then the Medellín Conference and again with the Conference of Puebla in the 1970s. . . . These were conferences where the bishops of Latin America came together and made a very great change. The dramatic point of this change is definitely there. The church has traditionally in Latin America—in many parts of the church, certainly not all of it—been allied with the ruling class, certainly with the crown under Spain. Then the church made a change toward what it calls the preferential options for the poor. That meant that the church decided that the basic area it felt it was important to both identify with, and at the same time serve, would be the poor masses of Latin America. . . . And I think that change also occurred because many of the people who were not only in the church hierarchy but ordained priests and sisters in the Catholic church began to go and live with the poor, move into their *barrios,* move out of the kind of institutions they had traditionally had of upper-class schools and really live with and see what the reality of the people is."

Sister Peggy speaks about how it was "for me, as a North American, coming down to Nicaragua" and becoming involved in the "reality of living with the poor in Nicaragua. Naturally, it makes you see the world from their point of view, it makes you see their reality, the political reality, their struggle for survival day after day, the reality of what they live. I think seeing it, that experience itself, moves the church in dramatic ways to take a new kind of stand." She adds, "It isn't accepted, let me tell you, across the board by everyone in the Catholic church—it's not to say there aren't divisions along that line."

The Nicaraguan revolution, I note, "involved violence, it involved killing. There's a commandment against killing. How do you equate your support of the revolution with that?"

She replies: "I think that in Nicaragua, first of all, we came to see through living with the poor the reality of murder in Central America. It doesn't just happen when one person takes out a gun and shoots another which, of course, I would consider a wrong thing to do. The reality is what's called institutionalized violence here, which is difficult for us in the United States to understand because of the standard of living we have. But for people who live in Central America and whose daily struggle, literally, is to survive, who watch their children grow up and know that their future is not going to be any better than theirs, they are actually living in a situation of what is known here as institutionalized violence—where the murder goes on not by shooting somebody but by, in fact, the social conditions in which they live. I think that any Christian person realizing that this is going on either within their own country, within their own reality, must act out of a situation of love for their brother and sister to deal with that.

"For many people in Nicaragua, for our sisters here, for example, our work was to help the refugees in Nicaragua. Our sisters stayed with the refugees during the whole part of the war. Others went and helped with the health care during the situation, helped to bury people who had been killed and so on. We did not ourselves physically fight in the revolution. A lot of people who were Christians made that choice because they felt like the only way they could change the situation was violence. They were pushed against a wall by violence of the powers of the Somoza government.

"In Nicaragua, people tried fasts, they had prayer vigils, they tried peaceful marches and every one of those steps that we participated in was met with bigger and bigger levels of violence from the Somoza government. The people made a decision which they felt was a Christian decision for themselves which said in this kind of situation we have to realize that the only alternative that was left—and they made that decision—was to overthrow this government so that they could go on with the process of eliminating the institutionalized violence."

I suggest that Mahatma Gandhi "wouldn't approve."

She says, "I don't think so. I'm not a student of Mahatma Gandhi so I can't compare those things directly. I was very moved by the film of 'Gandhi' that was just presented. I was deeply moved by that reality."

I ask, then the Gandhian message of non-violent civil disobedience wouldn't be relevant here?

Sister Peggy replies, "I'm not sure that it's not relevant here but I do think that the historical situations certainly are quite different. I would hope that message that Gandhi created could be more understood, could be better used all over the world. But I do also believe that . . . often we, from the United States, can't judge that from our point of view because we don't know what it's like to be hungry, to not have a future for your children, to see your children die of diarrhea. But I think the important thing for us to do is to try at every point to use the peaceful means and try not to judge others who, at least, are trying to change things for the betterment of other people. These are issues that still have to be dealt with. People are still studying them, and looking at them, and trying to look for alternatives."

About the United States' posture toward Nicaragua, Sister Peggy speaks about the "horrifying discovery" for her "as a citizen of the United States coming to Nicaragua . . . being with the people and trying to understand the situation and do something, that those taking my neighbors off to jail and torturing them were members of the National Guard, supported for over forty years by the United States. That is a discovery that makes you question what the United States has been doing for all those years, not just here but through all of Central America. I began to really question what is the policy of the United States, why is it that it has supported military dictatorships for years and years and years.

"And for me, the reality now as I watch the Reagan administration is that of a person critical of my government. The policy of the United States has been to provoke more violence, more bloodshed, more problems in Central America and certainly has not been one which has looked for peace."

I asked why she thought this was so.

"To me, that is a very difficult thing to understand. I've tried, to understand the mentality of the Reagan administration but I can neither understand it from a moral point of view, certainly not from a faith point of view, but I also can't understand it from a pragmatic point of view—in terms of a policy of the United States that is supposed to be looking for a security in Latin America in the future.

"I think that the policy of the United States has not only been directed at trying to stop basic change that needs to happen in Central America, but it has tried to do it in a way that has only provoked more polarization, more people's anger against the United States government—not the people of the United States but the government of the United States.

This has developed in Central America a very, very hostile feeling toward the United States government. I think the interests of the United States—security interests—would be better served by making friends in Central America than by trying to stop a process of history in which people are trying to change a very indecent and immoral living situation to one which provides more justice, more freedom."

As to what the U.S. government should do, Sister Peggy says: "I think the United States has to look for a policy all over the world which recognizes Third World countries in nationalistic revolutions need to change their realities. They're living in situations that are inhuman, unjust and basically unstable because of that reason. The United States has to adopt a pragmatic policy that doesn't fit all of these countries into the east-west prism, the Russia versus U.S. prism, but has to look at those situations, realize change has to occur, and make a policy that deals with that. In Central America, specifically, that means that it has to understand that change will occur in Central America, that these revolutions are not a product of the Cubans coming and telling people to revolt, or the Russians coming. This was a product of a national struggle by Nicaraguans to free themselves from a dictatorship.

"That's what's happening in Salvador and Guatemala. If the United States doesn't realize that change has to occur for stability in the region, and tries to stop that process, it will not stop it but polarize that process and then in the long run, there will only be more problems. In Central America the United States, I think, has to accept that change, Number One, and secondly, within that change realize that there are pragmatic relationships and good relationships that could exist. These are countries that are looking for new forms of economies.

"They've dealt with an economy that was modeled on the United States, but in these Central American countries the economy turns out to be one in which ten percent of the people own everything and 90 percent own nothing. It doesn't turn out like in the United States. So they're looking for new economic forms. They're looking for new political forms. They've had elections in Central America that have always been a sham, so they have an experience that is very different from the people of the United States in terms of these issues of elections and democracy. They're looking for new forms, and the United States, I think, should support those new forms rather than being antagonistic to governments like the government of Nicaragua, and other countries trying to change. If we keep supporting governments like the government in El Salvador, governments like the government of Efraín Ríos Montt in Guatemala, we're still going to be betting on the wrong horse, we're still going to be backing the wrong people. And the people of Central America are still going to be asking us, day after day, 'Why is your country doing what it's doing? What are we doing that merits this

*SISTER PEGGY HEALY: U.S. policy is "directed at trying to stop basic change that needs to happen in Central America."*

kind of treatment?' "

Is she is concerned about the Nicaraguan government changing from what she considers it to be now?

"First of all, I think that, of course, there's going to be evolution and there's going to be change in this revolution. It can't stay the revolution that it is. It's certainly a different revolution now, four years later. It evolves and it moves forward. Our experience of the revolution is that we've seen this government make a basic change in Nicaragua, and that is in the economic structure and in many of the other structures. The social structure has now been geared toward the majority, the economy geared toward basic needs that people have: food, housing, health, education. They've made enormous strides in a country that has very few resources.

"Secondly, the government in Nicaragua, we see, also provided for possibilities of change in Central America, and it provided some kind of model for that happening. And on a faith level, it's very important that it's been a revolution that has been generous. It hasn't slain its enemies, killed them. It's tried to treat them in a humanistic way. We've also seen, at the same time over the last four years, many difficulties and problems here. We've had our criticism of what's going on in Nicaragua, the Maryknoll Sisters have, and we feel free in this country to criticize. It's probably the only country in Central America where we are where we feel free to criticize its programs."

As to criticisms, she cites the treatment of the Miskito Indians by the revolution. Still, she said, the Maryknolls "were able to go and visit" the Miskitos on the Atlantic Coast "and talk to anybody we wanted of the Miskito Indian people, and we were able to criticize what we saw, what we felt was not correct" and to insist "we want an answer on this, what's been happening?" She says "we've gotten responses" from the Sandinista government on the Miskito situation. "Many times" it has "admitted" it was wrong, and conceded, " 'we messed it up, we did it wrong.' That's unheard of in Central America. It's not a reality that people normally live under.

"Certainly there have been human rights violations" in revolutionary Nicaragua. She speaks of reports of human rights violations in Nicaragua made by the Organization of American States and Amnesty International. But what you have to see in Nicaragua right now is the context in which it's living. It's a country that's not just operating within itself. It is now under attack from the CIA, from forces in Honduras that are supported by the CIA, the *Somocistas*, the former National Guard people that are supported by the CIA.

"There is real criticism and there is real opposition. I would say authentic. But at the same time Nicaragua is in a situation in which it is under direct attack from an outside power that's trying to destabilize and overthrow this government. The United States, the CIA, is trying to do that. And so it is a country that is reacting to that reality.

"In the United States, for example, (and I don't think that most people look at this as the proudest moment of the United States in World War II,) when there was the bombing of Pearl Harbor, a lot of Japanese people were put into prison, put into camps, letters were censored, and so on. I don't think people look at that as good, but I think they don't also mark that as Marxist-Leninist. I think they saw that as a country under attack needing to defend itself. In Nicaragua, with the press censorship, a lot of difficulties with political parties, the less and less freedom, the question is—is that a matter of Stalinism that's coming to Nicaragua, or is it the reflection of a country that is involved in a life-and-death struggle right now and it needs to limit, or at least feels that it needs to limit, those things in order to survive?"

She concludes that if the Reagan administration keeps pushing on its present course, "there's no doubt" these problems will increase because the government "will be under more and more pressure to defend this country and to defend the revolution and its reality. That just can't be helped. Nicaragua right now is a country at war. I just spent a month up on the border, in Jalapa. I saw thousands of refugees flow out of their own villages and towns that were bombed by forces from the other side in Honduras using U.S. rockets, weapons, mortar fire. The reality is that this country is at war, and so they feel that in order to defend themselves and to survive they have to do that. The more pressure there is from the United States, the more closed a society Nicaragua could become."

* * *

Peter Rosset, 28, originally from New York City and East Hampton on Long Island, has been in Nicaragua for two years working with the Ministry of Agriculture.

"I work in ecological agriculture," he is saying, "on ways of controlling pests using less chemicals, also ways of growing crops using less fertilizer."

A Ph. D. candidate in agricultural ecology at the University of Michigan with a masters in applied entemology from the University of London and a bachelors in biology from Brown University, he earlier was at an agricultural experiment station in Costa Rica but found "people who work as agronomists in government field stations, people who work in the Ministry of Agriculture in Costa Rica weren't all that interested in ecological agriculture. They are pretty much tied into the agri-business model of development for Third World countries. They're involved with multinational import-expert companies—the chemical companies—and they're not very much interested in seeing new ideas."

He made several visits to Nicaragua and "came in contact with people in similar jobs here" to those in Costa Rica who favored growing crops with the minimum of synthetic chemicals. "I was just amazed at how much more open people were to new ideas. People here were willing to acknowledge the fact that the system that was already in place, the same system here and in Costa Rica, wasn't working very well. There were tremendous problems with environmental contamination, massive poisoning of farm workers from insecticides, tremendous problems of insects developing resistance to the chemicals, and a huge dependence in terms of spending very scarce foreign exchange to import these chemicals. So people here acknowledged it didn't work and they were very anxious to hear about other alternatives. They didn't have very much experience themselves, but people were really open and really excited. That convinced me that I should change my site of work to a place where people were more interested in what I was working on."

As to how he got involved in ecological agriculture, Rosset relates, "I come from a background in basic ecology and had gotten interested through my studies in tropical ecology in general, and at some point I decided that basic ecology was just a little bit too esoteric and that I should be doing something socially useful with my life. The logical extension of ecology into useful applications is in agriculture, more ecological approaches to agriculture. So my interest in tropical ecology plus my new interest in agriculture meant that tropical agriculture was a very logical field for me to enter. And Central America is the closest tropical agricultural area to the United States." Further, "I've also been interested in Latin American politics and Latin American history for a long time."

What does he think of the Sandinista revolution?

"Well, speaking from a purely ecological agriculture point of view, I think it's absolutely fantastic. There's nowhere else in the world where I could be with my skills right now and be able to have my ideas put into effect as quickly as I can here. If I develop a new system, as I'm working on, to grow corn and beans together in the same field, I do one experiment and show people that there's less than 50 percent attack of insects and higher yields with the same amount of fertilizer, people say, 'Great! Let's do it on 100 hectares! Let's do it on 2,000 hectares!' And it's like whoa—hang on a minute, I'm not *that* sure that it works. But from that point of view, people are so open to these ideas that to me it's just a revelation. I can spend my entire life working in Costa Rica, working in the United States on non-chemical agriculture and never see my ideas put into action at any level, especially not a large-scale commercial level, so from my personal, professional viewpoint it's just a revelation to be here."

I note the claim of the chemical companies, for many years, that without their products the Third World would be hungry and that their products help feed the world.

Rosset laughs and quotes Monsanto's line that "without chemicals life itself would be impossible" and says "a very good example in Nicaragua of how untrue the chemical companies' claim that they are doing wonders for the Third World is cotton. Indeed, cotton in Nicaragua is now used as the classic case study in introductory entemology textbooks of an ecological disaster. Cotton was introduced into Nicaragua on a large scale in the 1950s. There were, more or less, three important pests that were so severe that with the products used then—early DDT, stuff like that—people had to apply pesticides between three and five times in a growing season in order to control these pests. Now what happened was there were a number of other insects that had not been a problem before, but these applications began to eliminate their natural enemies. These applications were effective in reducing two of the three principal pests in the beginning, but by the 1960s there had come into play another seven important pests, so by the mid 1960s there were eight important pests and the number of applications per season had gone to

*PETER ROSSET: "From a purely ecological agriculture point of view" revolution is "absolutely fantastic." Haskell Wexler*

from three and five to fifteen and twenty.

"And this process," he goes on, "continued through the 1970s, the 1979 revolution being a convenient point to measure it again, at which point there were thirty applications per field per season with individual fields receiving as many as sixty applications of insecticide. Some 96 kilograms of active ingredient of insecticide were being applied to every hectare of cotton field in Nicaragua, in addition to sixteen liters of liquid insecticide, an absolutely incredible amount. And by this point there were now fifteen major pests. We'd gone from the original three to eight in the 1960s to fifteen at the time the revolution triumphed. Just an incredible example.

"And then you look at the levels of DDT in people's blood," he declares. "Just within Nicaragua in the cotton-growing areas, they're thirty times higher than in the non-cotton-growing areas. On a worldwide basis, the level of DDT in people's blood is thirty-two times higher than the world average, the amount of DDT in mother's milk in Nicaragua is 80 times higher than would be permitted in cow's milk in the United States, just an all-around, complete, ecological disaster.

"Since the revolution, the government has launched a very ambitious program of ecological control of cotton pests," he says. "The principal pest right now is the boll weevil. The government this year had, on about 20,000 acres, a pilot project to ecologically manage the boll weevil. What they did was during the off-season—when normally everything is incorporated in the soil and the boll weevil hibernates in the soil—they left a strip about 50 meters long and three rows wide of cotton in every field. All the boll weevils, instead of hibernating come out and they sit on that one strip, and you can then kill them on that strip, and that can reduce the population by about 95 percent, the population that's ready to attack the field the following season. So within these 20,000 acres they had a net savings after the cost of the program of $2.14 million, and this is for a country which is extremely short of foreign exchange. That's just absolutely incredible. And they estimated that had the pilot area been all of the cotton region in Nicaragua, they would have saved $12 million which is more than twenty-five percent of the total insecticide imports of the country. The government junta has just declared the program a national program for next year. So we can expect even more spectacular results."

I note that insecticides restricted or outlawed in the United States—including DDT—are still imported into other countries like Nicaragua.

"Absolutely," says Rosset. "A perfect example is the substance which kills nematodes in the soil, DBCP. There was a tremendous scandal exposed by the *Los Angeles Times* in which all the workers in the factory in California where they were manufacturing DBCP were found to be sterile." Further, well water in "a large area" near the factory was contaminated "and there's a higher incidence of cancer" among the people who drink that water. DBCP manufacture as well as sale was banned in the U.S., Rosset continues, but the Dow Chemical Corporation—which owns the patent on the substance—allowed a company called Amvac Chemical Corporation to manufacture the substance at two factories that Amvac, based in Los Angeles, opened across the border in Mexico. "Amvac at this very moment is pressuring the Nicaraguan government to permit imports of DBCP. They're probably not going to approve it, but it's almost a touch-and-go situation because Amvac was sending them mountains of information lauding this product which is so totally banned in the United States that it not only cannot be sold, it cannot even be manufactured. Normally, these products can still be manufactured in the States but only sold to the Third World." For Amvac, "the only way they can sell that product is to penetrate new Third World markets, because it's banned in the U.S. and DBCP is also banned in Europe." Rosset thinks Amvac will "not be successful" in selling DBCP to Nicaragua "because the people here are on to them partially by me supplying them with background on this substance."

Currently, in Nicaragua, he continues, "they're debating a law in the Council of State which will almost undoubtedly be passed which is going to prohibit the import of chemicals to Nicaragua that are banned in their country of origin. They've banned the major ones: DDT, Dieldrin, Aldrin. But people are still permitted to use up the supplies that are already in the country which is about a one-year supply." These actions are "unlike almost any other Third World country."

Rosset regards the chemical companies as "doing exactly the same thing they do to U.S. farmers except, on a larger scale down here. It's called the pesticide treadmill. Once you start using a little bit it's like a drug addiction, because in the short run it kills the pest you want to kill but in the long run it leads to more problems because it kills the natural enemies of the pest and the pest becomes resistant. So each year you have to use more chemicals."

The political independence of Nicaragua gives the nation "a better chance to withstand the chemical companies," but it "definitely is not going to be easy. There's still a tremendous presence of the chemical companies," says Rosset. "In Nicaragua, Monsanto has a factory that does the final process of manufacturing Toxophene. The FMC Corporation is importing huge quantities of Furadan. Imperial Chemical Industries from England manufactures Paraquat here. These companies here, they're part of the mixed economy. The government is not about to kick them out. And so it's sort of a tug-of-war."

Usually, Third World revolutions do not have an ecological connection, I note. Why the difference in Nicaragua?

"The way I look at it," says Rosset, "is this revolution has, to a certain extent, changed the priorities. Under the previous government, under most of the governments in Third World countries and indeed in the United States—not so much under the government but under the system—the basic goal is to extract the maximum profit from a situation, say agriculture or a tropical rain forest, as quickly as possible, without regard to the long-term consequences, because the only interest at play is the corporation that's using that resource.

"Now the government in Nicaragua claims to be a government for the workers, for the peasants, for the poor people in the country and claims to be managing the country for their long-term, best interests. So if they are sincere in that claim, then it automatically follows that when they manage a resource, such as a tropical forest, such as the agricultural ecosystem, they'll manage it with the long-term stability, the long-range sustainability of productivity of the system in mind. And I've seen it here. There's been much more concern about managing forests: using them, doing some cutting, but making them last. And there is the same concern with destroying the agricultural systems.

"People in the government feel they have two factors at play: they need to maintain production, increase production in those critically important export crops such as cotton, coffee, beef cattle, sugar cane, etc.; given the general economic depression in the region they just cannot lose, afford to lose that foreign exchange. So their Number One goal is to maintain or increase production. However, at the same time, their secondary goals are: Number Two, decrease the dependency on imported chemical inputs because they don't have the foreign exchange, and Three, to protect the health and safety of agricultural workers and consumers. Now you put those three things together and that translates into a concern for ecological agriculture. There's no other way to achieve those three goals."

* * *

Mary Hamlin Zuñiga came to Nicaragua in 1968 as associate director of the U.S. Peace Corps contingent then in the country. (The U.S. pulled its Peace Corps personnel out of Nicaragua in 1979.) A native of Minneapolis, Minnesota, Mrs. Zuñiga has masters degrees in public health, with a speciality in health education, from the University of Minnesota and works in that field in Nicaragua operating an independent consulting firm in health and education.

She is married to a Nicaraguan—a Miskito Indian who is a veterinarian and works in Miskito communities. He has also acted as a representative for the Miskitos to the Sandinista government.

At the University of Minnesota she was active in the civil rights movement. "I think the people who were involved in civil rights could identify so easily with the principles of the Sandinista revolution if they knew truly what that was," she comments.

When she first came to Nicaragua, she coordinated activities of the Peace Corps with agencies of the Somoza government connected with development. She soon began to question the regime's "development" activities which, she says, involved things like assigning Peace Corps volunteers to collect debts from peasants. "It became obvious that this government was extremely repressive," she says. "It was not a limited democracy as we had been told in the United States."

In 1970, she moved to the Atlantic Coast to work at missions established by the Capuchin priests and the Sisters of St. Agnes of Fond du Lac, Wisconsin. It was there she met her husband, Marcelo, and stayed for almost five years helping with health and education and organizing in general in the Miskito country along the Coco River.

"But as we began to make the Indian more aware of his rights, it also became more difficult for us to work. We began to upset the power structure." Mrs. Zuñiga recalls one conflict involving school teachers who often failed to show up at distant schools until Tuesday and left on Thursday. She helped parents and village leaders demand that the teachers work a full week. "The authorities began asking, 'Why are you organizing these people to complain? They never complained before?' "

In 1975, she received threats from the Somoza security apparatus and left Nicaragua to join her husband who had begun studying in Guatemala. Between that period in Guatemala, her experiences under the Somoza regime in Nicaragua, and time spent in other Central American countries before that, Mrs. Zuñiga got a full taste of life under oppressive regimes in Central America.

She speaks of "the time in Guatemala when we encountered thirteen bodies hanging from the trees. They were farmers who had nothing to do with politics. I've worked with health workers in El Salvador who, the next day, were found dead. I've lived in virtual police states."

She and her husband returned to Nicaragua a few months after the Sandinistas triumphed. As to what she thinks of the Sandinista revolution, she declares: "Having lived here prior to the revolution and having lived fifteen years now in Central America, I believe in the Sandinista revolution. After having lived here and other places in Central America, I am able to evaluate perhaps something of what this revolution is trying to do for the Nicaraguan people and the real involvement of the people—their massive participation in this revolution, in trying to build a new society, in having the opportunity for the first time in generations to build a new nation. It's a very, very exciting place to be, especially knowing what's happening in other countries and having lived in repression both here and in those other countries."

Of charges that the Sandinistas have not been fair to the Miskito Indians, she says: "My husband is an Indian, and he's working with this government to try to improve the life of his people because he and others like him believe that the only way for the Miskito people to have involvement in the life of this nation is through this revolution. They lived isolation, they lived repression, they lived exploitation for all their existence since the time the British colonized the Atlantic Coast of Nicaragua, and so this is the first chance that they have had.

"That's not to say that in the course of this revolution, the Sandinistas haven't made mistakes. But I think that considering the historical development of this country and the feeling that the Atlantic Coast was separated from the Pacific, the Sandinistas being essentially people from the Pacific side,

*MARY HAMLIN ZUÑIGA: "It's a very exciting place to be."*

of Spanish origin, it was very difficult for them to even know and understand the Atlantic Coast.

"I remember when I was married; people said they didn't think it was possible that a North American could marry a Miskito Indian because they were 'savages.'" These were "Nicaraguans from the Pacific side" saying that "because there was no awareness of the life, the culture and the history of the people on the Atlantic coast. It is only since the revolution that there has been any effort to try to recuperate that history and that culture. There is a great deal that has to be done in building bridges, in destroying those many barriers that divided the people."

Of the changes in the Peace Corps through the years, Mrs. Zuñiga notes that she "started in a Democratic administration" with the Peace Corps and saw it go through a "substantial change" after the election of Richard Nixon, "and now there is no question that the Peace Corps is part of U.S. foreign policy." In the beginning of the Peace Corps, "it was not to be a part. In that initial conception, the Peace Corps would function separately from American foreign policy in the sense that its role would be to assist other peoples—independent of U.S. policy—and promote peace. That was the dream of people like [Hubert] Humphrey from my state who worked so hard for the people, and of [President John F.] Kennedy." But that has "been changed through the different years, and now Peace Corps volunteers are definitely a part of U.S. foreign policy."

I ask her what she thinks the American government should do in relation to Nicaragua.

"Stop its aggressive actions against the government of Nicaragua."

As to why the U.S. is taking such actions, she says: "They don't want a nation that can be an example to other nations of Latin America. They don't want to see the success of a government that works to eliminate exploitation, assures social benefits for all people and not a small number of people, that questions transnational companies and their influence throughout the world. They don't want to see a people work toward freedom and having all people involved in a popular way, participating in their destiny. It's against the interests of the United States—not against the citizens of the United States, but against the interests of big business that controls the United States. They don't want to see this revolution be successful because it can be an example to other struggles for liberation throughout Central America."

I ask her is she "not concerned about the claim that this is going to be Bulgaria in Central America, a Communist satellite?"

"I don't think so," she answers. "Nicaragua has a very unique revolution. It's a very exciting place to be because of the involvement of so many people. Compared to other revolutions, one thing that makes this particularly unique is the involvement of the Christian people and the whole Christian aspect of this revolution. This revolution and what you see in Nicaragua today are people who believe that God has given them the right to have a nation to call their own, to have land, to have education, to have health, to have social services—and they'll struggle for those."

Americans "don't understand" what it means to "have lived as slaves from generation to generation," for the many to be "oppressed by a very few," for "85 percent of the wealth to be in the hands of two or three percent of the people. We have a greater sharing of the wealth in the United States, so it's hard to understand the extremes of poverty that exist in this country. Most Americans are not exposed to those experiences in the United States, although some of them exist.

"And so I think that what Nicaragua is doing to make education and health and social services available to all and have land available to *campesinos*, to stop the exploitation of the factories—this is something that's infectious. And this can occur to people in other countries, and other people will want to have this, too, and the United States is afraid of that. It would be better if the United States would work with and help Nicaragua to develop, rather than try to destroy it because the destruction will only lead to a more firm conviction to keep building a new nation. They can't destroy the revolutionary spirit. The spirit that built our own nation wasn't able to be destroyed."

And what will happen if the United States "keeps pressuring?" I ask.

"The United States is a tremendous power and it can destroy this country, says Mrs. Zuñiga, "but it can't destroy the spirit of these people who have had a taste of freedom and who want to continue to live and build this new society."

# JALAPA: AT THE FRONT

We are in Ocotal waiting for a Nicaraguan Army truck to take us the two-and-a-half hours along the dirt road to the beseiged town of Jalapa.

Sister Lisa Fitzgerald, an attractive woman of simple dignity, wearing blue jeans and a plaid cotton shirt, a cross hanging from her neck, is speaking of how she used to take the bus to Jalapa where she and other nuns of the Sacred Heart order coordinate adult education programs and care for refugees from the fighting. "But it doesn't run very frequently now." Sister Lisa, an American and a former assistant attorney general of the Commonwealth of Massachusetts, says that the trip to Jalapa "is very dangerous either for a private vehicle or military vehicle or for a bus because of the number of ambushes which, I would say, average one or two a week."

Three times in recent months, says Sister Lisa, busses going to Jalapa have been ambushed. One time the *contras* "kidnapped all the men riding on the bus. They made everybody disembark and they took all the men. They let the driver go so he could continue on bringing the women and children who were left. Of the thirty-two who were kidnapped, five reappeared in a matter of days. They had escaped. Among the others, some were killed and most of the remainder forced into labor. The *contras* don't control any roads here so they have to carry their military supplies and their food supplies, and what happens frequently is that they kidnap peasants and force them to carry their supplies." One of those who had escaped on this occasion was "the English teacher in the high school in Jalapa who ran about twenty kilometers to Ocotal in his shorts."

In another incident, the bus was stopped and the *contras*

demanded to know if any Nicaraguan Sandinista soldiers were on it. "The driver said no but actually there was one, and he had taken off his military shirt, and the women sitting next to him sat on him so the *contras* wouldn't see his pants, and they allowed the bus to pass."

The third time, the driver of the bus "could see up on the road that there was an ambush taking place. They were ambushing whatever vehicles were going by. They had stopped a civilian jeep and had killed two of the people in the jeep already and were taking the other people hostage. The driver of the bus stopped and tried to turn it around in the middle of the road, and they opened fire on the bus wounding a woman and a child."

The nuns in Jalapa have "started a journal" to register kidnappings by the *contras,* says Sister Lisa, her blue eyes misty with sadness. In ten months, over 700 civilians have been abducted by the *contras* on the road to and from communities around Jalapa.

The *contras* have been zeroing in on Jalapa, she tells me, because it is among the richest farming areas in Nicaragua—taking it might affect the agricultural balance of Nicaragua—and because it is in a valley below Honduran mountains in which the *contras* have their camps. Indeed, one town in the Jalapa region, Teotecacinte, is in a cul-de-sac surrounded on three sides by Honduran mountains.

From their radio station in Honduras, notes Sister Lisa, the *contras* have broadcast that their aim is to "cut off" the Jalapa area from the rest of Nicaragua, occupy the region, declare a government-in-exile and ask for international recognition. Sister Lisa suggests that the U.S. and Honduras would be quick with recognition. From Jalapa they would then press on with their attempted overthrow of the Nicaraguan Sandinista government.

In Totogalpa, a village we passed through on the way to Ocotal, Father Enrique, a French-Canadian priest who before being sent to Nicaragua four years ago had a parish for twenty years in Honduras, spoke of why he now will not cross the border to return to the Honduran village where he once served. A year ago, twenty-five kilometers inside Honduras, he related, he was stopped by a band of blue-uniformed contras. Questioning him at length was a man with the *contras* who spoke Spanish but didn't appear to be

Nicaraguan, Honduran or Latin American at all. Several months ago Father Enrique came upon a photograph of that man in a Honduran newspaper.

He went to his study in the stone church and returned with the newspaper photo. "I'm sure this was the man," said the priest of the individual in the picture, a uniformed U.S. Army Ranger photographed at a U.S. military ceremony in Honduras. "He was this American."

On a subsequent trip to Honduras Father Enrique was stopped and interrogated for six hours by Honduran Army troops.

*SISTER LISA FITZGERALD: "Ambushes . . . average one or two a week."*

Totogalpa, he said, had been attacked by *contras* four times, most recently "last month." They struck then with mortars and machine guns, he said, and tried to destroy the village's grain storage bins before being driven back. In the Totogalpa village square that late afternoon, peasants with guns were preparing to guard their village for the night ahead.

"It's here," says Sister Lisa. The Nicaraguan Army truck has pulled up. A friendly-looking lieutenant in a camouflage uniform gets out, introduces himself as Lorenzo, and helps us get onto the open rear of the East German-made military vehicle. Lorenzo, 22, then takes a seat next to the driver up front, riding shotgun with an AK-47 machine rifle, the barrel of which he points out the window. Protecting us in the back are four regular Nicaraguan Army soldiers, all 16 to 19-year-olds, childhood still reflected in their pleasant faces, also carrying AK-47's.

Rumbling out of town, we leave behind the site of a carnival I had gone to the night before. It had been strange rolling into Ocotal (which is not on the front but is in the battle zone and was the scene of several *contra* attacks in recent months), having been concerned since Totogalpa about the possibility of ambush, and coming upon bright—very bright—lights strung over amusement rides, game tables and a small, rustic bull ring. It was a surrealistic sight.

At this fair were many Nicaraguan soldiers, along with people from Ocotal. They were warm to those of us from the U.S., they smiled at and appeared to like *Norteamericanos*—despite what the U.S. was doing. A 14-year-old boy told of his 18-year-old brother, who had been in the militia, being killed the month before by the *contras* at the front, not far off. I thought how it surely was a U.S. bullet that killed him.

A large bull rushed into the ring. Men hauled on a long rope tied around the bull's neck and pulled him to a pole dug into the ground of the ring. They tied more ropes to the bull and wrestled him to his knees. Then a young girl, a pretty girl with long brown hair streaked with gold, got on the bull's back and the men untied the lines. The bull bolted upwards and thundered around the ring, trying to throw the girl. She hung on. Men in the ring taunted the bull to charge at them, holding large pieces of burlap, primitive capes. It was not Madrid or Mexico City. It was a contest with a bull the likes of which I had never seen or heard of before. It was Ocotal in the midst of war, a war which I could not stop thinking was being organized by my own country.

The soldiers watching from the stands all were carrying weapons—AK-47's, rifles, sidearms. An attack could come at any time. And the pretty girl hung on under the bright lights as the bull bucked and charged. A companion commented that the contest was about "love and danger." Finally, after twenty minutes, the bull was lassoed and brought back to the ground. The girl seemed to have become caught underneath. Several minutes dragged by as men pushed against the bull. Then suddenly, the girl popped out from under the beast. She lifted her arms to cheers from the crowd. To applause, she walked rapidly off, although I noticed a slight limp.

Later that night I shared a room with a fellow journalist, who had been a G.I. in Vietnam, in a crude hotel where the water only ran cold and outside in a courtyard U.S. music could be heard. Themes from the movies "Saturday Night Fever" and "Grease" seemed to play over and over again. Lying in our beds in the darkened room, we spoke about how the Nicaraguans at the fair were so affable, open-eyed, trusting of Americans—even though. . . .

"It's just like Nam," he said just before we nodded off. "Nice people, poor people getting screwed again."

The army truck is moving through hilly passes. At some bends, two or three Nicaraguan troops are posted. I notice a Nicaraguan soldier, in camouflage, up in a tree, machine gun in hand. We pass three white crosses on the side of the road. "Three people were killed by the *contras* there," says Sister Lisa about the markings. We come upon patrols of four and five Nicaraguan soldiers, and waves are passed between the soldiers on the truck and the soldiers on patrol. People in front of and working near the houses we pass also wave at the army truck. Most of the houses have posters or writings on them: "*No Pasaran* (They Shall Not Pass), *Muerte a la Contra* (Death to the *Contras*), *Todos Las Armas Al Pueblo* (All The Arms To The People), and *Sandino Vive* (Sandino Lives).

"The village up there," says Sister Lisa, as we approach a community of little houses forty minutes out of Ocotal, "was attacked by the *contras* last month. They took 140 people. Two have returned. No one knows what happened to the others."

Occasionally, a jeep-load of soldiers, or another truck with soldiers, passes. All the soldiers are like those on our truck: young, helmetless. It is a youthful army, and like Sandino's force which preceded it, a peasant army.

The truck is carefully fording a river. "The *contras* blew up the bridge and that truck, too," says the sister. Pieces of timber and concrete from what once had been a bridge are scattered fifty feet from where the army truck is gingerly making its way across the waterway. The blackened hulk of a pick-up truck sits along the shore.

The landscape is now getting greener, flatter. We are in a highly fertile zone, the heart of the valley of Jalapa. It is verdant green, with the green-blue mountains of Honduras beyond. It looks like a tropical version of Vermont or Oregon. We pass fields of tall corn, rice, more corn where the fields are marked for some type of agricultural experiment evidently underway, and fields of beans, cotton, pineapple, coffee, coconuts, tobacco. They are rich, broad fields stretching on and on.

"That's Somoza's tobacco farm coming up." Sister Lisa points ahead. In front of us are a cluster of steel barns and a large house. "It was called *La Mia,*" says the nun. "For 'Mine.' "

She points out the "Somoza air strip" for the estate, one of several farm-estates the Somoza dynasty had in Nicaragua. By the time the Somoza dictatorship was ended, the family owned thirty percent of the arable land of Nicaragua—which is a country the size of the state of Pennsylvania. The runway is a macadam strip alongside the dirt road. Sister Lisa tells me that "when foreign dignitaries" came to *La Mia* to be entertained, "all the workers were ordered to leave." Out-of-sight, the mistreated workers would be out of a visitor's mind.

An army outpost is ahead. There are some small wood buildings, a few trucks and jeeps, surrounded by a fence. Overhead, the red and black flag of the FSLN ripples in the wind. Sentries with AK-47's stand out front.

"Nicaraguans are dying at this moment," said Deputy Commander Roberto Sánchez at a military briefing in Managua the morning before. "Foreign aggression is being launched against Nicaragua." The arms being supplies to the *contras* by the United States Central Intelligence Agency "are now qualitatively better, their military equipment overall is better." And, he said, there has been a general acceleration in recent months of U.S. involvement with the *contras* who "are mainly from the former National Guard of Somoza. There has also been an increase of U.S. advisors in Honduras" and U.S. military helicopters have been seen flying in and out of *contra* camps. Further, the Honduran Army was participating in *contra* attacks by having its artillery "soften up" targets.

With a pointer, he noted areas across the Nicaraguan border in Honduras where the *contras* have their camps. The camps make a wide semi-circle around Jalapa. He estimated the total number of *contras* at 12,000 and said that "when things go bad for them" they can fairly easily slip back to safe haven in Honduras. "We don't have the capability to discharge them. We don't have the helicopters."

He maintained that two U.S. reporters killed two months before along the Honduras-Nicaragua border died when Honduran artillery opened fire on their car. He suggested that the journalists might have gained "some kind of knowledge" about Honduran involvement with the *contras* that the Honduran Army did not want them to disclose.

Sánchez said the total number of "trained" Nicaraguan military is 80,000, which includes men, women and young boys. There are boys down to the age of 14 in the combat zone and the government was seeking to end this by limiting those entering the army to 17 and above. "Physically and psychologically, they are not prepared to understand the full magnitude of what's involved in war," he said of the young teenagers although youngsters, he noted, were extensively involved in the revolutionary struggle itself. (After years of deaths from malnutrition and hunger as well as terror under Somoza, and with the flight of many middle and upper-class people after the revolution, Nicaragua was left with a very young population, half under 14 years old.)

Sánchez stressed that with the country having a total population of but 2.7 million people, the hundreds of continuing casualties due to *contra* attacks constitute a heavy loss.

He spoke of the "southern front" where former Sandinista leader Edén Pastora is fighting with a far smaller band than the *contras* have in the north but "also with support from the CIA." He pointed to an area of Costa Rica from which, he said, Pastora's group operates. The Pastora band is engaged by the Nicaraguan Army about "once a week" and it functions as do the *contras* in the north, by "using sabotage, terrorism and ambush."

"Where the enemy is operating, we can't guarantee life to anybody," Sánchez added, so before leaving for Jalapa, I had to sign a declaration provided by the government saying I was "traveling to a zone of military emergency" and accepted full responsibility.

We are at the edge of Jalapa. We stop before a large sign as an oxcart approaches from the town. The sign, painted in bright colors, depicts a peasant plowing a field with an ox and Nicaraguan soldiers in combat, and declares: *Desde La Frontera Jalapa, Firmeza Revolutionaria* (From The Border Area of Jalapa, Revolutionary Strength).

The truck rumbles into the town which is clearly under seige. Soldiers are all over. Sister Lisa points out a hospital which has just been built. The streets are all of dirt. Muddy pigs and chickens wander. We stop at the modest house of the Sisters of Sacred Heart in Jalapa and have lunch: roasted chicken and mashed potatoes, made by the townspeople, and Coca-Cola.

"This area has been suffering an increasing amount of aggression against it since March of 1982," according to Sergio Lobo, a 30-year-old agronomist. "Since December 1982 the *contras* have made four attempts to take Jalapa."

Lobo is the civil administrator of Jalapa. Behind him, as he speaks, is a diagram outlining the defense of the town against an attack: to what buildings and on which streets people would go to fight.

"These forces receive the support of Ronald Reagan and the most reactionary elements in Honduras, and have as their base of operations Honduras itself," says Lobo, declaring he knows this is so because "their weapons, their boots, their clothes, everything to equip a soldier" are from the United States, with some material also Israeli-made. "They wouldn't have the capacity to confront the population without the support of the CIA." He states that the Honduran Army has routinely supported *contra* attacks with mortar and artillery fire.

The attacks that began in March 1982 have "seriously affected" the area, and the "escalation" of assaults in December 1982 "coincided with other factors. Jalapa is among the most productive areas in the country. It was not an accident that the attacks happened this way. It was part of the overall strategy of the counterrevolution." December, he notes, "is the harvest time for rice, beans and coffee and the period when cultivation of tobacco begins," and the *contras* mean to disrupt agricultural production.

He goes on about *contras* "creating terror" in the valley of Jalapa by "committing terrorists acts like cutting people's heads off and other terrible things." As a result, says Lobo, a native of Ocotal, people in smaller, scattered villages in the valley have been moved to larger communities so they can "work in the valley and we can protect the people in the valley from the counterrevolutionaries coming down from the mountains."

The violence has become constant. Three days before, in Sandino, twenty-two miles away, "nine *contras* were killed in a battle in the town and there were two of our *compas* (comrades) killed. One was the head of the militia here in Jalapa." The *contras* in the last three attacks on Jalapa seem to be attempting a pincer movement, striking at the north and south of the Jalapa valley in an attempt to "cut us off."

I walk around Jalapa and talk to people. Oscar Cascere, 22, sits on his horse talking to another man on a dusty Jalapa street. "They're not going to get in," says Cascere. "We will kill them if they try to get in."

Jorge Rivera, 18, is a soldier in the militia. "We're ready to do what we have to do," he says. I ask him about what he thinks of the revolution. "During the time of Somoza," he says, "we were exploited. Before the revolution very little was provided for the peasants." He has been in "many battles" against the *contras,* he says, and he is not frightened about combat. "I feel that I have valor and courage," says the young man who wears chinos and a civilian shirt of khaki and white. Marking his being a soldier is a khaki holder he wears on his chest loaded with AK-47 bullet clips. He comes from Estelí, has fifteen brothers and sisters, and was a mechanic before joining the militia. "I don't know when I will return," he says.

Soraya Safreán is a 19-year-old woman soldier. She speaks of being in battle, most recently at Teotecacinte. She says she fights with an AK-47. Of the revolution, she says: "Under Somoza there was tremendous exploitation. Now people from all social classes can participate. The imperialists and Somoza didn't want the *campesinos* to learn how to read and write." She is from Bluefields, in southeastern Nicaragua. Her family has a "small store" there. She says she's a student—and "I'm still a student. I would like to continue my studies but if the revolution needs defending, I'll postpone all of that and go wherever they send me to defend the revolution. As a woman I can participate in the whole revolution" including "fighting to protect it. It's all of the people, not just men, participating in defending the revolution," she says firmly.

There are children in the streets of Jalapa. Some look anxious.

*Soraya Safreán and Jorge Rivera*

*Children of Jalapa*

Meanwhile, coming off an army truck I see a Hollywood version of a Latin American *guerrillero* or revolutionary. Lt. Luis Enriquez, an AK-47 slung over his shoulder, bullet clips and hand grenades hanging from his chest, a .45 caliber sidearm and long knife "for emergency cases" on his belt, says from under his thick black mustache that he has been fighting "since 1976–1977. I am one of the founders of the army." He relates how "since I was eight years old I had to work, so since I was eight I saw exploitation of the people here, the crimes that were committed against our people, the injustices." He has been a truckdriver, an operator of heavy equipment, but since 1976 "this is the life I've been living . . . I have to do this until it is not necessary any more, until we can live in peace." He smiles as he is asked his name and comments that he often thinks of the name Juan before his real name. Juan, he explains, is the "nom de guerre," a code name he took during the revolution. He recalls it as a time "when we all knew each other." He now heads a squad which functions in the Japala region. "I am just off fifteen days of patrol." Holding a steaming cup of coffee in his hand, he grins broadly saying, "This is my first cup in two weeks."

Nearby, in the school in Jalapa an agricultural conference is being held involving 120 people divided into workshops in various classrooms. Roger Zeledon Torres, a primary school teacher who is coordinating the event, says it is being sponsored by the National Women's Organization, the Civil Defense Committee of Jalapa, the Association of Field Workers and the Farmers Union. He says the people are "evaluating the various agricultural programs that have begun, analyzing the situation as it relates to the production of rice, beans and grains." He tells of how, before the revolution, the Somoza family and other families economically "allied" with the regime owned much of the land in the valley of Jalapa. That land was "confiscated and given to the people." The government, he says, is trying to have the "most productive use" made of the land and it is its philosophy to have decisions "bubble up from the grassroots." That is the reason for this gathering and why similar meetings would be held to insure "massive participation" in decisions on how farming would be conducted in the valley. "There is no support at all here for the *contras,*" Zeledon says. He speaks of how it has been difficult in recent times because of the *contra* attacks. There were 122 villages in the Jalapa *municipio* or county but now, because of the situation, the 10,000 people in the *municipio* have been concentrated in twenty-seven of those villages. Returning to the agricultural conference and commenting about it being conducted in the midst of war, Torres says: "We can't afford to be afraid. We keep on going."

*LT. LUIS ENRIQUEZ: "I have to do this until it is not necessary any more."*

Liduvina Guitierez, 40, and her son are walking down the street outside. She is from Teotecacinte but has been in Jalapa for three months because of a series of recent attacks on Teotecacinte. Of the *contras,* she says: “They are a bunch of criminals. They try to kill us. We try to defend ourselves. I am taking refuge here with my family.” She has five children. Of the revolution Mrs. Guitierez declares, “It is excellent. A lot of good things happen for us all: education, there are good schools now; and medicine, there is medical help now.”

I am supposed to go to Estancia, a village with a large number of refugees from the *contras,* to interview some of them about their experiences. But the military command in Jalapa rules that out. Later I find out this is because Estancia has come under mortar and machine gun attack.

Instead, I am back on a Nicaraguan Army truck with a crew from Japan Radio and Television aboard heading, I only discover later, to Teotecacinte.

*Liduvina Guitierez and son*

Sister Lisa had advised that we return to Jalapa by 2:15, to make sure we would be traveling back to Ocotal before nightfall. As the truck rolls onward on a very poor road, a torrential rain begins, and the soldiers on the truck say we still have far to go. I am concerned about time. We pass an airfield and see the "air force" that defends Jalapa: a Piper Cub fitted with two rocket launchers and a biplane. It is 2, then 2:15, the time we are supposed to return, then 2:30, but the Japanese TV crew does not want to turn back. The Nicaraguan Army officer in charge on the truck complies with the Japanese urging to continue although time is very short. The patrols we pass along this road have the air of active combat. We are now riding at the front, and as I see the mountains of Honduras closing in on both sides, anxiety mounts. The hard rain continues. The open truck rumbles on. We are all thoroughly soaked. The Japanese still will not turn back, although I argue with them about the time. It is 3 when we arrive at Teotecacinte, and then we travel through the town to its very edge.

We are now 1,500 meters, I am told, from Honduras—the high ground of which surrounds us on all three sides. Someone on the truck hears a shot. We stop. There is talk among the thirty soldiers at this outpost about a Honduran helicopter landing close by a short time before. The correspondent with the Japanese TV crew, who is based in New York, has a New York City Police Department press card tied to a cord around his neck, and I emphasize to him that it is of no use here—we should leave as soon as possible. But he does not reply, and instead gets busy with his producer lining up Nicaraguan soldiers in a row, for no apparent reason. They are all in front of a thatched hut which has scrawled on it: *Muerte A Los Perros Yanquis Somocistas* (Death to the Yankee *Somocista* Dogs). The reason for the line-up suddenly becomes clear. The producer wants the soldiers to make a charge through a field laced with barbed wire fronting the Honduran mountains on the north. They do it, racing with their guns through the field, sliding under the barbed wire fences, all the while being chased by the Japanese reporter holding a microphone and his camera crew. It is a piece of media madness guaranteed, I fear, to draw fire.

I confront the producer at the thatched hut, telling him I will write an exposé in the *Columbia Journalism Review* about the fakery of his operation. I can think of no other source of pressure. It has no effect.

After an interminable twenty minutes, the shooting—fortunately it remains photographic shooting—ends. We are back on the truck, making a U-turn. It is then that I see black boots in several scattered piles—perhaps 100 boots in all—right along the border. A soldier explains that when a *contra* is killed, his boots are removed.

Still in the drenching rain, we rumble back on the truck. Much of the road is flooded. The truck, excruciatingly slowly, now must ford wash-outs. Several times the truck gets stuck, but the driver rocks it back and forth and moves it through the mud. It manages to get through. There are cheers on these occasions from the back of the truck: "Hooray East Germany." (The controversial Eastern Bloc trucks serve a good purpose after all. It is reported that the Nicaraguans have been disillusioned with their large purchase of East German trucks. The vehicles have proven unwieldy and sorely lacking on many levels. When the Nicaraguans tried to

*At Teotecacinte*

negotiate a cancellation of a second shipment, they were refused.)

We reach Jalapa a little before 4 p.m. We think of staying over in Jalapa but the military says no; an attack is feared that night. So again with Lorenzo in command and the same soldiers we had come with, still in a deluge, we start the two-and-a-half hour ride back to Ocotal.

As we leave Jalapa, we pass a small building in the middle of town which serves as its movie theatre. I see on it a sign noting the film for that evening, one about the town of Jews besieged by a Roman army many centuries before: "Masada."

*A young Sandinista soldier*

And on the wet return trip, I notice black boots every so often on stakes in front of the houses along the road: the boots of more dead *contras* in this beautiful but now bloody valley.

# THE *CONTRAS*

To speak to the leadership of the *contras* I go to South Florida. Latin America, indeed, begins these days just south of Fort Lauderdale. The road signs, the language of a major part of the population, the pace, takes on a thoroughly Spanish coloration. There are cities in America that resemble what they face: Boston in ways mirrors England and, of course, Ireland; San Francisco is America's echo of the Orient; and the greater Miami area, facing Latin America, in recent years has become a reflection of what it points towards.

There are no *barrios* of shacks and dire poverty in this outpost of Latin America. This Hispanic end of an appendage otherwise crammed with retirement condos, shopping centers, low-slung industry and highway national chain stores, is still the U.S. in its abundant wealth, but in culture a majority of people are very much Latin.

There is resentment to this Latin presence. On Interstate 95 a car passes with the bumper sticker: *Will The Last American Out of Miami Please Bring The Flag.* The dial on the car radio is full of stations playing Latin music. I come upon a talk show. It is two hours about what to do when something goes wrong with your television set. The guest is a TV repairman. He is telling callers how to best adjust the fine tuning dial. The program is interrupted for commercials for cruises and interments. One spot: "One-day delivery for burial back in the New York Metropolitan Area," says the barker. I cut off the interstate for a cup of coffee. I pass the office of *Anti-Aging News.* Only in South Florida. . .

The talk show I had been listening to is now dealing with the horizontal hold button—and how that can best be adjusted. I turn the dial to another talk show. This one is about how business could be better in Miami, with an emphasis on whether its hotels should be converted to gambling casinos—Las Vegas and Atlantic City style.

A caller has a different concern. "I can't go into a supermarket without hearing Spanish," the woman complains. "I'm moving."

I want to make contact with the *contras* leadership in Miami. It is reportedly from here that the war against the Sandinista government is being coordinated—under the guidance of Washington.

WTVJ-TV in Miami is a sister station to WSNL-TV on Long Island where I am a news anchor. Both are owned by the same company. From New York, before heading south, I had called the assignment desk at WTVJ-TV and asked whether they had information about Nicaraguan exiles in Miami, preferably those involved with the *contras.* Their list begins with the names of the Chamarro brothers—Eduardo and Edgar Chamarro and a Captain Wong, formerly a high officer with the National Guard under Somoza.

I roll into downtown Miami, driving through a very fancy area along South Miami Avenue looking for the office of Eduardo Chamorro. I find the address: a neat office building fronted by lush tropical foliage.

Eduardo greets me at the door. A white-haired man, he has a warm manner. "Meet my brother, Edgar," he says, of the somewhat more intense man beside him. "Edgar just came back last night from Central America." Edgar Chamorro Coronel, one of the seven directors of the *Fuerza Domecratica Nicarguenese* or FDN, the main *contra* group, says he has just returned from moving with a 50-member *contra* band within Nicaragua.

I have found whom I was looking for: Edgar, in 1977 was a member of the Nicaraguan delegation to the United Nations and he is often quoted as the FDN spokesman. (He and his brother are distantly related to the newspaper Chamorros.) Edgar, 52, was on the board of the Conservative Party of Nicaragua, was a director of the National Bank of Development, was a professor and dean at the National University and "operated his own advertising agency, Publicada Creativa," says his FDN biography, which adds: "He is skilled in communications and public relations." He has a bachelors degree from the Catholic University in Quito,

Ecuador, a masters in educational psychology from Marquette University in Wisconsin and did graduate work in philosophy, he tells me, for two-and-a-half years at Harvard. His FDN bio declares him to be "both a figure of loving and a man of action. He has very few personal material wants—yet fights always for the care and needs of others." It also says that upon coming to the U.S., he taught in the psychology department at the University of Miami and "later was active as an account executive in the field of commodity investments." Now, he says, he is working "full-time for the FDN."

Eduardo, 49, an architect and graduate of Notre Dame University in Indiana says that before he and his brother came to the U.S., he was the one "more involved" in politics in Nicaragua. He was a member of Congress in Nicaragua for six years, from 1971 to 1979, and political secretary of the Conservative Party. Indeed, he was one of the hostages in the FSLN attack on the National Palace in 1979 regarded as sufficiently prominent to be taken to the airport for the exchange of FSLN prisoners.

*Edgar Chamorro and Eduardo Chamorro*

"We left the day they took over," the day of the Sandinista triumph, Eduardo is saying at his desk in his architectural office.

Edgar, sitting alongside the desk, says that afterwards he and his brother met with Sandinista leaders in September of 1979—on an island off Nicaragua—"and didn't like what they were planning to do. They were acting like people dedicated to Marxism-Leninism. They had enjoyed a military victory and did not want to share any power with anyone. They were acting like they wanted to imitate the Cuban revolution and expand to El Salvador. We didn't feel any sense of democracy. They seemed very totalitarian from the beginning. They had no respect for any person, no respect for other parties. They wanted to change everything, to control everything, to be in complete charge."

Eduardo says he felt the Sandinistas wanted to immediately link with the Soviets and Cubans. "There's no such thing as a Marxist government in an abstraction," he says. "It depends on other Marxist governments: the Soviets, the Cubans."

At the center of the "very strict police state" the Sandinistas constructed, says Edgar, was "a security apparatus built by the Cubans in the Ministry of Interior." It had a "ripple effect" in chilling personal freedom throughout Nicaragua. It is the sort of mechanism, says Edgar, which is the "typical thing" in any totalitarian nation, "rightist or leftist—Haiti or Cuba. Borge is in charge of this apparatus. They were not going to let the revolution go democratic. They had a different script."

I ask the Chamorros about their relationship with Somoza. Somoza was "very arrogant, very decadent," says Edgar. He declares that he and his brother were "always opponents" of Somoza as members of the "opposition" Conservative Party. "Everybody knew that Somoza had to go," he continues, but "it is hard to listen when there is so much noise" and there was a failure "to find a peaceful solution" to removing Somoza. "We tried to find a solution."

He declares, "The real secret war was the one against Somoza, not against the Sandinistas—what the CIA did to throw out Somoza."

Edgar, who certainly is in close contact now with the CIA, says elements of the U.S. government—the CIA and "some of the planners in the State Department in the Carter administration"—decided that Somoza had to go. The decision was similar to one the same U.S. government elements made, he says, when they concluded that the Shah of Iran had to relinquish power. "They decided it was futile to go with the Shah, and the only way to counter Russia in Iran was with religious fanatics."

The same CIA officials and State Department planners who thought of Ayatollah Khomeini as a proper replacement, in 1979, for the shah, says the Chamorros, regarded the FSLN as appropriate to succeed Somoza.

"They were incredibly naive," says Eduardo. "They wanted to get rid of Somoza by any means. They thought they could moderate the Sandinista hard core with nice people. It was very smart but not real."

Working along these lines on the scene in Nicaragua, they say, was former Assistant Secretary of State William Bowdler and the U.S. ambassador to Nicaragua in the last few weeks of the Somoza regime in 1979, Lawrence Pezzullo.

Further, they claim, former U.S. Congressman Allard Lowenstein of New York was "very active" in 1977 on a visit to Nicaragua in "trying to de-stabilize" the Somoza regime. With Lowenstein's visit, "the whole thing began to change," says Edgar. He speaks of meeting with Lowenstein later that year while both served at the United Nations and how "Allard kept the *The Sandino Affair,*" a book by Neil Macaulay, "on his desk and was very much in favor" of the FSLN.

The men said they suspected Lowenstein was linked to the CIA because while he was in Nicaragua, although he only held the title of special ambassador to the U.N., after matters were raised with him there was extraordinarily quick action by the U.S. government. "Things happened fast," says Edgar. Eduardo adds: "The same things the CIA was working on, we saw Lowenstein working on."

The men say the CIA has two sides—a right and a left—and although both work in different ways, both have the same goal: countering Russia in international politics. They say the specialty of the left of the CIA is to try to facilitate moderate left governments taking power when revolutions are imminent rather than far left regimes linked with the Soviet Union.

Eduardo says Lowenstein, a noted U.S. liberal, could have "been part of the left of the CIA." (Lowenstein was killed by a former aide in 1980.)

Also, General Omar Torrijos, the president of Panama, was used as "a key person for America" in removing Somoza, says Edgar. Torrijos was seen as a "white guerrilla" by the U.S. government, a "revolutionary on the good side, anti-Castro." The U.S. worked closely with Torrijos in its anti-Somoza "effort." (Torrijos was killed in an airplane crash in 1982.)

Eduardo says the position of the U.S. government, including the CIA, toward the Nicaraguan revolution "very drastically changed" with the election of Ronald Reagan as president in 1980.

"I wouldn't be involved if Carter was in power," says Edgar, of his role in the *contras.* "Reagan means well. His administration believes what is happening is a menace. If Carter was still around, he'd be giving Florida to the Communists and I'd be in Alaska."

Of U.S. government support for the *contras,* Edgar will only say: "I'm not going to say we do or we don't get aid from the U.S. government." He does concede, however, that he visits Washington, D.C. and says he most recently was there for the Congressional debate about cutting off U.S. aid to the *contras.*

Edgar says the aim of the FDN is to "put pressure on the Sandinista government for them to have an election. We are involved in an effort to rescue the revolution." He speaks of the Sandinistas having created a "cult of death" in Nicaragua; "they've painted the towns red with slogans." He also complains about "inept incompetence" by the Sandinista government "in handling the economy."

The *contras* are able to "go very easily into the countryside of Nicaragua. We take precautions when we move. We have a lot of support." He has just returned from twenty-five days with a *contra* "column" and functioned as a "civilian, a political representative." He does not carry weapons because he has "no military training. There are democratic leaders in each squad to explain what we are fighting for so the people will know our program and our objectives, know our political goals, know why we want elections."

The FDN, Edgar asserts, is trying to "force" the Sandinistas "into reality, to make them accountable and to minimize Cuban and Soviet intervention."

I ask him about former Somoza National Guardsmen being

in the FDN. He says there are some but maintains that the FDN has "a very representative" membership. "People from all avenues have joined."

As for U.S. intervention, Edgar says he would be "very glad for direct intervention. I want to get the Americans involved. I say, 'Get the Americans back in Nicaragua. The Eagle has landed.'"

I ask him if he seriously wants this.

"Americans bring many things," he declares. "Hershey candy bars, 3.2 beer. They bring good things to life. I think we could become a state, like Hawaii."

Edgar sees no chance of Nicaragua becoming another Vietnam for America if it intervened directly in the country because "guerrilla forces have to have a pipeline." The Vietcong and North Vietnamese, he points out, were functioning on land bordering China and could get arms and supplies through China. "Nicaragua is in the middle of America. There's no way it can have a pipeline." If the U.S. invaded Nicaragua, it could "do it quickly" and win. The reason there has yet to be direct intervention by the U.S., he says, is because the Reagan administration has determined that "politically, it may not intervene." But, Edgar says, "if Reagan is re-elected" in 1984, he expects that determination to change, and a direct U.S. intervention—an invasion of Nicaragua by U.S. forces—would be possible.

An FDN declaration entitled "Principles and Objectives of the FDN" describes the group as "a nationalistic movement . . . organized to continue the historic struggle of the Nicaraguan people for its liberty, which after the overthrow of the Somoza dictatorship was ominously betrayed by the FSNL, imposing in the name of the Communist International, a totalitarian Marxist-Leninist system."

The declaration goes on: "Members of the FDN are Nicaraguans who from within or outside of the national territory, now under seige by the Sandinist regime, are tenaciously opposed to the Sovietization and Cubanization of their country and are now fighting in every way possible to free it from the tentacles of Marxist-Leninist imperialism. It is their aim to continue the original objectives of an authentic democratic revolution and the establishment of a type of government in accordance with the Western concept of man and society. After exhausting all pacific means, FDN proposed to invigorate resistance—armed insurrection—as a legitimate means in the struggle against the actual oppressors and in defense of the essential and fundamental values of the Nicaraguan nationality and Christian culture. The FDN has no intention of becoming a hegemonic political party nor a military or ideological vanguard and clearly states its mission as a liberation force to create the historical conditions needed for a rapid transition towards the institutionalization of democracy in Nicaragua and the establishment of a legitimate government in accordance with the spiritual and cultural heritage of the Nicaraguan people integrated with the free and democratic countries of the American continent."

The FDN puts out a slick magazine loaded with photographs of FDN guerrillas. Photos and stories about FDN combat activities are interspersed with full-page displays such as one urging *Eschuche Radio 15 de Septembre* (Listen to Radio 15th of September), the FDN radio station. On a back page is a photograph of Pope John Paul II and a headline: *El Papa Esta Con Nosotros* (The Pope Is With Us).

There is an essay by Edgar Chamorro in one issue. "Instead of the promised pluralistic, democratic and libertarian government which we all hoped for," he wrote, "what has been created is a Communist government with Stalinist enslaving tendencies. In the place of the patriotic nationalism symbolized by the figure of Sandino, we are living under an anti-Nicaragua regime, submissive, dominated by those who have made the country an instrument for extracontinental purposes foreign to our interest. A police state has been created maintained by force by a party-dominated army several times larger than the Somoza Guard or the armed forces of any neighboring country."

* * *

I am to meet Captain Wong at the restaurant he now owns in Miami, Los Ranchos—the same name as a famous Somoza-run restaurant in Managua. It is supposed to be a gathering spot for the Nicaraguan refugee community in Miami. It was more difficult arranging the meeting with Wong than with the Chamarros. In our first telephone conversation he said he was often "out of the country," but finally a rendezvous is set.

Wong, somewhat apprehensively, meets me at the front door of Los Ranchos which is in a shopping center. We sit at a table in the rear of the busy restaurant.

He is a Chinese-Nicaraguan. His father, he notes, came to Nicaragua from China in the 1930s "with a gold coin sewed in his pants" and parlayed that into a fortune in the grocery business. Wong, 40, says all his family's holdings were confiscated after the revolution. The Wongs were close with the Somozas. He received a bachelors at San Francisco State University and a masters at Harvard, both in business administration, and as a National Guard captain in Nicaragua was aide-de-camp of General José Somoza, inspector general of the National Guard and half-brother of the dictator. Wong says José Somoza, whom he has "loved like a father," also is a refugee in Miami.

Wong gives his version of the history of events in Nicaragua. He maintains that there was "literally no Sandinista movement." The FSLN was just "a little radical group" up almost until the fall of Somoza. It consisted of a few dozen people and was comparable to "the Symbionese Liberation Army or the Black Panthers in the United States." In 1976, he says, the areas the FSLN was active in were "just a few little dots on the map" at National Guard headquarters.

The election of Jimmy Carter as the U.S. president that year marked the beginning of the end of the Somoza regime and the rise of the FSLN. The "turning point," he claims, was the assassination of Pedro Chamorro. He speaks of Carter as a product of the David Rockefeller-organized Trilateral Commission. "It orchestrated Carter's rise to the presidency. He was a good-intentioned, religious man," says Wong, and had "many liberals" in his administration who wanted to "do an exercise in bringing socialism" to Nicaragua and to oust Somoza.

Pedro Chamorro, meanwhile, was leading a drive to remove Somoza, he notes. Wong speaks of the Chamorro family as "the ruling family in Nicaragua long before Somoza. They owned the wealth and the means of production."

Wong says the threats to Somoza's leadership—particularly the pull-back in support of the United States after decades of backing for his family—"transformed Somoza overnight." This "happy, charismatic West Point graduate became a harsh man."

The assassination of Chamorro made the newspaperman a "national martyr," notes Wong, and caused chaos in Nicaragua on which the FSLN capitalized by advancing itself as the mechanism to replace Somoza. The FSLN had a "ruling hard-core which was financed, educated and trained in Havana. It was 100 percent Communist." But "people of good intentions supported the Sandinistas"—people in Nicaragua and in the Carter administration—as a way to eliminate Somoza with Chamorro gone.

"They were tricked. They were fools," says Wong. "They thought they could control them." But the FSLN leaders, he asserts, were "hard-core Marxists with their own agenda."

As to brutality by the National Guard, Wong says: "Yeah, when you win a war, you get medals for bravery. When you lose they accuse you of brutality, genocide, you go to jail." He charges that the FSLN "used children as hostages" in conflicts with the National Guard. Meanwhile, Wong says some of "my best friends are still in jail in Nicaragua. They're rotting in jail." Also in jail, he says, are other members of the Wong family.

Of the potential for democracy in Nicaragua, Wong says "you can't give the vote to people who can't read or write, who never saw a toilet." He gives an example of why he thinks many Nicaraguan people can't handle much in the way of modern civilization: what he says happened in the days after the revolution when confiscated Mercedes-Benz autos were taken, and in short order "half the Mercedes in Nicaragua were demolished in crashes." He continues, "I believe in evolution. Changes must be made in the whole region. You have to educate people first."

He attacks what he describes as the "left-wing Congress" of the U.S. and the "liberals" in it who "can't give help to friends. The Communists don't hesitate to help their friends."

He warns of Communism spreading in Central America from Nicaragua. "The domino effect exists," he says. "That's why the liberals attack it so much. Reagan wants to do something, but not Congress."

Wong says he came to the United States after the revolution succeeded in 1979 "with no money. I was washing dishes." He insists he is "just a restauranteur now," not involved in guerrilla activity although he urges that the *contra* groups "try to consolidate, have a common force, or we're never going to get back."

He recommends the U.S. Army book, *Nicaragua: An Area*

*Study*, to me, and I follow his Mazda sports car to his Miami condominium apartment to see his copy. The walls of the condominium are lined with photographs of Wong and fellow National Guard officers—including José Somoza. It is a gallery of dour, mostly sun-glassed, some rather frightening Central American military figures, but Wong looks at the photos warmly and points out some of those who are now in jail in Nicaragua.

* * *

How the *contras* are allegedly carrying out their U.S.-supported campaign to overthrow the Sandinista government by making use of the sort of terrorism long associated with the Somoza National Guard is chronicled in a lawsuit, currently before the United States District Court for the District of Columbia. The suit, filed in 1983, begins with a listing of plaintiffs—which includes U.S. Congressman Ronald Dellums of California—and then lists defendants beginning with President Reagan and including John Negroponte, the U.S. ambassador to Honduras, and all the *contra* groups. It was prepared by the Center for Constitutional Rights in New York and the National Lawyers Guild in San Francisco.

The suit is yet to be decided, but the case it presents on the nature of the campaign the U.S. is supervising to overthrow the government of Nicaragua is horrifying.

Here are segments of that action:

JAVIER SANCHEZ-ESPINOZA, resident of the village of San Francisco de Guajiniquilapa, Department of Chinandega, Republic of Nicaragua;
MYRNA CUNNINGHAM, resident of Bluefields, Department of Zelaya, Republic of Nicaragua;
BRENDA ROCHA, resident of the village of Bonanza, Department of Zelaya, Republic of Nicaragua;
MARIA ESPINAL-MONDRAGON (VIUDA DE GUEVARA), individually and as personal representative of Victorino Guevara-Centeno, resident of the village of San Francisco de Guajiniquilapa, Department of Chinandega, Republic of Nicaragua;
VICTORINO HERNANDEZ-AGUILERA, resident of the village of San Francisco de Guajiniquilapa, Department of Chinandega, Republic of Nicaragua;

JOSE SANTOS-BARRERA, individually and as personal representative of Evilio Baquedano Barrera, resident of the village of San Francisco de Guajiniquilapa, Department of Chinandega, Republic of Nicaragua;
ELIA MARIA ESPINOZA (VIUDA DE MONCADA), individually and as personal representative of Ramon Aristides Moncada, resident of the village of San Francisco de Guajiniquilapa, Department of Chinandega, Republic of Nicaragua;
RONALD V. DELLUMS, in his capacity as a member of the United States House of Representatives, 213 Rayburn House Office Building, Washington, D.C. 20515;
ELEANOR GINSBERG, *ex rel.* State of Florida 9500 Southwest 60th Court, Miami, Florida, 33156; and
LARRY O'TOOLE, *ex rel.* State of Florida, 15625 Southwest 102nd Place, Miami, Florida 33157,

Plaintiffs,
-against-

RONALD WILSON REAGAN, individually and in his official capacity as President of the United States;
WILLIAM CASEY, individually and in his official capacity as Director of Central Intelligence;
ALEXANDER M. HAIG, JR.;
GEORGE P. SHULTZ, individually and in his official capacity as United States Secretary of State;
THOMAS O. ENDERS, individually and in his official capacity as United States Assistant Secretary of State;
VERNON WALTERS, individually and in his official capacity as United States Ambassador-at-Large;
CASPAR WEINBERGER, individually and in his official capacity as United States Secretary of Defense;
NESTOR SANCHEZ, individually and in his official capacity as United States Assistant Secretary of Defense;
JOHN D. NEGROPONTE, individually and in his official capacity as United States Ambassador to Honduras;
FRANK GRANIZO, individually and in his capacity as an official of the Central Intelligence Agency;
JORGE GONZALEZ;
HECTOR ALFONSO;
INTER-AMERICAN DEFENSE FORCE, an unincorporated association;

EDMUNDO CHAMORRO;
FERNANDO CHAMORRO;
MAX VARGAS;
DAVID STADTHAGEN;
NICARAGUAN DEMOCRATIC UNION—REVOLUTIONARY ARMED FORCES OF NICARAGUA, an unincorporated association;
NICARAGUAN DEMOCRATIC FRONT, an unincorporated association;
STEADMAN FAGOTH-MUELLER;
PEDRO ORTEGA;
NICARAGUAN LIBERATION ARMY, an unincorporated association;
ENRIQUE BERMUDEZ;
15th OF SEPTEMBER LEGION, an unincorporated association;
JOSE FRANCISCO CARDENAL;
NICARAGUAN DEMOCRATIC FORCE, an unincorporated association;
ALPHA 66, an unincorporated association; and
ASSOCIATION OF BAY OF PIGS VETERANS-BRIGADE 2506, an unincorporated association,

Defendants.

INTRODUCTORY STATEMENT

1. This action is brought *inter alia* on behalf of various Nicaraguan citizens who have been murdered, tortured, mutilated, wounded, kidnapped and/or raped as a result of U.S. sponsored paramilitary activities designed to ravage the civilian population of Nicaragua and to destroy its economy. Plaintiffs sue for damages caused by these acts of terror and for an injunction to prevent such attacks in the future. These United States sponsored raids against the people of Nicaragua violate fundamental principles of human rights established under international law and the Constitution of the United States.

2. This suit also seeks to enjoin the operation of U.S. sponsored and condoned paramilitary training camps operating in Florida, California and elsewhere. People trained in these camps engage in terrorist attacks on civilians in Nicaragua. The maintenance and sponsorship of these camps,

which are in the United States and which violate U.S. neutrality laws, constitute a nuisance under Florida law. Plaintiffs Eleanor Ginsberg and Larry O'Toole, residents of Dade County, Florida, sue under Florida law to close these camps.

3. Plaintiff Ronald V. Dellums, a member of Congress, sues to stop the undeclared war waged by defendants against the people of Nicaragua. Such an undeclared war conducted by the U.S. government, sometimes using a proxy army, violates plaintiff's authority as a member of Congress to declare war under Article I, Section 8, Clause 11 of the United States Constitution and the Neutrality Act. . . .

## FACTS

40. United States government defendants, acting in conspiracy with other defendants and others unknown, have authorized, financed, trained, and directed activities which terrorize and otherwise injure the civilian population of the Republic of Nicaragua. As an intended or foreseeable result of these activities, plaintiffs herein have suffered and continue to be threatened with torture, murder, kidnapping, mutilation, rape, wounding and other injuries.

41. In addition to harming individual civilians, the defendants' conspiracy and their activities include:

a. Destroying hospitals, bombing bridges, razing communities, destroying crops, stealing cattle, and cutting communications lines; and,
b. Destroying the livelihood of thousands of innocent Nicaraguan civilians and leaving them homeless refugees.

42. Among the goals of the defendants' conspiracy is the terrorizing of the civilian population of Nicaragua as a means of destabilizing the Nicaraguan government. In furtherance of this goal defendants are:

a. Supporting, arming and training former Somoza National Guardsmen and other terrorist groups to enable them to attack innocent civilians;
b. Assisting the Honduran armed forces to provide military assistance to such groups;
c. Utilizing economic means including withdrawal of promised U.S. aid and discouraging financial aid by other countries;

d. Covertly supporting opposition parties; and,
e. Manipulating the press in Nicaragua and elsewhere.

43. This conspiracy is directed against the people of Nicaragua, a country with which the United States is at peace.

44. In November of 1981, as part of the conspiracy, pursuant to a Reagan Administration request, the CIA presented an option plan covering covert activities which would result in terrorizing and otherwise harming the people of Nicaragua.

45. On information and belief, the plan set forth above was reviewed and aspects of it were approved by various members of the National Security Council and others, including, but not limited to defendant President Ronald Reagan, defendant Director of Central Intelligence William Casey, defendant former Secretary of State Alexander M. Haig, former National Security Adviser Richard Allen, defendant Assistant Secretary of State Thomas O. Enders, defendant Secretary of Defense Caspar Weinberger, defendant Deputy Assistant Secretary of Defense Nestor Sanchez, and Edwin Meese, Counsel to the President. The approved plan is hereinafter referred to as the "Plan". . . .

52. Defendants acting in concert, support, train and direct terrorist training camps in Honduras (see Appendix I) and Nicaragua (see Appendix II). On information and belief, there are up to 10,000 terrorists operating out of these camps.

53. Defendants, acting in concert, launched hundreds of raids from these camps against innocent Nicaraguan civilians and against economic targets which had provided Nicaraguans with the basic necessities of life, causing grievous injury to the plaintiffs and other civilians.

54. On or about November 1, 1982, U.S. defendants or their agents admitted that the U.S. was supporting clandestine military operations against the people of Nicaragua. They admitted that the CIA provides money, military equipment and military training to the "anti-Nicaraguan" forces and that this support is part of the covert military operation plan approved by defendant Reagan.

55. Upon information and belief, the appropriate members of Congress have never been fully and accurately informed about the extent of the Plan, as required by law. . . .

84. The above described terrorist organization, financed, trained and otherwise supported by the U.S. government defendants have carried out, in furtherance of the conspiracy, scores of attacks upon innocent Nicaraguan civilians. These attacks, some of which are described below, resulted in summary execution, murder, abduction, torture, rape, wounding, and the destruction of private property and public facilities.

85. On November 22, 1981, terrorist forces kidnapped security officer Granicio Eden Tom in the community of Krasa. He was taken to Honduras, tortured and killed. The Nicaraguan Democratic Force claimed responsibility for his murder.

86. On November 23, 1981, four terrorists raided the Cerro Dorado mine and took three hostages to Honduras. The three, Jose Medina, Juan Spelman Zuniga and Norman Castro, were later murdered.

87. On November 30, 1981 terrorists attacked Nicaraguans near Asang. Julio Cesar Granados and Edgard Espinoza Gonzalez were killed. Ignacio Ortega Sequeira and Juan Rugama Duarte were taken to Honduras where they were assassinated.

88. On December 2, 1981, terrorists attacked San Jeronimo, kidnapped health official Benigno Romero, and abducted him to Honduras where he was tortured and murdered.

89. On December 7, 1981, terrorists from Honduras crossed the border and attacked several towns in Nicaragua. In Asang, stores were raided and Genaro Williams and Arles Escobar were kidnapped, taken to Honduras and tortured and murdered. The towns of Andres and Tara were raided and Fabio Barrera, Bacileo Barrera, and his son were murderd. In Ulwas, Agustin Brismon Lopez was kidnapped and murdered. The terrorists then raided the community of Krasa kidnapping Elmos and Hernando Ralf who were taken to Honduras and murdered.

90. On December 13, 1981, in a brutal attack on San Carlos, 12 Nicaraguans were kidnapped, taken to Honduras and murderd. On information and belief, Efrain Omier Wilson led this attack. Numerous other Nicaraguans were tortured.

91. On December 18, 1981, as Nicaraguans searched for those captured at San Carlos, four of the searchers were ambushed and murdered including Rafael Gomez Rios, Jose Antonio Torres and Bernabe Perez Solis.

92. On December 21, 1981, several Nicaraguans were killed by terrorists at San Carlos. Others were wounded, tortured and mutilated. Naked bodies were thrown in a common grave, with hands tied behind backs. A man whose legs had been broken and who had been shot in the stomach was still alive, and was then taken by the terrorists, tied to a post, stabbed in the chest, and killed.

93. On December 28, 1981, the village of Bilwaskarma was attacked. Terrorist forces ransacked the hospital. Plaintiff Dr. Myrna Cunningham, Regina Lewis, a nurse, and two hospital administrators were kidnapped. The two women were raped as were 13 other women from the town.

94. On December 31, 1981, 25 terrorists attacked the village of Anorestara, kidnapping Jose Morales. Morales was subsequently found decapitated, with his eyes removed from their sockets.

95. On March 14, 1982, terrorists invading Nicaragua from camps in Honduras blew up a bridge on the Rio Negro on the highway leading to El Guasaule, a town on the Nicaraguan-Honduran border. They also caused substantial damage to another bridge. After the explosions, a U.S. made M-18 anti-personnel mine and U.S. made rolls of detonation cable were found. Defendant National Liberation Army claimed responsibility for destruction of the bridges.

96. On July 3, 1982 terrorists, with the support of the Honduran Army, attacked the village of Seven Benk, Province of Zelaya. There were 200 attackers armed with FAL and M-16 rifles, rocket launchers and M-79 grenade launchers. The attack lasted for three days and resulted in 30 civilian dead, 12 wounded and 11 kidnapped. Captured weapons included automatic rifles, disposable rocket launchers and grenades, all made in the United States.

97. On July 24, 1982, plaintiff Brenda Rocha was at the village of Salto, in the Province of Zelaya, about 20 kilometers from her home in the village of Bonanza. Salto was attacked by about 100 terrorists, and she and seven other townspeople took cover in a trench. The seven others were killed, and plaintiff Rocha was wounded in the arm. She

pretended to be dead until the attackers departed. She was later rescued, but her wound was so serious that her arm had to be amputated.

98. On the same day, July 24, 1982, approximately 130 armed terrorists who, upon information and belief, were members of defendant Nicaraguan Democratic Front, attacked the small rural farming town of San Francisco de Guajiniquilapa (Norte), Province of Chinandega, Nicaragua at about 6 a.m. The town is located about 12 kilometers from the Honduran border. On information and belief, the attacks were launched from camps in Honduras.

99. The attackers were dressed in two types of uniforms—some wore dark blue uniforms similar to those of FUSEP, a special unit of the Honduran Army, and others wore olive green uniforms. They attacked the town with FAL and Galil rifles, mortars, rocket launchers and machine guns.

100. Townspeople tried to defend the town for about two and one half hours. Fifteen villagers were killed: Walter Baquedano-Espinoza, Reynoldo Barrera-Carrazco, Evelio Barrera-Baquedano, Justo Espinal-Moreno, Victorino Espinal-Moreno, Alfredo Espinoza-Aguilera, Luis Alberto Espinoza-Moncada (15 years old), Donald Espinoza, Victorino Guevara-Centeno, Reymundo Garcia-Montenegro, Domingo Lainez, Hugo Martinez-Espinoza, Ramon Aristides Moncada, Angel Sanchez-Perez and Felix Pedro Sanchez-Guido. Four villagers were wounded: Aristides Espinoza-Aguilera, Armando Espinoza-Hernandez, Arturo Espinoza-Sanchez and plaintiff Victorino Hernandez-Aguilera.

101. After the battle, the attackers ran through the town painting "FDN" on buildings and shouting "Long Live the Nicaraguan Democratic Front," and "With God and Patriotism We'll Defeat Communism." People were told to come out of their houses or the soldiers would break down the doors.

102. Some of the attackers then ransacked homes, stores and the town's municipal building. They took food, clothing, money and horses and destroyed the telephone system.

103. Eight people were kidnapped, including a fifteen year old boy, plaintiff Javier Sanchez-Espinoza, who was seized from his home. The others were: Oscar Espinal Benavides, Constantino Espinoza, Santiago Espinoza-Betanco (who was wounded), Jose Santos Gomez, Ismael Meza Castellon,

Timoteo Moreno (who is blind), and Felix Pedro Moncada-Neyra.

104. After the attackers left the town, plaintiff Jose Santos-Barrera found the body of his son, Evelio Baquedano-Barrera. He was lying face up, his legs destroyed, his chest bullet-ridden. His watch had been taken and his pockets turned inside out.

105. Plaintiff Elia Maria Espinoza discovered the body of her husband, Ramon Aristides-Moncada. His head had been destroyed; his brains were falling out. His chest had a hole in it that appeared to have been made with a knife and a knife handle was protruding from his back. Plaintiff Espinoza lost seven members of her family in the attack, including her brother, nephew, uncle, and cousin, as well as her husband.

106. Plaintiff Maria Espinal Mondragan found the body of her husband, Victorino Guevara Centeno, with holes in his neck, stomach and right leg. His throat, as well as the throats of other victims lying near him, had been slit.

107. About 80 mortar shells were left behind bearing the marking "Made in USA." In one home, the attackers left matches and pills marked "Made in USA." The pills were later found to be poison.

108. On information and belief, this attack was carried out by defendant Nicaraguan Democratic Front, which took credit for the attack. . . .

* * *

127. The aforesaid conspiracy and acts of defendants constitute torts in violation of the law of nations and treaties of the United States including, but not limited to: the U.N. Charter, the Universal Declaration of Human Rights, the U.N. Declaration Against Torture, the American Declaration of the Rights and duties of Man, the O.A.S. Charter, the American Convention on Human Rights, the Charter of the International Military Tribunal (Nuremberg Charter), the General Assembly Resolution adopting the Nuremberg Charter Principles, the Geneva Convention (IV) Relative to the Protection of Civilian Persons, the Inter-American Treaty of Reciprocal Assistance, the General Assembly Resolution, "Declaration on Principles of International Law Concerning Friendly Relations and Cooperation Among States," the Treaty of Friendship, Commerce and Navigation between the United States and Nicaragua, and other pertinent declarations, documents and practices

constituting the customary international law of human rights and the law of nations . . .

131. The aforesaid conspiracy and acts of the defendants are carried out in violation of the Fourth and Fifth Amendments to the United States Constitution; the National Security Act of 1947, 50 U.S.C. §§401 *et seq.*; the Hughes-Ryan Amendment, 50 U.S.C. §413; the Neutrality Act, 18 U.S.C. §960; the War Powers Resolution, 50 U.S.C. §§1541 *et seq.*; and Article I, Section 8, Clause 11 of the United States Constitution, giving Congress the power to declare war. . . .

## APPENDIX I

### *Border Training Camps in Honduras*

1. San Judas Base—14 kilometers west of San Pedro de Potrero Grande. Weaponry at the base includes hand grenades, M-79 grenade launchers, 60 and 81 mm mortars, bazookas and helicopters.
2. Cerro Baldoquin Base—11 kilometers northwest of San Pedro de Potrero Grands. Approximately 700 people at the camp. Armaments at the camp similar to San Judas camp.
3. San Marcos de Colon—400 to 600 people at the camp.
4. Cacamuya Base—600 ex-Somoza guardsmen at the camp led by Alcides Espinoza. Weapons similar to San Judas.
5. Trojes Base—10 kilometers northeast of Teotecacinte. 400 to 600 ex-Somoza guardsmen at the camp. Operations center on Jalapa area.
6. La Ladoza—(also called "Nicaragua Military Training Base".) This camp is a school for ex-Somoza guardsmen who are transferred to other camps or sent directly to Nicaragua to operate as paramilitary bands. Approximately 130 to 150 ex-guardsmen led by Benito Bravo. Weapons similar to San Judas.
7. Monte de Aguila Base—10 kilometers northeast of Jalapa. Approximately 250 guardsmen at the camp. Armaments similar to San Judas.
8. Hacienda La Estrella Base—12 kilometers southwest of Jalapa. Approximately 250 ex-guardsmen at this camp.

Armaments similar to San Judas.

9. Cerro Los Nubarrones Base—10 kilometers west of Jalapa. Approximately 200 ex-guardsmen. Armaments similar to San Judas.
10. Auka Base—36 kilometers northeast of Leymus. Approximately 400 ex-guardsmen at the camp. Armaments include FAL and M-16 rifles, M-79 grenade launchers and rocket launchers.

*FDN COMMANDO SCHOOL IN HONDURAS: Photo courtesy* Patria Libre

11. Rus Base—37 kilometers northwest of Leymus. Approximately 400 ex-guardsmen. Armaments similar to San Judas.

# CONCLUSION

What the United States is up to in Nicaragua is illegal, immoral and impractical. And if it escalates—and the Reagan administration seems to have a compulsive desire to have it escalate—a Vietnam-style war is what would be ahead.

## *Illegality*

U.S. activities in trying to overthrow the Sandinista government of Nicaragua are in violation of America's own Neutrality Act—enacted in 1794 shortly after the birth of the republic and a bedrock of American law affirmed by the courts on numerous occasions. The actions are also in violation of the charters of the Organization of American States, the United Nations, and the Rio Treaty, all of which the U.S. signed.

One section of the Neutrality Act— which is in Title 18 of the U.S. Code—declares: "It is unlawful to provide or prepare the means for or to furnish money for any kind of military enterprise against a foreign government with which the U.S. has diplomatic relations."

Another section of the act states: "Whoever, within the U.S., knowingly begins or sets on foot, or provides or prepares a means for or furnishes the money for, or takes part in, any military or naval expedition or enterprise to be carried on from thence against the territory or dominion of any foreign prince or state, or of any colony, district or people, with whom the U.S. is at peace, shall be fined not more than $3,000 or imprisoned not more than three years, or both."

A lawsuit centered on the contention that the Reagan administration and the CIA are violating the Neutrality Act by their use of the *contras* to try to overthrow the government of Nicaragua is now before the U.S. District Court for the Northern District of California.

An important ruling has been handed down in this case. Despite strong opposition to the suit by the U.S. attorney general, Judge Stanley A. Weigel in November 1983 "ordered that the attorney general shall conduct a preliminary investigation . . . into the conduct of any person presently covered by the Ethics in Government Act named in the information submitted by plaintiffs relating to violations of the Neutrality Act arising out of the actions connected to paramilitary expeditions against Nicaragua. . . . It is hereby further ordered that if the attorney general" finds indications of Reagan administration and CIA violations of the Neutrality Act," he shall apply for the appointment of an independent counsel," a special prosecutor.

This suit also involves U.S. Congressman Dellums as one of the plaintiffs and also was brought in 1983 by the Center for Constitutional Rights in New York and the National Lawyers Guild in San Francisco.

It holds that not only are the Reagan administration and CIA breaking the Neutrality Act by their activities against Nicaragua, but that U.S. Attorney General William French Smith and his office are in violation of the Ethics in Government Act. The Ethics in Government Act, a 1978 law which was a product of the Watergate scandal, requires that the attorney general launch a "preliminary investigation" upon receiving information that a serious crime has been committed by a high official. "As soon as there is any indication whatsoever that the allegations involving a high-level official may be serious or have any potential chance of substantiation, a special prosecutor should be appointed to take over the investigation." This provision is intended "in order to eliminate the conflict of interest inherent when the Department of Justice must investigate and prosecute high-level executive branch officials."

Earlier, Dellums and the other plaintiffs had written to the attorney general listing Reagan administration and CIA acts in using the *contras* against the Nicaraguan government, citing them as illegal under the Neutrality Act and asking for an inquiry under the Ethics in Government Act.

An assistant attorney general replied in a letter that the

material presented "does not constitute specific information of a federal offense sufficient to constitute grounds to investigate."

The suit, however, declares that "plaintiffs presented in considerable detail facts which demonstrate that high government officials have violated the Neutrality Act," that the information presented "is both specific and credible" and "satisfies many times over" the requirements of the Ethics in Government Act. The attorney general, it is charged, is acting "unlawfully" and "refusing to perform his clear statutory duty."

The suit makes these points:

10. U.S. government officials identified by plaintiffs in their letter to the Attorney General as having violated the Neutrality Act and other criminal statutes and specifically covered by §591(b) include: Ronald Reagan, President; Alexander Haig, Jr., former Secretary of State; George Shultz, Secretary of State; Caspar Weinberger, Secretary of Defense; and William Casey, Director of the Central Intelligence Agency.

11. In November 1981, pursuant to a request from Ronald Reagan and other persons in his Administration, the CIA presented a plan to covertly aid, fund and participate in a military expedition and enterprise utilizing Nicaraguan exiles for the purpose of attacking and overthrowing the government of Nicaragua, a country with which the United States is officially at peace.

12. That plan was reviewed and approved in November 1981, by various members of the National Security Council including, but not limited to, Ronald Reagan, William Casey, Alexander Haig, Jr., Thomas Enders, Caspar Weinberger and Nestor Sanchez.

13. That plan was and is being implemented and includes:

(a) providing at least $19 million to finance covert paramilitary operations against the people and property of Nicaragua;

(b) financing the training of invasionary forces in the United States and Honduras, including former Somoza National Guardsmen, various terrorist groups and others;

(c) conducting intelligence activities by the CIA to determine the specific targets for such anti-Nicaraguan terrorist forces;

(d) using Honduras as a base for invasionary forces;

(e) supporting organizations of Nicaraguan and Cuban exiles based in the United States which, in turn, train and support invasionary forces on United States soil;

(f) sending hundreds of CIA officers and agents and other U.S. government agents to Honduras and Costa Rica to participate and assist in covert military operations against the people and government of Nicaragua.

(g) sending at least 96 members of United States military "mobile training teams" to advise and train terrorists, many of whom were initially trained and recruited in the U.S. to attack Nicaraguan towns and citizens.

14. In furtherance of this conspiracy and plan, John Negroponte, U.S. Ambassador to Honduras, and Nestor Sanchez, Assistant Secretary of Defense, were placed in charge of local implementation of the plan. They are in charge of paramilitary activities and direct Honduran support for those activities.

15. Pursuant to the plan and conspiracy, the government officials named herein have provided and are providing financial, technical and other support to paramilitary groups training in camps in the United States for the purpose of attacking and overthrowing the Nicaraguan government.

16. Groups and individuals from the U.S.-based paramilitary camps, by arrangement or agreement, have been and are being sent to participate in military raids against Nicaragua.

17. Upon information and belief, the U.S. camps are located in California, Florida, Texas, Georgia, Virginia and New Jersey.

18. At least five paramilitary training camps are located in Dade County, Florida, Among these are: Camp Cuba y Nicaragua located at S.W. 40th Street and 158th Avenue; a camp run by the Association of Bay of Pigs Veterans-Brigade 2506, located near 58th Street and 102nd Avenue N.W.; and a camp run by Alpha 66. The function of these camps is to train, prepare and arm men to invade Nicaragua with the aid of the U.S. officials named herein, or their agents.

The legal action goes on to tell how the U.S. financed "the formation of a united front by the various paramilitary groups," and in August 1981 "representatives from a number of paramilitary groups . . . met in Miami to form such an alliance. At that meeting an alliance was formed called the Nicaraguan Democratic Front (FDN). The purpose for forming this alliance was to further a military expedition and enterprise against Nicaragua. The FDN, which uses southern Florida as a base of operation, is a leading insurgent force, and is responsible for numerous attacks on Nicaragua."

The suit speaks of other financial payments to the *contras* by the U.S. government sometimes "delivered by Argentinian officials acting in concert with the U.S.," and of direct CIA agent support. It names "one such agent, Frank Granizano, acting with William Casey's approval" who works with *contra* leaders, "meets regularly with them, and supplies them with cash."

It also outlines *contra* purchase of arms including a load of "machine guns, handguns and ammunition in Miami with money received from agents of the U.S. officials named herein. The weapons and ammunition were shipped from Miami, regular air cargo, and picked up in Honduras by the Honduran Army's Public Security Force. . . . The arms were then delivered to the Honduran home" of a *contra* leader identified as Rodolfo Mendez and taken to a *contra* "paramilitary camp near El Paradiso, Honduras."

The suit tells of CIA personnel "and a number of retired military and intelligence officers" of the U.S. "serving in Honduras in support of the insurgent anti-Nicaraguan forces."

And it notes President Reagan's acknowledgement of U.S. support of anti-government guerrillas against the Nicaraguan government both in "a public news conference" on April 14, 1983 and in a second one on May 4, 1983 at which he "again admitted that covert aid was being provided to anti-Nicaraguan paramilitary forces. Calling the insurgent forces 'freedom fighters,' Reagan admitted that the insurgent forces' purpose is to challenge the Nicaraguan government, and Reagan himself questioned the legitimacy of the ruling Nicaraguan regime."

The suit gives this summary of the situation:

"The United States government has been funding, encouraging and conducting a secret war against Nicaragua utilizing Nicaraguan exiles trained, organized and armed in paramilitary camps located in the United States. This war, which has never been declared or mandated by Congress, has resulted in the death of hundreds of Nicaraguan citizens, as well as the rape and torture of many more, including Doctor Myrna Cunningham, a plaintiff in this lawsuit. The actions of these executive officials were taken in disregard and contravention of the Neutrality Act, a criminal statute forbidding the organizing or launching of a paramilitary expedition against a country with which the United States is at peace. This statute was enacted to protect congressional war powers from unauthorized usurpation."

The legal action stresses that "the history of the Neutrality Act, statements of its framers, and judicial precedent all insist that the act applies to all citizens, including the president."

Thomas Jefferson was the U.S. secretary of state when the act was passed and, it is noted, he said: "If one citizen has a right to go to war of his own authority, every citizen has the same." The U.S. Constitution, Jefferson emphasized, gives the power to declare and make war "to Congress alone and not citizens individually."

In the nearly two centuries since the Neutrality Act became U.S. law, there have been several attempts to amend it, the suit points out, including a try in the U.S. Senate in the 1850s during the takeover of Nicaragua by William Walker's private army. But "all such attempts" to "permit presidential support for private expeditions . . . failed and the Neutrality Act has remained substantially unamended to the present time."

A key U.S. Supreme Court decision on the act came in 1806 and involved a move by a Francisco de Miranda to "launch an expedition against Spanish America. As part of their defense," those charged with violation of the Neutrality Act in that case "asserted that their acts had been authorized by President Jefferson and his cabinet." U.S. Supreme Court Justice William Patterson, "a participant in the Constitutional Convention who presided over the trial," ruled that even if the president had authorized the expedition, "the president of the United States cannot control the statute, nor dispense with its execution, and still less can he authorize a person to do what the law forbids. If he could, it would render the execution of the laws dependent on his will and pleasure. The law is paramount. Who has the dominion over it? None but the legislature. It is the exclusive province of Congress to change a state of peace into a state of war. . . . The organ entrusted with the power to declare war, should first decide, whether it is expedient to go to war, or to continue in peace, and until such a decision is made, no individual ought to assume a hostile attitude; and to pronounce, contrary to the constitutional will, that the nation is at war, and that he will shape his conduct and act according to such a state of things."

As for the U.S. Congress on Nicaragua in our day, in 1982 the House of Representatives passed the Boland Amendment—by a vote of 411-to-0—specifically forbidding any action by the U.S. government aimed at overthrowing the Sandinista government of Nicaragua.

The amendment by U.S. Congressman Edward Boland of Massachusetts to the Department of Defense appropriations bill for 1983 declares: "None of the funds provided in this act may be used by the Central Intelligence Agency or the Department of Defense to furnish military equipment, military training or advice, or other support for military services to any group or individual, not part of a country's armed services, for the purpose of overthrowing the government of Nicaragua or provoking a military exchange between Nicaragua and Honduras."

The law authored by Boland—chairman of the House Permanent Select Committee on Intelligence—was ignored by the Reagan administration. Robert Pastor, a former National Security Council advisor during the Carter administration, commented that the vote was really 411-to-1 with the one being Reagan who prevailed.

In 1983, Congress voted to have another amendment concerning U.S. government efforts to overthrow the government of Nicaragua added to the Department of Defense appropriations bill—this one for 1984. Called the Boland-Zablocki-Wright amendment, it states that "during fiscal year 1984, not more than $24 million of funds available to the Central Intelligence Agency, the Department of Defense, or any other agency or entity of the United States involved in intelligence activities may be obligated or expended for the purpose or which would have the effect of supporting, directly or indirectly, military or paramilitary operations in Nicaragua by any nation, group, organization, movement or individual."

The Charter of the Organization of American States says: "The territory of state is inviolable; it may not be the object, even temporarily, of military occupation or of other measures of force taken by another state, directly or indirectly, on any grounds whatsoever."

The United Nations Charter declares: "All members shall refrain in their international relations from the threat or use of force against the territorial integrity or political independence of any state."

Article 18 of the Rio Treaty states: "No state or group of states has the right to intervene directly or indirectly for any reason whatever in the internal or external affairs of any other state. The foregoing principle prohibits not only armed force but also any other form of interference or attempted threat against the personality of the state or against its political, economic and cultural elements."

The attorney general's office claimed to Congressman Dellums and the others in the suit charging the Reagan administration and CIA with violating the Neutrality Act that "specific information" was not provided. Beyond it being apparent that enough information was provided, all the attorney general's office had to do to see evidence of the illegal war—under the Neutrality Act—by the U.S. government against the government of Nicaragua was to look at the front pages of most U.S. newspapers in recent times.

A sampling:

ITEM: (*Newsweek,* August 1, 1983) "When Gen. John W. Vessey, Jr., chairman of the Joint Chiefs of Staff, arrives in Tegucigalpa this week, he will find the sleepy capital of a onetime banana republic changing rapidly—to an American military nerve center. From the U.S. Embassy, now the largest in the area with 149 staffers, U.S. Ambassador John D. Negroponte supervises about 300 technicians, engineers and advisers who are building roads and airstrips around the country and training as many as 2,000 Salvadoran soldiers at a new U.S.-built facility at Puerto Castilla. The CIA, with more than 150 operatives, runs at least 5,000 anti-Nicaraguan rebels along Honduras's frontier with Nicaragua. And from a radar base outside the capital, the U.S. Air Force monitors air traffic and guides secret reconnaissance flights over the region."

ITEM: (*The Wall Street Journal,* August 29, 1983) "WASHINGTON—the U.S. financed counterrevolutionary army in Nicaragua is growing bigger and more potent, as it demonstrated by launching a series of new attacks against the Nicaraguan government last week."

ITEM: (*Washington Post,* September 29, 1983) "SAN JOSE, Costa Rica—The sudden new burst of guerrilla activity against Nicaragua's government this month is the result of a new strategy imposed on the Nicaraguan rebels by the Central Intelligence Agency that funds them, according to U.S. and rebel sources interviewed in recent weeks. . . . With Congress threatening to cancel funding for the not-so-secret 'covert' operations, the CIA is reported to have told its leading Nicaraguan surrogate group, the Honduras-based Nicaraguan Democratic Force (FDN) . . . that unless it 'shaped up' funds would be cut off. . . . According to a senior FDN official . . . so serious was the CIA pressure that, by April, supplies to their forces in the field had dried up—leaving units deep inside Nicaragua without the support imperative for their survival. . . . The FDN official said, 'Our people in Nicaragua were in such bad shape that some of them straggled back to their bases literally without shoes.' "

ITEM: (*The New York Times,* October 2, 1983) "MIAMI—The Central Intelligence Agency is using a Salvadoran Air Force base and some Salvadoran pilots to supply United States-backed rebels in Nicaragua, according to United States officials in Central America."

ITEM: (*The New York Times,* October 16, 1983) "WASHINGTON—The Central Intelligence Agency recommended and helped plan recent rebel attacks against an oil storage depot and other industrial targets in Nicaragua, according to Reagan administration officials."

Father D'Escoto, the Nicaraguan foreign minister, while in America recently noted that the U.S. government was devoting "millions of dollars to the destabilization of another country," and asked: "Is this a government of laws?"

### *Immorality*

How can the United States denounce terrorism when it is centrally involved in managing what is one of the largest terrorist organizations in the world today: the *contras?*

As Congressman Jim Wright of Texas, the House majority leader, said during the debate in 1983 on the Boland-Zablocki-Wright amendment, "Contrary to the president's claims, the *contras* are not 'freedom fighers.' They are terrorists, pure and simple. They offer Nicaraguans a return to the nightmare of the Somoza regime, of campaigns of mass killings."

I will never in my life forget riding on that Nicaraguan Army truck on the way to Jalapa with Sister Lisa explaining how the crosses along the side of the road marked where people had been slain by the *contras,* pointing out a village to which the *contras* had recently come and kidnapped 140. And all along the American nun and I had been concerned that we could be ambushed this day—by American-supervised terrorists with U.S. weaponry purchased with the tax dollars of us all. Of U.S. backing of the *contras,* Sister Lisa commented sadly: "I think we all share the responsibility." Indeed we do.

The scene in Jalapa, a community under seige by the U.S.-organized terrorists, is also etched in my mind: the faces of anxiety on the children, the young men and women under arms fighting to preserve a revolution they so deeply believe in. And, appropriately, "Masada" at the Jalapa movie.

The lawsuit filed against President Reagan, other high U.S. officials and the *contra* groups, is graphic enough in describing details of *contra* brutality. There is abundant corroboration. Amando Lopez of the National Commission for the Protection and Promotion of Human Rights gave a similar accounting.

Alexander Cockburn and James Ridgeway of the *Village Voice* of New York wrote, after a trip to Nicaragua in December 1983, an article entitled "What Reagan is giving Nicaragua for Christmas." It is about a *contra* attack on the village of Boaco: "The *contras'* mission, as always, was economic sabotage—and most importantly—terror. A typical example involved a Nicaraguan woman who had been involved with a Cuban doctor. Along with two agricultural technicians she was kidnapped by a *contra* band. The dead agricultural technicians were found within two days. The woman's body was found nine days later. Her agony had lasted far longer. Her hands had been cut off, along with her breasts which were hung on a nearby tree. She had been raped repeatedly and finally by a bayonet. Her remains were suspended from a branch. The *contras* later murdered the rest of her family."

Chapters chronicling *contra* savagery could fill another book. Not incidentally, it is identical to the sort of savagery practiced by the Somoza National Guard of which so many *contras* were members.

Sister Lisa spoke of a training routine—which I've since seen confirmed in writings about the National Guard—in which an instructor would scream to Guardsmen: "*Quines somos?*" (Who are we?). The answer: "*Somos tigres!*" (We are tigers!) "*Que comen los tigres?*" (What do tigers eat?) "*Sangre!*" (Blood!) "*Sangre de quien?*" (Whose blood?) "*Sangre del pueblo!*" (The blood of the people!) This army, backed by the U.S., its officers trained in the U.S., would sometimes roll around in jeeps stencilled with a skull and crossbones as it enforced state terrorism.

What was the United States ever doing supporting this kind of horror? Why do we continue doing it?

## *Impracticality*

ITEM: (*Washington Post,* November 25, 1983) WASHINGTON—The CIA has concluded that the U.S.-backed rebels fighting Nicaragua cannot achieve a military or political victory over the Sandinista government, according to congressional sources. . . . In a National Intelligence Estimate provided in September to the congressional committees that monitor U.S. intelligence activities . . . the Central Intelligence Agency said: The U.S.-backed *contra* forces of 10,000 to 12,000 guerrilla lack the military capability, financing, training and political support to overthrow the powerful and well-entrenched Sandinista government. . . . The document, a presidential 'finding' under the National Security Act, was presented to the congressional committees by Secretary of State George Shultz and CIA Director William Casey."

Additional reasons as to why the U.S. effort to overthrow the government of Nicaragua is impractical were provided in a speech during the 1983 debate in the Senate on U.S. efforts to overthrow the Nicaragua government given by Senator Patrick Leahy of Vermont.

Leahy began by saying, "I hold no brief for the Sandinista regime, but whatever anyone thinks about it, it is the internationally-recognized government of a sovereign nation. It should not be the function of the United States to overthrow regimes because it does not like their ideological character."

Beyond that, he emphasized, "there are many reasons why the covert paramilitary action program is contrary to our national interests. Let us look at this operation not from the standpoint of what is in the best interests of Central America or Nicaragua or anywhere else, but purely in our own national interests. I should like to list what I see as the four most important reasons why it is contrary to our national interests.

"First, Nicaragua is yet another example of this administration's substitution of covert action and military force for a sophisticated foreign policy. Someone should remind the president that he has other nonmilitary tools at his disposal to further our national interests. Covert action is never an adequate substitute for foreign policy. . . .

"Second, military pressure against Nicaragua is bringing about results completely opposite to what the administration tells us it is seeking. Instead of promoting pluralism and democracy in Nicaragua, the covert action program is strengthening the hand of Sandinista radicals for bringing in Cuban and Soviet military assistance. It unites the Nicaraguan people, even those who fear the Sandinistas, against a common enemy. Whatever their differences, most Nicaraguans are against the hated *Somocistas* who control the insurgents. They also remember the painful history of American military occupation of Nicaragua in the 1920s and 1930s, and our support for the brutal Somoza dictatorship. It undermines regional stability by increasing tensions between Nicaragua and Honduras. This is not a situation which involves just the United States and Nicaragua. We should not overlook what happens to other countries in the area as a consequence of what we do. . . . Nicaragua may be goaded into attacking Honduras. If it does, the United States will be asked to intervene with military force to defend our ally. This will be a catastrophe. The American people will not support a Central American War.

"Third, the president's course of action is illegal. The U.N. Charter, the OAS Treaty, and the Rio Treaty, all of which we have signed, commit us not to intervene in the affairs of sovereign countries." And, he cited the 1982 and "still valid" Boland amendment.

"Fourth, is that often mocked but real force in America—morality. It is against our best traditions to compel others to believe as we believe, to live as we live, to govern themselves as we govern ourselves. We are a nation founded on diversity and toleration. That is our ideal, and we have to live up to it, however often we may fall short. It is not good enough to say that because the Soviets flout international law and decent behavior, we must do the same. I like to think that America lives by a standard different from that of the Soviet Union."

Leahy also posed "a few questions" including what would happen if with U.S. help the *contras* somehow managed to "win and seize power in Managua? Does anyone really think the Sandinistas would simply quit and become model citizens or that the insurgents would install a reformist democracy dedicated to eradicating centuries of social and political injustice? Is it not more likely that the Sandinistas will go back into the hills and brutal war would continue? How would a new regime survive unless the United States provides massive military backing, probably for decades?" and "Where do we draw the line in Nicaragua? When do we decide that enough pressure has been exerted and it is time to stop?. . . . Is Congress ready to support American participation in a much wider war in Central America if that is where the covert action program leads?"

*The Potential for a Vietnam-style War*

It is widely recognized that if the U.S. directly intervenes in Nicaragua—if it invades that nation—a Vietnam-style war is ahead. The Sandinistas pledge this, and they speak from nearly two decades of guerrilla war experience based on the principles of a man who successfully stood off the U.S. military in a conflict often described as the most similar war to Vietnam in which the U.S. has ever been involved.

Now, however, the scale would be different. *Todos Las Armas Al Pueblo* (All The Arms To The People) is more than just a revolutionary slogan. Fearing a U.S. invasion, the Sandinistas have distributed and hidden in caches hundreds of thousands of weapons around the nation so weapons for resistance would be abundant.

And the people to use those weapons are also plentiful.

Even if the U.S. "sent 500,000 soldiers, as in Vietnam," Father D'Escoto said, "they won't obtain their goal" because the resulting struggle would not be conventional but a guerrilla war in which "every Nicaraguan, including my 84-year-old mother, will fight." He went on that such a war would embroil the U.S. for years and destroy America's image even further in Latin America and the rest of the Third World. And, he said, every American "not for love of Nicaragua but for love of your own country . . . should be interested in helping the United States not make a mistake that would be a source of embarrassment and shame for years to come."

It would not be like the invasion of the twenty-mile long island of Grenada. An invasion by the U.S. of Nicaragua would be a war against a well-armed and committed populace of a substantial nation defending a generally popular revolution.

Pleading for the U.S. not to invade, Edén Pastora in a visit to the U.S. in November 1983 warned that if the U.S. did invade it would find not only Sandinista troops but "the whole Nicaraguan people" fighting back. "Military intervention in Nicaragua," he said, "would be the biggest mistake that Reagan could make. In Grenada you got in and out quickly. In Nicaragua you could get in, but getting out would be another matter."

Observers of the situation from U.S. establishment institutions, political figures not associated with anything remotely close to the left, and even the U.S. military have been warning about the same thing: a Vietnam-style war if there is direct U.S. military intervention in Nicaragua.

A U.S. military force invading Nicaragua "would certainly drive the Sandinista leadership out of Managua in short order," wrote Steven Kinzer in *The New York Times Magazine* in August 1983. "Such an attack, however, would guarantee that Sandinistas take to the hills by the thousands to fight on. In fact, the Sandinistas are already preparing for this eventuality by hiding stores of weapons, ammunition and fuel at clandestine depots around the country. An American military victory would have to be followed by a protracted occupation marked by intense guerrilla warfare and heavy American casualties."

"Unless he is stopped by Congress—and only Congress and the force of public opinion can stop him," John B. Oakes, former editorial page editor of *The New York Times,* wrote also in August 1983, "Ronald Reagan could plunge this country into the most unwanted, unconscionable, unnecessary and unwinnable war in its history, not excepting Vietnam." The column was headed "Reagan's Path to War." Oakes also commented that there is no sense in the United States functioning "by mirroring the Soviet Union, by competing with it as arms suppliers, as agents provocateurs and interventionists, and even—as in the case of Nicaragua—as armed subversives. The way to undercut what influence the Soviet Union and its satellites have is not to ape them, nor to send arms to every tin-pot dictator who calls himself an anti-Communist. It is to accept the inevitability of social revolution in countries such as El Salvador and Nicaragua that are ripe for it—and try to guide it along democratic lines, not fight it along undemocratic ones."

McGeorge Bundy, national security adviser under Presidents Kennedy and Johnson, in a column in January 1984 in *The Times* warned that a U.S. military invasion of Nicaragua would be "a self-inflicted wound" and the Grenada invasion should be no example. "The armed forces of Grenada were almost nonexistent, and dissolved immediately; those of Nicaragua are numerous, with a demonstrated capacity for survival. . . . As a target of a military invasion, Nicaragua is to Grenada as a hand grenade is to a marshmallow."

Bundy said that "the controlling issues in Central America are political, not military" and an invasion "could be justified only if there were a serious military threat to the United States itself. But the realities of relative strength make it totally clear that no one is going to make war on us from Central America. There is something genuinely zany in thinking about the area in such terms."

Edward L. King, a retired Army lieutenant colonel and former member of the U.S. delegation to the Inter-American Defense Board, also warned strongly in 1983 against a U.S. invasion of Nicaragua. "Military action against Nicaragua would require a large United States ground combat force from the outset. At least two divisions with supporting troops—roughly 55,000 men—would be needed even for a multinational Condeca force. And this commitment might have to grow quickly as the fighting developed. The Sandinista army has hidden stockpiles of arms and supplies throughout Nicaragua in preparation for guerrilla warfare. . . . The 30,000 regular Sandinista soldiers would probably fight a short initial delaying action before retreating into the hills to reinforce the 75,000 armed militia members fighting in both rural and urban areas. . . . The Sandinista objective would be to bog down United States units in the same type of guerrilla warfare that Augusto César Sandino used against Marines in Nicaragua in the 1930s. The Sandinistas believe that casualties and international opposition would cause a humiliating United States defeat and withdrawal." Congress and the U.S. people should not "be confused about the cost of military involvement in Central America. It would be some billions of dollars, much reducing our ability to meet our commitments in the North Atlantic Treaty Organization and the Persian Gulf. Battle casualties might well require reintroduction of the draft to provide replacements for men and wounded."

General John W. Vessey, Jr., chairman of the Joint Chiefs of Staff, said in a 1983 speech that "neither I, nor any member of the Joint Chiefs of Staff, nor the civilian leaders in the Department of Defense advocate introducing U.S. combat forces to try to implement an American military solution to the problems of Central America."

Indeed, Drew Middleton, the veteran military correspondent of *The New York Times,* wrote in an article in June 1983 headlined "U.S. Generals Are Leery of Latin Intervention," that "with unusual unanimity, senior generals of the United States Army say they oppose any military intervention in Central America. . . . The generals and staff officers in the Pentagon do not see the Central American situation as a peculiarly military one. Rather, they stress that the region's problems are economic, political, social and military." And agreeing with those views, said Middleton, was General William Westmoreland, the retired former American commander of U.S. troops in Vietnam.

But the Reagan administration sees things otherwise.

Says U.S. Congressman Michael Barnes of Maryland, chairman of the House Subcommittee on Western Hemisphere Affairs: "I think very significant elements within the administration have decided that the only answer is a military solution."

In opening a hearing on "U.S. Policy in Honduras and Nicaragua" in March 1983, Barnes declared: "In Nicaragua current U.S. policy, I think, is making a bad situation into what could be a disaster."

One of the things the Reagan administration has been trying to do is organize joint military action against Nicaragua by El Salvador, Guatemala, Panama and Honduras. The Reagan administration has been attempting to do this by reviving a regional defense alliance called Central American Defense Council or Condeca—but excluding Nicaragua, one of the founders of the group when it was established in 1963. A "secret meeting" was held in October 1983 of 14 top military leaders of El Salvador, Guatemala, Panama and Honduras on the plan, *The New York Times* later disclosed. It quoted from a report issued at the Tegucigalpa gathering which asserted that "a war situation is predictable" and there should be study on what "legal instruments" may "permit the security and armed forces of Panama and other Central American countries to participate in the action for the pacification of Nicaragua." The report said that "opposition forces" fighting the Nicaraguan government "can establish a government somewhere in its territory, and, once recognized internationally, can ask for aid from Condeca." A wide range of military aid from the U.S. was proposed including "in case of extreme crisis, direct participation by the United States, with all its resources."

Meanwhile, the Reagan administration continues to push Honduras toward conflict with Nicaragua. Honduran armed forces chief General Alvarez is excited about the prospect. If the U.S. helps Central American countries "that are fighting for democracy, there won't be any need to send American troops," he says.

Lt. Colonel John H. Buchanan, a retired Marine Corps officer who became director of area studies at the Center for Development Policy in Washington, D.C., warned the House Subcommittee on Inter-American Affairs in 1982 of "the intent of General Alvarez and other hardliners to lead Honduras into a war with Nicaragua." Buchanan, after an extensive tour of Central America, testified: "Such a war would truly be a 'war without winners.' It seems a terrible price to pay for this administration's determination to seek a military solution to what are deeply-seated social, economic and political problems. Such a war could easily spark off a regional conflagration involving all the nations of Central America, and perhaps the U.S. and Mexico—on opposing sides. It would exact a terrible price from the people of Honduras and Nicaragua, and stain the name of the United States in the eyes of all of Latin America and the world." The Marine Corps Vietnam combat veteran scored "the present administration's policy toward Central America. It is a misguided policy and if it is not soon reversed, the people of this land and the rest of this continent will suffer for decades from its grave consequences. It is not in our interests as a nation."

And the world worries about what the U.S. is doing. The prime minister of Spain, Felipe Gonzáles, after a tour of Latin America in 1983, declared: "Let us imagine that there is a war, as is sometimes feared, between Nicaragua and Honduras. What would the outcome be? Would it spread from Nicaragua and Honduras to El Salvador, Guatemala and, who knows, even to Costa Rica? How will Panama be affected? What repercussions would it have in Mexico? I believe that the road to a possible armed confrontation has at this moment unforeseeable consequences from the political and historical points of view. Therefore, I believe that the interests of the people in the region and of the United States is to avoid at all costs the triggering of a general conflict."

Why, then, the great push by the U.S. government to go to war in Central America? What is the Reagan administration's fixation on overthrowing the Nicaraguan government?

"Nicaragua Is Not An Enemy" was the title of an article by the Rev. William Sloane Coffin, senior minister of the Riverside Church of New York, after he visited Nicaragua in 1983. "The administration," he wrote, "appears totally out of touch with reality." As for its insistence on a quick election, Rev. Coffin noted "that thirteen years passed from the time of our own revolution to our first elections." Most of Nicaragua's economy is "in private hands. To be sure the banks in Nicaragua have been nationalized, but so too have those in Mexico, as well as the Mexican oil industry. Yet the president never refers to 'Marxist-Leninist' Mexico." As to Nicaragua being any kind of threat to U.S. security, "A single American plane flying out of southern California, Texas or Florida could obliterate Nicaragua in twenty minutes and every Nicaraguan knows it. As for the charge that the Sandinistas are exporting violence, isn't that a little like accusing France of starting the American Revolution? Anyone with common sense knows you can't have a revolt without revolting conditions." Rev.

Coffin concluded: "Obsessed with Communism, the Reagan administration sees a 'Marxist-Leninist' under every Central American bush. The result is a policy without wisdom or conscience. What the Reagan administration is doing in the name of America and with American money is a disgrace," he said, especially the "arming and training" of counter-revolutionaries who "not only kidnap and kill, they torture and mutilate."

Nicaragua has never been a center of major U.S. economic activity, the kind that has developed in other Central American nations and has been the reason the U.S. has used its military to invade these lands—to keep them safe for U.S. interests.

According to statistics I received from the U.S. Embassy in Nicaragua, the trade Nicaragua has had with the U.S.—imports and exports—was exceeded by other markets. Interestingly, the change in U.S.-Nicaragua trade before and after the revolution has not been drastic. In 1978, according to the statistics, Nicaragua imported $186 million from the United States in goods. In 1982—after the revolution and despite the Reagan administration's attempts to isolate Nicaragua economically—it imported $147 million from the U.S. Its main source of imports have been other Third World countries ($257 million in 1978 and $366 in 1982) and Japan, Canada and Western Europe ($146 million in 1978 and $172 million in 1982). Imports from socialist countries were listed as $3.6 million in 1978 and $89 million in 1982, still a good deal less still than from the U.S. As for exports, the highest amounts have gone to Japan, Canada and Western Europe ($245 million in 1978 and $175 million in 1982), other Third World countries ($248 million in 1978 and $104 million in 1982), the U.S. ($150 million in 1978 and $96 million in 1982) and finally the socialist countries ($1 million in 1978 to $31 million in 1982).

No, it hasn't been economics that has been the U.S. concern involving Nicaragua. Through many decades, the central U.S. concern has been interest in Nicaragua's placement as a route for an Atlantic-to-Pacific canal.

That was the reason for the U.S. focus on the nation in the 1800s—to possibly use it for a U.S. canal route. That is the reason why the U.S. first invaded Nicaragua in 1909 and overthrew the government of José Zelaya. Having dug the

Panama Canal, the U.S. wanted to make sure no other country would use Nicaragua as the route of a competing canal.

Are we to be really concerned today that Nicaragua, in the age of air transport, is going to turn around and give a concession to some other nation to dig up the nation and compete with the Panama Canal?

Are we to be concerned that the Russians are going to use Nicaragua as a site for missiles? Beyond the Nicaraguan insistence that they don't want their country to serve as a platform for Soviet missiles, there are Russian missiles aimed at every major city in the U.S. sitting in Russian submarines a few dozen miles off our coasts and in silos in Russia. What do the Soviets need Nicaragua for?

Are we to be worried that Nicaragua is going to be "another Cuba," but on the mainland? The differences between the Cuban and Nicaraguan revolutions are striking. An attempt is being made in Nicaragua to create a new government form, not in the Cuban model, not in the Soviet model, not in any standard model. It's a laid-back revolution to a Latin beat making unique links between religion and revolution; it's the first revolution in history to so combine socialist economic and political theory with religious ideals. Pluralism is being sought. In many ways, Nicaraguan society is less socialistic than that of Mexico which, not too incidentally, is Nicaragua's closest ally—not Cuba or Russia. People in Nicaragua are trying to build a new society after over four decades of having a nightmare imposed on them. They are working hard and creatively to try to avoid the pitfalls and tragedies that have mired and destroyed revolutions that have occurred before.

"A lot of time is spent trying to label the revolution," says Sandinista government leader Sergio Ramírez. Some would like to label it Communist, or Social Democrat, or Eurocommunist "or whatever," he says, but essentially "it's Sandinista. . . . We don't claim we've invented anything, but we are trying to give this process some new dimension, a local quality, if not a universal one. We don't claim to substitute universal doctrines, but we do claim the right to lead this process along a truly creative path."

Are we to be worried because Marxism is a central component of the Sandinista philosophy? Is this supposed to make us ready to go to war? Over half of the world's people today live in countries with governments with Marxist points of view—and some are our friends and some are our enemies. Our government under Ronald Reagan makes the Cold War with the Soviets ever more frigid, but meanwhile the U.S. government gets closer and closer to Communist China and Yugoslavia. We have no difficulty in dealing with socialist governments in Greece, Spain, and France. The issue here is not whether a country is Marxist or socialist or Communist. There are obviously other factors at work.

Are we to be worried that a revolutionary government in Nicaragua will mean the export of revolution to the rest of Central America—into Latin America? As Gautama Fonseca said in Honduras: "The fire doesn't spread to where there is no dry wood." People of all views in the U.S. who have taken the time to carefully study the issue have come to the conclusion that critical social and economic problems, not subversion, are responsible for revolution in Latin America—and around the world. The University of Miami's Graduate School of International Studies, for instance, issued a 35,000-page report in the beginning of 1984 culminating an eight-month study in which 200 bankers, corporate executives, economists, investors, international lawyers and scholars took part. It declared that "there is a real danger in seeing . . . rural peasant movements in opposition to a oligarchic regime . . . as only a result of 'enemy' actions, which view tends to support responses such as military aid, as opposed to aid aimed at eradication of some of the basic economic and social problems of the affected societies." The report urged "a long-term commitment by the United States to political independence, economic viability and human rights within the region."

A group of U.S. scholars in a group called Policy Alternatives for the Caribbean and Central America issued a report, also early in 1984, entitled: "Changing Course: Blueprint for Peace in Central America and the Caribbean." It concluded: "Successful revolutions in Central America need not threaten U.S. national security. A sensible U.S. policy would be to assist post-revolutionary governments, not force them to rely upon the Soviet Union and Eastern Europe." The report stressed: "The revolutions and civil wars in Central America have indigenous roots. They are not products of a Soviet-Cuban conspiracy."

Mexican diplomat and writer Carlos Fuentes addressed this issue in a commencement speech in 1983 at Harvard: "The daybreak of a movement of social and political renewal cannot be set by calendars other than those of the people involved. Revolutions cannot be exported. With Walesa and Solidarity, it was the internal clock of the people of Poland that struck the morning hour. So it has always been: with the people of Massachusetts in 1776; with the people of my country during our revolutionary experience; with the people of Central America in the hour we are all living. The dawn of revolution reveals the total history of a community. This is self-knowledge that a society cannot be deprived of without grave consequences."

In his speech, entitled "High Noon in Latin America," Fuentes declared: "The source of change in Latin America is not in Moscow or Havana: it is in history."

And of Nicaragua, he said: "Why is the United States so impatient with four years of *Sandinismo,* when it was so tolerant of forty-five years of *Somocismo?* Why is it so worried about free elections in Nicaragua, but so indifferent to free elections in Chile?

"Nicaragua is being attacked and invaded by forces sponsored by the United States. It is being invaded by counterrevolutionary bands led by former commanders of Somoza's National Guard who are out to overthrow the revolutionary government and reinstate the old tyranny." Fuentes said that "these are not freedom fighters" as Reagan has claimed. "They are Benedict Arnolds." He continued: "Everything can be negotiated in Central America." There could be nonaggression pacts, and reduction of armies. What is necessary is "the respect of the United States . . . for the integrity and autonomy of all the states in the region, including normalization of relations with all of them."

Yes, respect—for the dignity of other peoples.

Asks the Nicaraguan housing minister, Dr. Miguel Ernesto Vigil Icaza in Managua, "Why doesn't the U.S. treat Nicaragua with dignity? Why has the U.S. treated Nicaragua through the many years with contempt, with a lack of respect?" Indeed, he asks, why has this been the way the U.S. has generally treated Latin America? There are problems that neighbors inevitably have with each other. But if one has a problem with a neighbor, "you don't put a tank in front of his house and aim the barrel at his front porch." Icaza's two sons, 14 and 16, were at the border with the Nicaraguan militia facing the *contras* as he spoke.

The answer to why the Reagan administration is ready to go to war in Central America, why it has a fixation on overthrowing the Nicaraguan government, stems not from economics nor international trade nor security nor geopolitics—nothing so measurable or more-or-less rational.

Reagan and his associates have become trapped in a "web their paranoia has spun," is the way Princeton Professor of International Affairs Richard H. Ullman explained it in the Fall 1983 edition of *Foreign Affairs.* In the article, "At War With Nicaragua," he stressed that "Nicaragua today strikes a visitor as being no more easily comparable with Cuba or Czechoslovakia than with Mexico—whose revolution a generation and a half ago (we too often forget) also seemed profoundingly frightening to North Americans. . . . Certainly Nicaragua now is not the repressive communist dictatorship that figures in so many of President Reagan's speeches." And, he added, "Sandinist Nicaragua is likely to remain a magnet and a model for men and women elsewhere in Central America who would transform repressive oligarchical societies. Those who fear the force of that model should be constrained to look at the inequities in their own societies, rather than—as would Honduras' General Alvarez—seek temporary safety in a holy war."

"The Reagan administration's hostility toward Nicaragua appears to be fundamentally ideological. Its policy cannot be understood simply as a response to real or potential security threats from Nicaragua," Jorge I. Dominguez, a Harvard professor and former president of the Latin American Studies Association, explains. "The main reason for the Reagan administration's policies is that the president and his political advisers simply do not like the regime and would like to avoid any steps that would help its consolidation. Thus, the prospects for negotiations remain poor—not because such talks are impossible, not because U.S. security interests cannot be identified and defended through negotiations, but because this administration will not countenance the thought that it might live in peace with a regime it despises so much."

And despite the repeated warnings of the U.S. military to direct intervention of the U.S. in Central America, there are "officials in the White House," Barbara Rehm reported in the *New York Daily News* in October 1983, who "argue that Nicaragua is the one place where the U.S. can regain its honor, lost in Vietnam. They see it as the place where a real win against Communism is possible. In strategic terms, they say, Nicaragua is easily isolated. The country is tiny, and a simultaneous sweep from the northern mountains and southern swamps could put victorious Marines inside Managua within a week."

And then what?

Fred C. Iklé, U.S. undersecretary of defense for policy and a chief architect of the Reagan administration's Nicaragua policy, called in a 1983 speech for a military victory in Central America, saying negotiations cannot resolve current conflicts. "We can no more negotiate an acceptable political solution with these people than the social democrats in revolutionary Russia could have talked Lenin into giving up totalitarian Bolshevism," he proclaimed. "We do not seek a military defeat for our friends. We do not seek a military stalemate. We seek victory for the forces of democracy."

*The Wall Street Journal* reported as 1983 ended that "the hard-liners are winning" in the Reagan administration on Nicaragua. "So, the more the Sandinistas promise, the more the administration raises the ante, in an effort to see how far it can push Managua." There may be a temporary modification of policy. "With an election year approaching," *The Journal* reported, "the administration must decide whether the ideological beliefs that have dominated Central American policy should temporarily give way to political consideration. To appease a restive Congress and avoid criticisms that Mr. Reagan is a trigger-happy president, the U.S. may stress its interest in negotiations." But that's not the long-range plan. "Says one administration analyst," *The Journal* continued, " 'The general view, if we're talking about living with a regime continuing along the line we've seen over the last couple of years, is that it's going to be very difficult if not impossible to live with them.' "

Edgar Chamorro of the FDN had said that "if Reagan is reelected" his administration would be "politically" freed to do what Chamorro wants: a direct intervention by the U.S. in Nicaragua.

And in early 1984, the commission appointed by Reagan to

study Central American issues—headed by Henry Kissinger, the designer of so much of the U.S. war strategy in Vietnam and Southeast Asia and the architect of the U.S.-organized overthrow of the Allende regime in Chile—came out with a report supporting continued U.S. backing of the *contras.*

It said, "We do not believe that it would be wise to dismantle existing incentives and pressures on the Managua regime." The report of the National Bipartisan Commission on Central America charged that "in Nicaragua, we have seen the tragedy of a revolution betrayed," and declared: "The use of Nicaragua as a base for Soviet and Cuban efforts to penetrate the rest of the Central American isthmus, with El Salvador the target of first opportunity, gives the conflict there a major strategic dimension. The direct involvement of aggressive external forces makes it a challenge to the system of hemispheric security and, quite specifically, to the security interests of the United States. This is a challenge to which the United States must respond." The report said direct U.S. military action should be "only a course of last resort" but warned that "Nicaragua must be aware that force remains an ultimate recourse" for the United States. Two commission members, Mayor Henry G. Cisneros of San Antonio and Yale University Professor Carlos F. Diaz-Alejandro, opposed continuing U.S. aid to the *contras.* Dr. Diaz-Alejandro said "the possibility of accidental war is . . . increased by the covert operations, which otherwise show little prospect of overthrowing the Sandinista regime," and "covert aid probably makes successful negotiations with Managua less likely—raising unsettling questions about what Washington will do if they fail."

The Kissinger panel's action came as no surprise. "The choice of Kissinger as chairman further guarantees that the commission will fullfill its political mandate," said American University government Professor William LeoGrande when Kissinger was appointed by Reagan. Senator Christopher Dodd of Connecticut described Kissinger as "a symbol for a foreign policy many would rather forget than repeat."

How is it that the U.S., born of revolution, is not only now managing the *contras* but has been a principal antirevolutionary force globally? Why is its passion to support murderous regimes and thrust them down the throats of the populace?

In a speech in Managua in 1983, Ramírez told of the impact

of the American revolution on Latin America. "The revolution which gave rise to the United States' nationhood has been the most exported revolution in modern history and the one which employed the greatest number of imported ideologial elements as the basis for its thinking, its liberation war and its innovative laws."

It is the U.S., he said, which has "betrayed their original revolutionary project. . . . We believe that the United States is the one which should return to its original project of liberty and democracy, the project of Washington and Jefferson, that beautiful revolutionary project that was betrayed by capitalist greed, by the wanton accumulation of riches and by this perverse expansionist will that has forced the United States borders so many times to our borders, like they are once again doing by pushing it to the Honduran border."

Ramírez concluded: "We are not a people chosen by God to fulfill any manifest destiny, we don't have capital to export or transnational corporations to defend beyond our borders. Our dreams are not to dominate, expand or conquer but rather our dreams are the humble dreams of a humble people who aspire to true justice and independence."

The man who led the American revolution, George Washington, offered some advice in his "Farewell Address" on avoiding the hatred in which the Reagan administration is caught up.

"These will be offered to you with the more freedom as you can only see in them the dissinterested warnings of a parting friend who can possibly have no personal motive to bias his counsels," said Washington.

"Observe good faith and justice toward all nations. Cultivate peace and harmony with all. Religion and morality enjoin this conduct; and can it be that good policy does not equally enjoin it? It will be worthy of a free, enlightened, and, at no distant period, a great nation to give to mankind the magnanimous and too novel example of a people always guided by an exalted justice and benevolence. Who can doubt that in the course of time and things the fruits of such a plan would richly repay any temporary advantages which might be lost by a steady adherence to it? Can it be that Providence has not connected the permanent felicity of a nation with its virtue? The experiment, at least, is recommended by every sentiment which ennobles human nature."

Washington continued: "In the execution of such a plan nothing is more essential than that permanent, inveterate antipathies against particular nations and passionate attachments for others should be excluded and that in place of them just and amicable feelings toward all should be cultivated. The nation which indulges toward another an habitual hatred or an habitual fondness is in some degree a slave. It is a slave to its animosity or its affection, either of which is sufficent to lead it astray from its duty and interest. Antipathy in one nation against another disposes each more readily to offer insult and injury to lay hold of slight cause or umbrage, and to be haughty and intractable when accidental or trifling occasions of dispute occur. Hence, frequent collisions, obstinate, envenomed, and bloody contests. The nation prompted by ill will and resentment sometimes impels to war the government, contrary to the best calculations of policy. The government sometimes participates in the national propensity, and adopts, through passion, what reason would reject; at other times, it makes the animosity of the nation subservient to projects of hostility instigated by pride, ambition, and other sinister and pernicious motives. The peace often, sometimes perhaps the liberty, of nations has been the victim."

He closed hoping his words of advice "may be productive of some partial benefit, some occasional good; that they may now and then recur to moderate the fury of party-spirit, to warn against the mischief of foreign intrigue, to guard against the impostures of pretended patriotism; this hope will be a full recompense for the solicitude for your welfare by which they have been dictated."

The Sandinista revolution is far from perfect; I have noted its faults in this work. But, again, neither was the American revolution perfect. It, like the American revolution, is a humanitarian undertaking, and is one attempting to evolve and improve.

What right does the United States have to try and stop it? Can't we take the counsel of our revolutionary leader and "observe good faith and justice toward all nations" rather than send terrorists to savage the Nicaraguan populace? U.S. Congressman Tom Downey of New York told of how, in 1983, "as our gunboats steam toward the Central American coast, Americans understand the terrifying *déja vu* of too many ill-fated military decisions of our recent past. They are witnessing the choice of military solutions when peaceful alternatives . . . are still at our disposal. They are watching in fear as the administration continues to defy international and domestic law, as well as elemental principles of democracy and respect for human life. . . . Our self-restraint and explorations of peace are not indications of weakness, but the ultimate recognition of the responsibility of our might. For it remains our adherence to ideals, and not our abandonment of them, that offers our most successful strategy for competing with adversaries."

The Nicaraguan Sandinista revolution grew out of the poverty, hunger and misery of masses of people and the murderous, oppressive policies and actions of a horrendous dictatorship. That chemistry is not extraordinary: it is common, although Nicaragua was among the countries where these elements existed in the extreme. Such pressures can be expected to culminate in revolution again and again. It is an historical process of humanity seeking to be fed, to be healthy, to be free, to live in dignity and pursue happiness and peace. Some of these same ingredients led, of course, to the American revolution.

These same ideals led the people of the United States in World War II, exactly forty years ago, to sacrifice their own lives in order to liberate people being trampled under the heavy heel of terror and tyranny. America was seen as a bulwark of freedom then.

What has happened to the United States since?

As American Penny Lernoux writes from Colombia in *Cry of the People:* "It isn't pleasant to be called an oppressor, yet that is how many people in Latin America see the United States. And there is considerable documented evidence to support the Latin American's point of view—in the Pentagon's encouragement of military regimes, in the CIA's interferences in Latin American political affairs, and in corporate industry's business practices." This view of America, the bad, is not confined only to Latin America.

The United States, a child of revolution, has regularly committed itself against revolution around the world. Is that because revolution in the undeveloped world would mean independent governments which might end a world economic and political system that gives the U.S. an extremely disproportionate share of the wealth? Is it because, as Ramírez says, the

U.S. has "betrayed" its own revolution? Is it because the U.S. has been caught in the syndrome into which Rome fell in its last years: becoming too powerful, imperial, a U.S. Empire, treating other peoples with contempt? Or does the U.S. government just automatically ally itself with dictators who pledge allegience to the fortunes of U.S. multinational corporations operating in their countries?

This pattern is not consistent. The U.S. sided with independence movements in India and Indonesia. But in most years before and after World War II, the U.S. did not act on the international stage as the bulwark of democracy for which it was known during that war.

Today the U.S. conducts a not-very-covert war to overthrow the revolutionary government of Nicaragua. It could easily become a Latin American version of the Vietnam war, another drawn-out, heavily destructive guerrilla conflict. Or the U.S. can start changing its general ways and adopt a policy in harmony with those people in the world who are attempting to liberate themselves from oppression. Nicaragua is a country where the people like the U.S.: its music, its blue jeans, its writers, its baseball, its people (but not its Marines and CIA). By dismissing what has been going on there as some sort of Communist takeover, a smokescreen frequently used by our leaders, or as a Cuban or Russian export, the U.S. government is not only wrong but isolates and alienates Nicaragua even more than it is now and forces that incorrect perception to become a self-fulfilling prophecy.

Daniel Ortega went to the Security Council of the United Nations in 1983 because the U.S.'s "waging of covert aggression against our revolution has now intensified to the point at which the imminence of intervention in Central America" is likely.

Said Ortega: "Throughout history, humanity has engaged in a constant struggle to achieve better and more just ways of life. As part of this historical process, the Central American region in recent times has been in upheaval because of the constant action of its people, who have so long been oppressed and who are determined to free themselves, in the face of the resistence of privileged minorities which are at pains to halt the changes which, sooner or later, must come to these unjust societies.

"When our revolution triumphed, notwithstanding the historical inconsistency of United States policy, we felt—and indeed proposed—that it was necessary to normalize relations with the United States within a new framework of respect and cooperation." That move "underwent a sharp change when in January 1981 the new administration assumed the presidency of the United States.

"We can affirm at this time that the policy of the present United States administration is still out of step with the realities in the region and that despite what some had predicted, the threats made against the region in the government's platform were not mere campaign rhetoric but are increasingly becoming a dreadful fact."

Ortega asserted: "I want to say to you with the utmost sincerity and simplicity, and with the moral support of our entire people, that if our fervent efforts for peace should fail, neither imperial will, nor threats, nor blockades, nor invasions will be able to put an end to the historic struggle we are prepared to wage to safeguard our legitimate rights to self-determination, fighting to the last man and shedding the last drop of our blood. But it is not confrontation that we desire, but peace and tranquility; that is why we have come here before you. . . .

"Nicaragua can in no way represent a threat to the security of the United States. We are a small country, a dignified and poor country that pursues a policy of international non-alignment."

He asked for "direct and frank conversation with the government of the United States," saying that Nicaragua "is willing immediately to sign non-aggression pacts with all neighboring countries of the Central American area." He requested that "the United States government officially and explicitly . . . voice its commitment not to attack Nicaragua, nor to initiate or promote any direct, indirect or covert intervention in Central America." He called on the United Nations to "reject any acts of force or threats and to repudiate any direct, indirect or covert intervention in Central America.

"In memory of the millions of people killed in wars throughout history," he concluded, "in memory of the millions tortured and murdered in the Nazi concentration camps in the Second World War, in memory of the thousands of patriots who fell in the struggles for liberation and against colonialism, racism and all kinds of oppression, in memory of the Central American patriots who have fallen in the fight for independence, justice and peace, for the right of peoples to be free, sovereign and independent, for the right of humanity to desire peace and to demand peace—let there be peace in Central America."

Yes, let there be peace in Central America. Let it be that my sons and the Nicaraguan young men on the cover of this book, and all the many young men and women of both nations don't have to shoot one another, kill and wound each other, and be victims of the political madness which sends the U.S. farther and farther from its ideals and hurtles the nation toward another Vietnam.

*A Nicaraguan girl*

# ACKNOWLEDGEMENTS

With grateful appreciation to: the professors at the *Universidad de Guanajuato* in Mexico who as part of an Antioch College Education Abroad program first made me aware of the dynamics and history of revolution and U.S. intervention in Latin America; the Nicaraguan Education Project of Washington, D.C. and Valerie Miller and Mary Ely Christie of N.E.P.: Jackson Baker, Tom Beraden, John Betancourt, William P. Cheshire, Bert Emke, Elaine Ruth Fletcher, David Lowery, Edward Shanahan, John Workman; Lorna and Eric Salzman, Congressional staffer Jon Donner, Rev. John Long, Marty Grossman, Richard Elman, Peter Rosset; Dr. Martin and Judith Shepard, my supportive publishers at Permanent Press, and Judy Wolfe of Permanent Press; Janet Grossman, my editor and wife.

# RECOMMENDED READING

*Cocktails at Somoza's: A Reporter's Sketchbook of Events in Revolutionary Nicaragua* by Richard Elman, Apple-wood Books, Cambridge, Mass, 1981.

*Cry of the People: United States Involvement in the Rise of Fascism, Torture, and the Persecution of the Catholic Church in Latin America* by Penny Lernoux, Penguin, New York, 1980.

*Intervention and Revolution, America's Confrontation with Insurgent Movements Around the World* by Richard J. Barnet, New American Library, New York, Revised edition 1980.

*Nicaragua,* photography by Susan Meisalas, Pantheon Books, New York, 1981.

*Nicaragua: A Country Study* edited by James D. Rudolph, Department of the Army, Washington, D.C., 1982.

*Nicaragua: A People's Revolution* by EPICA Task Force, EPICA Task Force, 1470 Irving Street, N.W., Washington, D.C., 1980.

*Nicaragua in Revolution* edited by Thomas Walker, Praeger, New York, 1982.

*Nicaragua: The Sandinist Revolution* by Henri Weber, Verso Editions and NLB, 15 Greek Street, London, 1981.

*Now We Can Speak, A Journey Through the New Nicaragua* by Frances Moore Lappe and Joseph Collins, Institute for Food Development Policy, 1885 Mission Street, San Francisco, 1982.

*Revolution and Intervention in Central America* edited by Marlene Dixon and Susanne Jonas, Synthesis Publications, San Francisco, 1983.

*Sandinistas Speak,* Tomás Borge, Carlos Fonseca, Daniel Ortega, Humberto Ortega, Jaime Wheelock, Pathfinder Press, New York, 1982.

*The Nicaragua Reader, Documents of a Revolution under Fire* edited by Peter Rosset and John Vandermeer, Grove Press, New York, 1983.

*Triumph of the People: The Sandinista Revolution in Nicaragua* by George Black, Zed Press, London, 1981.

*Under the Eagle: U.S. Intervention in Central America and the Caribbean* by Jenny Pearce, South End Press, Boston, 1982.

*What Difference Could a Revolution Make? Food and Farming in the New Nicaragua* by Joseph Collins, Institute for Food Development Policy, 1885 Mission Street, San Francisco, 1982.